THE OTHER AMERICAN REVOLUTION

Afro-American Culture and Society
A CAAS Monograph Series
Volume 4

Publications Committee
Baruch Elimelech
Pierre-Michel Fontaine
Romey Keys
Lewis Langness
Claudia Mitchell-Kernan
Richard Yarborough

The Editor for this Monograph
was Robert A. Hill

For Sandra O'Neal

Continue teaching and learning
The best is yet to come.
Vincent Harding
5/27/85

THE
OTHER AMERICAN
REVOLUTION

Vincent Harding

Center for Afro-American Studies
University of California, Los Angeles
and
Institute of the Black World
Atlanta, Georgia

Library of Congress Cataloging in Publication Data

Harding, Vincent.
    The other American revolution.

    (Afro-American culture and society; v. 4)
    Bibliography: p.
    Includes index.
    1. Afro-Americans—History.   2.   Afro-Americans—
Civil rights.   I.   Title.   II.   Series.
E185.H28   973′.0496073   79–54307
ISBN 0-934934-10-X
ISBN 0-934934-06-1 (pbk.)

Center for Afro-American Studies
University of California, Los Angeles

Institute of the Black World
Atlanta, Georgia

Library of Congress Catalog Card Number 79–54307
ISBN 0-934934-10-X
ISBN 0-934934-06-1 (pbk.)
Printed in the United States of America

Second Printing, December 1982

For my family
 Rosemarie, Rachel, Jonathan, and Mabel—and that extended clan,
   both living and dead
   Who have nurtured and loved me
   Every step of the way.

For my people, everywhere
 Whose name is legion
 Whose struggle is the soul of this work.

For my comrades and companions
 in the continuing movement toward a new humanity.

Remembering Gordon McDonald Broome
 Uncle, Father, and Friend.

Letter to the Editor

Dear Bobby,

In ways that I did not anticipate, your request for an account of the origins of my manuscript, *The Other American Revolution*, actually proved to be a most helpful and stimulating inquiry. It sent me to the files, stirred up a period of recollection and reflection, evoked experiences that I had nearly forgotten, and reminded me that this particular part of our struggle for freedom does indeed have a unique history of its own, one that reflects many aspects of the larger story of our people's movement in this land.

Without burdening you with too much detail, let me try to summarize the major developments that led to the creation of *The Other American Revolution*, as well as those that now bring it to the Center for Afro-American Studies as a joint publication with the Institute of the Black World.

The beginnings were in another, larger manuscript, *There Is A River*, a two-volume history of the Afro-American quest for freedom, a work that has been engaging much of my time and thought since the death of my friend and comrade, Martin King. As you know, my work in Atlanta as the first director of the King Memorial Center, and as co-creator of the Institute of the Black World (IBW), often made it necessary for me to put aside the longer manuscript. At the same time, our work at IBW (and I remember your own time there with great joy and appreciation, Bobby) kept me at the eye of that storm that was the black power/black identity movement and the struggle for black history and black studies. That exhilarating cultural/political movement was the context for this work.

Early in the seventies, at the height of the recurring battle for hegemony over the interpretation of the history and the future of black people in America, many local community groups began to organize to challenge the local mass media outlets, especially television stations. Their central concerns were the lack of black programming, personnel, and power. One such local battle over the black presence on the airwaves provided the immediate occasion for the creation of *The Other American Revolution*. In 1971, WMAL, then the Washington *Star*-owned station in the District of Columbia, began to respond to black community pressure in a variety of ways. One was to seek help in the development of a series of programs on what was defined broadly as "black history and black culture." In the course of this search WMAL turned to Professor Stephen Henderson, who had been one of IBW's founding fellows, and who was then director of Howard University's Institute of the Humanities. Steve, in turn, called on IBW.

At the time, we had developed what was essentially a "paper" consortium among our institution and Howard and Fisk Universities. For a while we thought that the creation of a major television series might present an excellent opportunity to inspire the consortium with some real life. Without going into *that* story (which is a history in itself), it is enough to say here that early in 1972, after many months of negotiations, what finally developed was a proposal that would give IBW primary responsibility for developing a book to be used as the basis for a television series on the black struggle for freedom in the United States. Under the arrangement, WMAL would provide funding for the research and writing of the book and would also take major responsibility for seeking out a commercial broadcast outlet and one or more sponsors for the series. (It was their intention to begin at the network level, and to drop back to their local grouping only if the larger goal proved impossible to achieve.)

The agreement was finally signed in January, 1973. When it was executed, all of us, especially the IBW group, were very excited about the possibility that we might actually develop a vehicle for mass commercial television which would convey with integrity the centuries-long movement of our people towards justice, freedom, and a new society. Remembering what some of us had done with the CBS *Black Heritage* series in 1969, we looked forward to growth and development.

We decided at the institute that I would have the basic responsibility for producing the book. Since I had been working for some time on the research and early drafting of *There Is A River*, the document for WMAL actually grew out of my engagement with that larger body of material. Written between the spring and fall of 1973, constantly benefiting from the insights of the community of intellectual workers in the struggle at IBW, *The Other American Revolution* was completed in December, 1973. (But it should be noted, Bobby, that the introduction that now appears with the work was actually written in 1976.)

In essence, *OAR*—as we called it at the institute—became a condensation of *There Is A River* (to be published by Harcourt Brace Jovanovich). But in 1973 it was geared especially towards a television schedule, which would have placed it on the air sometime between 1975 and 1976, the year of the Bicentennial. That is part of the significance of its title. That is the reason for the particular focus of its original introduction. At the same time, there is little I would change if I were rewriting a summary work like *The Other American Revolution* today.

Of course, it is natural for you (and anyone less familiar with my life and times) to ask what happened to the television series that was to be based on this work? Well, Bobby, at least three things happened. First, our friend John Oliver Killens, the novelist and movie script writer, agreed to prepare a treatment for the script of an initial pilot program. But by the time John had completed his work, WMAL and its parent company had run into problems with the Federal Communications Commission, problems that eventually led to the requirement that the *Star* divest itself of its television and radio outlets. Finally, by 1974, the advance promotion for *Roots* had begun, and many persons in the television industry apparently assumed that *that* would be the medium's big black history thing for the rest of the decade. By the end of 1975, these latter factors, plus the sale of the parent company—and the fading of black chic—all led WMAL to drop its plans for the series.

Nevertheless, like our struggle, the book continued to have a life of its own. For instance, in 1975 I was asked to make a series of thirty audio tapes that essentially consisted of my oral presentation of *The Other American Revolution*. Originally developed for Shaw University's Seminary Without Walls, the series is now part of IBW's expanding set of audio tape offerings. At the same time, several persons, including the filmmaker, St. Clair Bourne, began a long campaign to find funding that might make it possible for *OAR* to become a series for national public television. Then, during 1976–1977, IBW serialized parts of the work in its *Black-World-View* periodical publication; and recently the possibility of a national public television airing has taken on new life. (Meanwhile, *There Is A River*, the parent manuscript, continues to move on its own way.)

So, friend, there is the story. Out of that cauldron of struggle *The Other American Revolution* has emerged; and now I am very glad that IBW and I are able to share a full-scale publication of the work with friends, colleagues, and comrades like you at UCLA's Center for Afro-American Studies. To have come finally to this point seems to me not only a witness to the stubborn endurance of the work, but it is also a testimony to the power of cooperative endeavors to overcome the most difficult obstacles. Those, of course, are lessons that we have learned many times, in many ways, in the course of the other American revolution.

Yours in hope and solidarity,

Vincent Harding

December, 1979

P.S. Bobby, in an attempt both to round out the text—which ends with Martin King's assassination—and to offer some perspective on the modern period of our struggle, I have added two other documents from my more recent work. They are "The Black Wedge in America" (1975), and "A Long, Hard Winter to Endure" (1979). Together, they now comprise the last chapter of this book.

Contents

Introduction: Of History, Revolutions, and Hope   xiii

Chapters

1. The African Roots   1
2. Mainland and Middle Passage: The First Struggles for
   Freedom   5
3. Laying the Foundations in North America
   (Prerevolutionary Years)   11
4. Revolution within the Revolution (1770–1790)   15
5. The Revolution That Failed: Searching for Models
   (1790–1800)   19
6. "Death or Liberty": Black Style (1801–1822)   23
7. Freedom Struggle in the North: Intimations of Things
   to Come (1820–1830)   29
8. "Slay My Enemies with Their Own Weapons"—Nat
   Turner (1825–1835)   33
9. Resistance, Rebellion, and Flight: The Unmaking of
   Slaves (1830–1840)   37
10. Vigilance and Disobedience: The Northern Duties
    (1830–1840)   43
11. Black Abolitionism—and Beyond (1830–1850)   47
12. White Compromise, Black Struggle: The Search for
    "Our Country" (1850–1854)   51
13. Black Slavery and White Freedom: The Impossible
    Peace (1850–1861)   59
14. Civil War and the Surge toward Freedom: What Did the
    Handwriting Say? (1861–1865)   63
15. Reconstruction: Struggle, Hope, and Betrayal
    (1865–1877)   71

16. Beyond the "New South": Searching for a Way
    (1875–1900)   79
17. Towards a New Century: "To Protest Forever" or "To
    Possess this Land"? (1900–1914)   87
18. World War I and the Exploding Revolutions
    (1914–1918)   93
19. After Three Hundred Years: "If We Must Die . . ."
    (1919)   101
20. Look for Me in the Whirlwind: The Rise and Fall—and
    Rise—of Marcus Garvey (1919–1925)   107
21. Black and Red Together: The Broken Hope of the
    Communist Party (1919–1936)   115
22. Depression and Struggle: Towards "The Last Great
    Battle of the West" (1929–1939)   123
23. World War, World Revolution, and Black Struggle
    (1939–1945)   131
24. Cold War and Black Freedom: A Time for Paradox
    (1945–1954)   137
25. Beginning in Montgomery: The Rise of the Southern
    Movement (1954–1960)   147
26. ". . . Want My Freedom Now": The Student
    Revolutionaries (1960–1963)   157
27. From Birmingham to Atlantic City: The Testing of
    America (1963–1964)   167
28. Black Power and Urban Rebellion: The Struggle
    Transformed (1964–1967)   177
29. Vietnam, Detroit, and Memphis: The Indivisible
    Movement, the Indivisible Man (1967–1968)   189
30. The Wedge and the Winter: Reflections on the   201
    Search for Meaning
    Bibliography   233
    Index   253

Introduction:
Of History, Revolutions, and Hope

The situation is filled with paradox and irony. A nation's bicentennial approaches, and, except for a few paid promoters, no one seems prepared to admit it, to possess it, certainly not to celebrate it. Equally afraid of passion and hope, disavowing and subverting revolution and self-determination at home and abroad, America espies the two-hundredth anniversary of its own revolution and turns away.

Meanwhile, miasmic clouds of cynicism and despair hang heavy over the land, threatening to stifle all conviction and belief, casting every humane ideal in the meanest possible light. In such a situation (now code-named "Watergate"), only a stupendous act of the imagination can convey any vital connection between these days and a time when men dared say of their political struggle, "The sun never shone on a cause of greater worth." When all the past and present tragedies of the nation threaten to overwhelm any expectation of a better time, who can recognize this revolutionary history, much less celebrate it?

Yet there was a time, not very long ago, when humane passion and revolutionary commitment seemed to flood the streets of America. There was a time when men, women, and children believed in the imminent coming of radical, compassionate change in this country, and gave their lives, their fortunes, and their honor for it. There was a time when ambivalent American presidents were forced to take up the marching songs of a freedom-possessed black people. There was a time, not very long ago, when talk of revolution and justice was as common as discussion of apathy, corruption, and fear are now. In those days dreamers rose up from the heart of Georgia, Alabama, and Mississippi, pursued visions of a new society, and at the same time fought for the fulfillment of the best, great hopes of the first American revolution.

We called it the time of the black revolt, the Negro revolution, the civil rights movement. (To its participants, it was mostly "the movement.") We trembled and thrilled as the defiant young ones demanded "Freedom Now!" "Black Power!" and "The Fire This Time!" Because of television's intrinsic sense of immediacy, we sometimes thought we were really present when the demonstrators set out from the churches, when the dogs snarled and the fire hoses blasted the marching people down.

We felt the dank chill of the prison cells and the searing heat of the cattle prods. We fell under the clubs of the state troopers and wiped the blood off the faces of our comrades. We sang the freedom songs and let the tears flow like rivers of hope and longing. We saw ourselves in the crowds as King and Malcolm and Stokely poured out their variations of the same revolutionary summons to a new society of justice and truth.

We trembled as we watched the Panthers' men-children and their guns. We felt the fires burning; we faced the bared bayonets of the soldiers. We died in the hail of their bullets. But even while dying in the darkness, we still believed in the coming revolution, in the bursting of a new sun.

It was a magnificent time. It was a tumultuous time. It was a terrifying time—like all times of radical upheaval. No social movement of the twentieth century possessed the nation so completely for so long. Nothing divided it so deeply. Nothing called forth so much sheer heroism and undreamed of courage, especially from people who were so recently considered "invisible." Nothing elicited such passion and belief, such chaos and hope. Nothing more fully revealed the glory and the promise of the black community, the possibilities of a new America, the vision of a world transformed.

In the 1950s and 1960s, when we saw the dramatic, contemporary manifestations of this struggle for a transformed society, we thought we knew it fully, but we did not. For the very immediacy of the electronic media misled us, and we were encouraged to believe that the black movement for freedom had no past, that it had sprung full-blown out of Montgomery, Birmingham, Watts, and Detroit in our own time. That is why so many of us now think it has no future. But we were terribly wrong on the first count, and will just as surely be wrong on the second.

For the fact is that every line of freedom marchers in this generation had its echoes and precedents along the way, in Georgia chain gangs, in Marcus Garvey's parades, in the underground railroad, in the harrowing treks of slave coffles from Africa's interior to the European ships along the coast. Every group of demonstrators singing in jails was joined in song and in struggle to southern sharecroppers of the 1930s, to captured black fugitives of the 1830s, and finally to the multitudes who created songs and struggle in the barracoons and slave castles along the Guinea coast.

No black fire leaped out in Watts and Detroit in the 1960s without having burned before in the depression days of Harlem, in the 1919 racial warfare of Chicago, in the cotton-filled warehouses of the antebellum South, on the ships waiting for human cargoes at the mouth of the Senegal River. No word was spoken by Malcolm, Stokely, King, or Fannie Lou Hamer which had not been raised earlier by Paul Robeson, W. E. B. Du Bois, Garvey, Ida B. Wells-Barnett, Bishop Henry McNeill Turner, and David Walker in this country, and by a host of nameless spokesmen on the ships of the middle passage.

This black struggle for freedom, this insistent black movement towards justice, this centuries-long black search for a new America—all this is The Other American Revolution. Every serious challenge to the system of white domination and exploitation, each act of resistance and rebellion, each attempt to fashion an independent black vision of new humans and a new society has been an element of the continuing revolutionary tradition. (Indeed, it is part of the ironic reality of a white racist society that even the simplest claims of black humanity—like the privilege of sitting where one pleases on a bus—have tended to become radical threats to those in power.)

What any careful historical study eventually reveals is that, in spite of its recurring periods of quiescence, intimidation, and uncertainty, this Other American Revolution is the longest, unbroken, active struggle for freedom ever carried on in the annals of American history. Covering more than three hundred years, costing untold thousands of lives, its continuing existence is at once a monument to the human spirit and a rebuke to all those who believe that the only American revolution was a temporary struggle that began and ended two centuries ago. Of course, it is no credit to white America that such a freedom struggle should need to continue, but it is certainly part of the agonizing glory of black life on these shores that The Other American Revolution has not died.

Now, in this moment, when so many men and women no longer dare to hope, refuse the will to struggle, and are afraid to believe in the possibility of radical change for society or for themselves, the history of this Other American Revolution may be crucial.

For black people, a serious reappraisal of their continuing revolution may serve as a reinvigorating summons, a call away from the deadly paths of America's cynicism and compartmentalized deaths. It may sustain encounters with their ancestors in the long black freedom struggle. It may suggest a reason for living, beyond the fantasies of Hollywood and television, or the latest life styles of a lifeless society.

For other nonwhites, some spark of inspiration and hope may be taken from this history, just as they have been able to find strength from the black movement itself. Eventually, of course, whatever is found by Chicanos, Native Americans, Puerto Ricans, and others must be fed back to provide new levels of hope and power for us all.

For whites, it may be good to face this alternative revolutionary tradition and its implications. For the struggle for black freedom has been tied to their history by cords of anguish and rivers of blood. Indeed the centuries-old black quest for justice has relentlessly challenged the white nation to complete its own best work, to fulfill the broken promises of the Declaration of Independence, to join the thrust for black freedom and bring forth what is indeed a new, human nation. But at the hard, critical edges of decision, the leaders and the people of white America have chosen piecemeal solutions, or turned back from the tremendous costs of the new way.

So, if white men and women encounter the history of the other American revolution, if they grasp its current life, they may know why their own revolution has been so often aborted, so terribly incomplete. Perhaps they will even understand why they now avoid that first revolution in fear and shame, why its unrealized future has been smashed back into their uneasy, unsatisfying lives.

Ultimately, it may be that a serious look at the other American revolution will mean a rediscovery and a transformation of both traditions, of both hopes. Then the two struggles may meet on the paths that lead to the embattled frontiers of a new society. At that juncture we may begin to discover what it means to "turn over a new leaf, [to] . . . work out new concepts, and try to set afoot a new man."

Chapter 1

The African Roots

I

The struggle for black freedom in America has roots that reach far back through time and space, moving past centuries, stretching over thousands of miles. Ultimately, the beginnings are in Africa, second largest of the earth's continents, the place where humankind engaged in its own earliest struggles to be free from the domination of the sub-human past. It was at the edges of this vast land mass, along its undulating shores, at the mouths of its great rivers, that the Europeans and Africans whose progeny would create other nations and worlds first met each other.

In the fifteenth and early sixteenth centuries, when the white men from the north made their initial sustained contacts with the people of the coasts of Africa, these Europeans had no way of imagining the immense wealth of history, land, and humanity they had encountered. (For instance, it would have boggled their minds to consider the distinct possibility that somewhere in this land of black men and women there may have been the historical prototype for the mythical Garden of Eden of their Christian faith.) Indeed, although all of the peoples of Africa had a profound sense of their own history and traditions, few of them could have any real conception of the full depth and grandeur of the continent and the variety of its traditions.

Fortunately, we have been released from many of the limitations of time, space, and, perhaps, imagination under which our forebears lived, and it is possible to gain some idea of the sweep of the African experiences that fed into the struggles of the New World. Now we know something of the antiquity of Africa and its peoples, reaching

1

back into the scores of millenia. This gives us some sense of the time scale in which men and women developed traditions of life and death, work and love, religion and warfare, and helps us to understand how and why these men and women and their children might engage in mortal struggles to regain control over their lives, to reconnect themselves to their vividly experienced past.

II

We now understand more about the development of many kinds of political structures, from strong central governments with their kings, courts, civil services, and thriving cities, to the loosest confederations of tribes and clans, living nomadic, internally self-sufficient lives. Thus the obscene myth of the "civilizing" function of slavery is swept away, and we are no longer surprised by the capacity of blacks, from the earliest moment of their arrival on these American shores, to organize and govern themselves whenever it was possible. Nor can we be surprised by the many manifestations of that desire for self-government and independence.

A sense of the African past provides at least some minimal understanding of the centrality of religion in the life of the community, of its informing presence in all of the activities of existence, from birth to death, and beyond. Again this offers a pathway for understanding the critical role of religion in the resistance movements of Africans in the New World, and the specific functions of the religious leaders in the struggle for freedom, from Nat Turner to Martin Luther King, Jr.

Inextricably involved in the issues of life and religion were the tasks of the artists, and Africa was filled with their skills. They worked in gold, silver, ivory, and wood, fashioning the masks, stools, and statues for the ceremonies of the people and their rulers, creating forms and shapes that still thrust their vitality into the modern world. They worked by the waters in clay, creating bowls for food, bricks for homes. They worked with the trees and animal skins, creating instruments and music of great inventiveness. They worked with the spirits and with their bodies and created dances destined for the whole of humanity. Men and women with thousands of years of such creative, artistic traditions behind them could not be samboized or Christianized within a few decades, could not be stripped clean of the will to create, to be human. Instead, this driving will formed still another element of the background of the struggle.

Obviously, then, any serious exploration of the Africa met by the Europeans would suggest the variety of work being done by its inhabitants. In addition to the artists, it would include the extensive traditions and communities of its trading peoples, who traversed many parts of the continent, and who developed early links with Asia and India. It would note the vast stretches of farming areas, the significant development of iron working, the mining of gold and copper, the role of the fisherman (and fisherwomen) along the seemingly endless stretches of coastline and in the rivers and lakes of the interior. Of course, these and other skills were transferable to the land of their enslavement, and blacks could not brook the lie that they had been delivered from an idle savagery and taught to work. Indeed, among the continual justifications they gave for their struggle for justice and freedom were the extensive contributions their skills had made to the creation of a new society in America. This claim to America as a right of black creation, rather than as a gift of white benevolence, became a key to black struggle, and it may be traced back to the traditions of work, to the creativity of the African past.

III

Finally, if there is any single element of the African past which strikes even the casual observer and which may summarize much of its life, it is the great variety of experience and existence that marked the continent. On this stretch of land about twice as large as the present continental United States, a vast set of possibilities existed, beginning with its natural settings. These ranged from deserts and arid plains to some of the world's highest mountains and its largest lake. On the continent, men and animals moved through broad, grassy savannahs, tropical forests, and rich alluvial plains. The people were Kikuyu, Fulani, Zulu, Dinka, Ewe, Bakongo, Mandinka, and thousands more.

Their dwellings were constructed of terra cotta, stone, wood, straw, cloth, or animal skins, or combinations of these. Their work, their play, their worship, and their laws, all testified to the same variety. They knew good and evil, freedom and oppression, despots and great, creative leaders. They lived in many states of society, including slavery. (But their slavery bore no essential relationship to the bondage they would soon experience. For in most of Africa, the ancient institution of slavery had not developed primarily for profit, had not been cast along lines of race. It had not cursed the children of the slaves with the condition of their parents; and in many places slaves were known to join the ruling families which had originally captured and enslaved them.)

In sum, then, within the limitations of their particular tropical world, and recognizing the many significant continuities of their cultures, the peoples of Africa lived out their lives with all the variety of humankind. Thus, when the cruel days of the European slave trade broke upon them, they had every reason to struggle for their freedom, to fight for the right of their humanity.

IV

Of course, this history and its meanings were largely inaccessible to the Europeans who came sailing up to the African coasts in the fifteenth century. Moreover, there is no reason to believe that it would have influenced the nature of their errand, for Europeans brought with them their own history, their own driving forces of life and death.

At the outset, European traders were in search of a new route to the dazzling opportunities of Asia, a route that would avoid the soldiers and the heavy trading duties imposed by the Ottoman Turks who had taken control of the overland routes. For a long time, such an ocean journey around the African mainland had not been possible. It was only recently that the builders and sailors of European ships had sufficiently mastered the technology of North African vessels and the theory and practice of North African navigational instruments. Just about the same time, the rise of strong nation-states was making available to explorers the royal patronage and the considerable financing that were necessary for such tremendous ventures. Then, when to the technology and the financing were added the overwhelming lust for new wealth and the thirst for new adventures, the stage was set for the clash of two histories. The ground was prepared for the coming of the struggle for black freedom.

Chapter 2
Mainland and Middle Passage: The First Struggles for Freedom

I

At first, Africa was to be no more to the Europeans than a means to the end of the Orient's great trade. Its coasts would be a haven from the storms, a source of supplies, perhaps a place of rest on the seemingly endless journey around the Cape of Good Hope. The ships of Portugal were the first to discover that Africa was much more. They found its people, were often stunned by the beauty and order of its cities, but were moved more than anything else by its gold.

Then the trade began, and Africa became an end in itself. Gold, ivory, pepper, fish, were obtained from the West Coast, sugar from the offshore islands. These were the first objects of the European trade. In return, the sun-stained men from the north brought their horses, silks from the Barbary states, brassware, beads, handkerchiefs, and wine. Unintentionally, they also introduced new foods from the Americas and the East Indies, like maize, rice, tomatoes, cassava, and oranges. For a time, all things considered, the encounter seemed to serve some significant, helpful purposes for both peoples.

But that time was not long. Early in the trading experience, the Europeans began to purchase and capture Africans, first in small numbers, but then in ever increasing supplies. Through the establishment of its "plantations" in the Western Hemisphere, Europe had begun the pillage of the New World. By the second decade of the sixteenth century, direct shipments of African captives across the Atlantic had begun. From that point on, captured Africans were marked for three

5

uses: as a source of profit from their sale in the Americas, as a source of unpaid labor in the physical upbuilding of the new lands, and as an object of the racism of the European world.

We may safely assume that the Africans who were actively engaged in this trade had no precise idea of the nature of the slavery that Europeans had in mind, could conceive of no image that would adequately describe the killing grounds of Brazil, Barbados, Cuba, and Carolina. Still, they may have had certain suspicions, for a kind of degradation was entering their own life right there on the Continent.

As the Europeans traded guns for human beings, the balance of life and the traditional relationships between peoples were deeply affected. Power arrangements were transformed. Those who had the new weapons were now great threats to those who did not, and most often the weapons could only be gained by way of the slave trade. Eventually entire tribes were corrupted as they organized their lives around their role in the slave trade. But no one was more intimately affected by the trade than the captives themselves. Ultimately it is to their threatened lives that we trace the struggle for black freedom. They produced its first participants.

II

Often the captives were forced to march many miles from the interior areas to the coast. On many occasions the slaving ships were not there when they arrived, or the captains were waiting for the full consignment of Africans to be brought in before loading them on board. At such times the weary marchers would be held in guarded clearings by the riversides, or in the dungeons known as castles and barracoons near the beach. In these places, where groups of Africans from many scattered areas were often brought together, some of the earliest plans for Pan-African struggle were laid. Men and women broke past the barriers of language and nation to organize for freedom. Sometimes, the struggles began right in those castles and riverside clearings, and the waiting captives broke free, streaking off towards the bush, leaping into the river, attacking the guards, seeking a way to break their bonds.

Then the ships came, from Lisbon and Barcelona, from Bristol and Liverpool, from Nantes and Rotterdam, eventually from Newport and Boston. They bore strange, deceptive names, like *Brotherhood, Charity, Gift of God, Morningstar,* and *Jesus.* But from the moment the

Africans stepped on board they knew that they were in prisons. In effect such prisons were their introduction to the Western world.

One captain described his ship, and provided a picture of hundreds more like his. He said,

> When our slaves are aboard we shackle the men two and two, while we lie in port, and in sight of their own country, for 'tis then they attempt to make their escape and mutiny; to prevent which we always keep centinels *(sic)* upon the hatchways, and have a chest full of small arms, ready loaden and primed, constantly lying at hand upon the quarterdeck, together with some granada shells; and two of our quarter-deck guns, pointing on the deck . . . and two more in steerage.

On such prison ships, in the face of such arsenals of guns and fear, the early struggles for black freedom were waged. Sometimes the action was simply verbal protest. Often it ranged along a spectrum from protest to armed rebellion. As long as the slave trade lasted, so long did the Africans continue to do battle for their humanity. Breaking out from the gloomy, fetid dungeons below deck, they struck towards freedom and light.

III

Most often unarmed, save for their chains and pieces of wood and steel they had secreted among them, the captives rose up repeatedly on these ships near the shores of the homeland. Women fought as well as men. Priests and other religious leaders were regularly at the forefront of the struggles. Together they battled to remain in Africa, to continue the history and traditions they had created, to resist the breaking up of their families and the chain of their existence. They fought desperately for release from the power of the European intruders.

Considering the odds faced by these unarmed and manacled people, it was not surprising that most of their rebellions did not succeed. But some did, especially those that began in the coastal waters. For instance, a substantial number of shipboard struggles ended like the one on the South Carolina-bound vessel, *Clare*. That ship had hardly got thirty miles out to sea when

> the Negroes rose and making themselves Masters of the Gun power and Fire Arms, the Captain and Ships crew took to their Long Boat and got

ashore. . . . The Negroes ran the Ship on Shore . . . and made their escape.

Even after the ships had left the shores, even after the birds of the coasts were no longer with them, the blood of African martyrs streaked the decks of *Jesus* and *Mary*. Many persons leaped from the sides of the ships, preferring to take their lives than to give them to their captors, believing that a new life was surely at hand beyond the depths of the ocean. Others starved themselves to death, resisting even the burning coals and white hot tongs against their lips. In a few cases, victorious Africans brought ships back to the homeland shores even after more than a week at sea.

Some captains said they could not understand this resistance, this willingness of the black people to fight and die, even far out on the ocean. When one group of rebels was temporarily subdued, the ship's captain asked, through an interpreter, "What had induced them to mutiny?" Without hesitation the Africans replied that the captain was "a great rogue to buy them, in order to carry them away from their own country, and they were resolved to regain their Liberty if possible."

IV

There is no way to know what percentage of the thousands of voyages across the middle passage were marked by such rebellions. Nevertheless, the available evidence indicates that although they were usually unsuccessful in their ultimate goal of mastering the ship, these uprisings erupted with significant frequency. Moreover, there was a valor and a determination inherent in the slave ship struggles which could not be denied, even by those who finally put them down. So among the nameless host of forerunners in the other revolution, few images are more clearly etched than that of the young African who was later described by a white sailor who fought against him. The seaman wrote,

I could not but admire the courage of a fine young black who, though his partner in irons lay dead at his feet, would not surrender but fought with his billet of wood until a (pistol) ball finished his existence. The others fought as well as they could but what could they do against fire-arms?

The sailor's last question summed up much of the first stage of the struggle for black freedom. The issue was never a matter of superior

white cultures, more satisfying ways of life, democracy, or higher
civilizations. The seaman's account reminds us that always, beneath
the surface of these shibboleths of black captivity, there were the
demonic forces of white racism and Euro-American capitalism, fueled
and protected by Europe's more highly developed engines of fear, destruction, and warfare. Still the struggle for black freedom continued.

Chapter 3

Laying the Foundations in North America (Prerevolutionary Years)

I

Resistance and rebellion on the prison ships continued right to the shores of the New World. In some cases, when the Africans sighted the new coastlines, they made their last attempts to take over the vessels. Then, failing that, they leaped overboard into the strange waters of the Western Hemisphere. Of course, most of the captives on most of the ships were landed on shore; and we are told that the struggles of barracoons and the slaveships were immediately renewed on the North American mainland. (Of course it was taken up everywhere in the Americas, but from this point on, our focus will be on those hundreds of thousands of Africans who landed in the territory which would become the United States of America.)

The earliest recorded settlement that included Africans in the North American mainland was in what would eventually become South Carolina. In the fall of 1526 it also became the first clear location of black rebellion. Those Africans who participated struck for their freedom and fled to the surrounding Native Americans in search of safety. This was an understandable move, one repeated many times in the centuries that followed, for the blacks discovered early that there were many grounds for a natural alliance with the original settlers of this land. In fact, on many occasions, that alliance with the Indians became a significant element in the struggle for black freedom.

In spite of the earlier records of black presence in the North American settlements, the year 1619 is often chosen as the commemorative

11

date for the arrival of the Africans at Jamestown, in the British colony of Virginia. Interestingly enough, there is evidence that conflict did not develop immediately. Rather, the earliest Africans who arrived in Virginia and other English colonies seem to have met a surprising level of civility and fairness.

But as the number of blacks increased, changes came with them. Many of the Africans indicated their firm desire for the privileges of freemen. In contrast, many whites began to see more clearly the great profits that could be obtained from permanently unpaid labor. Even in those early days, most of the whites were steeped enough in the poison of racism to find it impossible to give up a source of profits and domination in exchange for the voluntary sharing of the newly plundered land with the children of Africa.

Soon the imported legal system of Anglo-America, with its accompanying military sanctions, was brought to bear on behalf of white domination. In the course of the seventeenth century, the English colonies introduced laws prohibiting intermarriage between whites and Africans, laws against the ownership of property by Africans, laws against all rituals connected with African religious practices, laws against the sanctity of marriage between Africans, laws against the free status of African children born in slavery, and many more. Though they sometimes varied in severity and extent from colony to colony, the basic intent of the laws was the same: to give permanent legal sanction and moral justification to the white economic exploitation and the white political and social domination of the captives from Africa, to set the poorer whites against their black fellow laborers.

II

Under such repressive circumstances, it was inevitable that black resistance and struggle should continue and expand. Black people fought in a variety of ways. Some raised verbal protests, using the laws and the beliefs espoused by the colonists to support their own call for freedom. Petitions of many kinds appeared in the black community, ranging from painfully misspelled, but honorable scrawlings to elegantly executed statements of rights. In certain places, Africans actually tried to go to court against the injustices they faced, and in the earlier periods they won a few cases.

But there were more than words. Black struggle often took the form of individual acts of resistance, from arson and poisoning to suicides and voluntary abortions. And the trail of runaways was continuous, regularly marked by blood. While some of these individuals fled to the Indians, or to Canada, Florida, and elsewhere, many others stood their ground. Soon, a class of what were called "outlyers" (or "maroons") began to develop among those Africans who had broken out from the bonds of slavery, but who then banded together as independent out-laws. Sometimes these became aggressive, guerrilla bands, attacking the plantations and other white possessions.

In addition to these other forms of struggle, there were always cases of significant armed uprisings. They took place in the North as well as in the South, for slavery, racism, and exploitation existed in both sec-tors of the colonies. For instance, in New York City in 1712, a group of blacks allied with Indians organized a plot that was supposed to "de-stroy all the whites in the town." Setting fires, killing whites who came to extinguish the blazes, the insurrectionaries succeeded for a short time, but the group was ultimately routed by the colony's military forces. Most of them were executed, but some members of the rebel group took their own lives first, including one husband and wife who made a pact that they would not allow themselves to be captured alive by the forces of white oppression.

III

One of the most striking examples of the open southern struggles took place in 1739 near Stono, South Carolina, a place some twenty miles west of Charleston. There, a group of enslaved Africans planned an uprising, broke into a weapons warehouse, and finally gathered a company of some seventy to eighty men who were determined to march from Stono toward refuge in Florida, then a Spanish possession. For a time they did march, with two drums beating and flags waving and shouts of "liberty" breaking through the air. Part of their struggle was obviously for the repossession of their own identity, for though the world called them slaves, they clearly saw themselves as soldiers of liberty, and they were determined to act on their own vision. But again they finally had to contend with the militia, and after a pitched battle, another hope for freedom was smashed.

Though such hopes were dashed, the black will to struggle could not be destroyed. All through the colonial period, in North and South, in every conceivable form and situation, the struggle for black freedom continued. Almost invariably, the price for open, armed resistance was high. In Louisiana two leaders of a rebellion were "dragged (to the gallows) from the tail of a pack-horse with an . . . halter tied to the neck, feet and hands." Another of the rebels was destined to "remain on the gibbet and have his hands cut off and nailed on the public roads." So, even on the public roads, no one could miss the announcement of the price of freedom. Many counted the cost and stood back. Others, many others, continued the struggle, in every possible way.

Chapter 4

Revolution within the Revolution (1770 – 1790)

I

For some persons, the paradox was painfully obvious. Here were the colonists, moving toward revolution, calling for freedom and justice, pledging to seek liberty or death. And here were their enslaved Africans.

The patriots of New England were based in the major slave ship center of North America. The patriots of Virginia were surrounded by one of the largest populations of captive Africans in the colonies. Together the slaveholding patriots and the slave-trading patriots were planning to make a revolution based on liberty.

The intellectual and moral arguments that the colonists most often used to support their right to revolution against the British crown were based on a three-part foundation: the enlightenment philosophy of Europe; a fascinating religious mixture of Protestant Christianity and rationalist Deism; and the common law of the English state. The essence of their revolutionary power was summed up in the Declaration of Independence, with its affirmation of the equality of mankind before God, the need for the consent of the governed to any government, and the inherent right of revolution against sustained oppression.

In theory, all of these doctrines and frames of thought could be brought to bear against the oppression being carried on by the white American patriot slaveholders as well, and could be used as justification for the revolution of their captives. That was part of the paradox of the American revolutionary period, and there were many children of Africa who saw it very clearly. As a result, black people seized on both

15

the general confusion of the wartime period and the explosive implications of the revolutionary doctrines and put them to the service of the struggle for their own freedom.

II

At the level of verbal protest and affirmation, hundreds of petitions were drawn up in various parts of the black community, especially in the North, based largely on the doctrines of the "Fathers" of the Revolution. For instance, during the war, a group of enslaved blacks in Connecticut petitioned the state's general assembly, saying,

> Reason and Revelation join to declare that we are the creatures of that God, who made of one Blood, and kindred, all the nations of the Earth; we perceive by our own Reflection, that we are endowed with the same faculties as our masters, and there is nothing that leads us to a Belief . . . that we are more obliged to serve them, than they us, and the more we consider of this matter, the more we are convinced of our Right . . . to be free . . . and can never be convinced that we were made to be slaves.

Therefore, when they pressed for emancipation, they said that "we ask for nothing, but what we are fully persuaded is ours to claim." Obviously, men and women who knew they had a *right* to freedom had already made the first, revolutionary break with a system that sought to crush every recognition of their truest human potential. Without such a vision of themselves, there could be no authentic struggle for freedom.

In both the North and the South, tens of thousands of other captive Africans went beyond the initial consciousness, beyond even petitions for freedom. Rather, they made the physical break, using the alarums of the war to cover their flight into the wilderness, to Canada, to Florida. In the course of the Revolution, Thomas Jefferson claimed that thousands of blacks had broken free in one year in Virginia alone. Thus, the other revolution was alive, right in the heart of the Old Dominion.

In Philadelphia, while the Second Continental Congress worked on the task of creating a new nation, black people continued to struggle for their own newness and sense of self-determination. There, Richard Allen and a group of comrades took their stand after they were literally pulled from their knees in the white church where they had worshipped for years. Moving to assert their manhood and dignity, they left the jurisdiction of the white Methodist church, formed the Free African

Society, and eventually laid the foundation for the development of independent black churches in the North.

The struggle for self-determination in the churches became an integral part of the movement for black freedom. For in spite of many weaknesses and faults, those churches evolved as the bases of operation and the training grounds for many of the forces of black struggle. For instance, during the Revolution, African people in Georgia were engaged in critical struggles similar to those in Philadelphia. Especially in and around Savannah, black Baptists who had been gathered into white churches, under the oversight of white pastors and missionaries, seized the time and established independent black churches. When the war was over, whites engaged in a campaign of intimidation, seeking to coerce the black people back into white-controlled churches. In spite of jailings and beatings, the blacks generally held fast, and the independent black Baptist churches that eventually spawned a man named King were firmly established in Georgia. This, too, was part of the other revolution.

III

There were, of course, thousands of black men who fought with the American revolutionary forces. (Even here, they were admitted to military service only after the British had invited blacks to join the ranks of the crown—which thousands did—and after the military situation of the colonists became critical.) Many of them probably thought that their service would contribute to the freedom of their people, that this might bring a coalescence of the two movements for freedom. But they were wrong. Although some of them were granted their own legal freedom in exchange for service in the revolutionary armies, the sacrifices they made did not affect the status of the vast majority of their enslaved people. And their own status as "free" blacks was questionable in a land of black slavery.

They were, of course, only the first of a vast company of black American soldiers to discover such sad paradoxes. As the American revolutionary war ended, the shape of the struggle for black freedom was just beginning to be clear.

Chapter 5

The Revolution That Failed:
Searching for Models (1970 — 1800)

I

It had been a most unusual war of liberation, one that left some seven hundred thousand persons in bondage. Then, as the new nation was developed by the white patriots, the ironies only deepened. For instance, during their struggle with England, slaveholding Founding Fathers like Thomas Jefferson had complained that the mother country forced the well-meaning Americans to participate in the slave trade, against their will. In 1774, the revolutionary First Continental Congress had announced,

> We will neither import nor purchase any slave imported after the first day of December next, after which we will wholly discontinue the slave trade and will neither be concerned in it ourselves nor will we hire our vessels nor sell our commodities or manufactures to those who are concerned in it.

But by the time the constitutional convention went to work some thirteen years later, they had put aside such revolutionary resolutions and instead wrote a stern protection of slavery into the nation's constitution. In the document, both civil and military guarantees against the rise of any black freedom struggle were invoked. White Southerners were permitted to use the bodies of black people when counting for representation in Congress, but they were also allowed to deny all rights of these blacks to their own freedom and representation. Besides, every postwar report from the Gold Coast, the Bay of Biafra, and the entire slaving area, testified that American participation in the

19

slave trade had actually increased since the Revolution. Indeed in many places, these revolutionaries were providing the main strength of the trade in human lives.

II

In a very important sense, then, the revolution had freed the white population to intensify its aggression against black people. As a result, there were two kinds of responses within the ongoing movement of the black freedom struggle. First, a tradition developed which attempted to draw on the best principles and ideals of the American Revolution, sometimes hoping that those principles could be separated from the patriot slaveholders and slave traders who espoused them. Within that tradition of the freedom struggle, black people continued to use the language of the Revolution, especially the liberty or death words of Patrick Henry, and the power of the Declaration of Independence as justifications for black struggle. (Actually, they were trying to call the white American people to see the grandest possibilities of their own revolution, rather than to be satisfied at its meanest levels.)

The other major response of the period was for black people to seek for other, more useful, more viable revolutionary models for their own struggle. (For them, for instance, the liberty-loving words of Patrick Henry and Thomas Jefferson were drowned out by their slaveholding deeds.) Some turned to the literature of the Bible and found hope in the freedom movement of the Hebrew people. Others reached into the rich traditions within their own history, in Africa and America. Before the eighteenth century was over, however, blacks in America were presented with a contemporary model of black revolutionary struggle which bore tremendous force and power, and which was succeeding in overcoming the domination of white power.

Beginning early in the decade of the 1790s, the Africans of San Domingo (Haiti), had begun a series of revolutionary uprisings, first against their Spanish and then their French oppressors. In 1794, Toussaint L'Ouverture assumed leadership of the struggle, and from that time on his name and the news of his people's rebellion spread like wildfire through the black community in America. From their perspective, here was a true revolution. So, for the next decade of the Haitian revolution, and in the decades of Haitian independence, this model was of great inspirational importance to black freedom struggle on these shores.

III

It should be clear, however, that most participants in the other American revolution were well aware of the uniqueness of their own situation, and realized that no single model could serve them. They were not a majority white population separated by an ocean from a king, nor were they a majority black population, separated by the same ocean from deputies, consuls, and emperors. And, in spite of the songs, Bible verses, and sermons, they knew that they were not Israelites either. Rather, as it developed in the nineteenth century, the struggle for black freedom tended to be creatively eclectic, and sought to call upon each of these models and more, at one time or another.

For instance, in the course of the planning for the first attempt at large-scale black insurrection in the nineteenth century, three tall, stalwart brothers in their twenties, Solomon, Martin, and Gabriel Prosser, engaged all these traditions, as well as the powers of African religion. Living in a rural area near Richmond, Virginia, their plan was to capture that capital city and spur a general uprising of black captives throughout the state. Late in August, 1800, after having organized hundreds—some say thousands—of their fellow Africans for the freedom struggle, the young leaders saw their plans shattered by betrayals and the coming of the heaviest rainstorm the area had ever known.

While this level of the movement for black freedom continued, and while there were constant attempts at smaller uprisings, other black people sought alternate means of struggle toward freedom. Constantly, in many parts of the black community, men and women spoke of and planned for a return to Africa. Some, working with leaders like Paul Cuffee, actually made the trip back. For them, this was the way to reconstitute their lives and their history, this was the pathway to the self-determination and independence that they considered impossible to find in America. This "new nation" was not theirs, nor was it dedicated to their freedom. Only black people could create the freedom they needed.

Chapter 6
"Death or Liberty":
Black Style (1801 — 1822)

I

As the first decade of the new century developed, it was obvious that the whites who had made revolution in North America were desperately afraid of the revolution that still stretched its bloody way across the life of Haiti. Having denied black people in this country any real access to the American Revolution, they then searched wildly for ways to cut them off from this African revolution so near at hand. Its successes were too inviting., Its implications were far too clear and sanguinary.

So, for example, in 1804, shortly after the completion of the Louisiana Purchase, the new governor of the Louisiana territory reported on the special precautions he had taken against any revolutionary infiltration that might come by way of the historical lines of contact between his area and the other former French colony in the Caribbean. He said,

> All vessels with slaves on bord (sic) are stopped at Plaquemine, and are not permitted to pass without my consent. This is done to prevent the bringing of slaves that have been concerned in the insurrections of St. Domingo; but while any importations are admitted, many bad characters will be introduced.

In the reversal of definitions that takes place in any struggle for freedom, "bad characters" for the white governor were revolutionary heroes for the black captives, and they were everywhere. While the Louisiana official watched the ships, Governor Richard Byrd of Virginia complained about "slave preachers (who use) their religious meetings as veils for revolutionary schemes." Indeed, he was specifically

23

concerned about one charismatic black religious leader named "General Peter," who was leading a guerrilla force based in the state's Isle of Wight County. Other black characters in North Carolina were organizing rebellion and sending messages saying, "Freedom we want and will have, for we have served this cruel land enuff."

Such bad characters were at the heart of the struggle for black freedom, and finally not even the governor's watch on the coast could keep them out of Louisiana. In January, 1811, hundreds of black men were involved in a movement in the outlying parishes which sent wagons and cartloads of whites fleeing to New Orleans. Unfortunately, this strike for freedom did not work. Among its opponents were three hundred soldiers of the United States Army, who were determined that no black people should ever make the mistake of appropriating the Declaration of Independence to themselves.

II

Still, black men and women did their own reading and thinking, and decided to continue with the struggle. During the War of 1812, blacks again sought to take advantage of the crisis created by white warfare. In 1813, on the Sea Islands along the South Carolina coast, there were heavy rumors of an impending invasion by the British against that area. Blacks began to make serious preparations for a major insurrection, which would coincide with the British invasion. It was said that the black revolutionaries sang a song at the beginning and end of each planning session which included these words:

> Hail! all hail! ye Afric clan
> Hail! ye oppressed, ye Afric band,
> Who toil and sweat in Slavery bound;
>   . . .
> Let *independence* be your aim,
> Ever mindful what 'tis worth.
> Pledge your bodies for the prize
> Pile them even to the skies!

And the chorus clearly voiced the American revolutionary sentiments. It said,

> Firm, united let us be,
> Resolved on death or liberty
> As a band of Patriots joined
> Peace and Plenty we shall find.

The British invasion never came, and as far as we know the black uprising did not take place. But the tradition of struggle was enlarged, and who is to say which of those singers in the South Carolina night eventually joined Denmark Vesey's band?

Of course, even without the immediate availability of another organized insurrectionary movement, there were other avenues of struggle available to black men and women who were "resolved on death or liberty." For instance, in the course of the War of 1812, thousands of black fugitives from slavery fled to the Florida wilderness and many allied themselves with the Indians who were based there. Then, in 1816, one group of approximately three hundred of these black fugitives—including women and children—found an abandoned English fort (Fort Appalachiola), which a group of Seminole Indians had occupied, and which the Seminoles now turned over to their black allies. Repeatedly, the group of outlyers—aided by their Native American allies—used the fort on the northwest coast of Florida not only as a sanctuary from slavery, but as a base for continued attacks against the slaveholders. As knowledge of this freedom outpost spread, it attracted blacks from Georgia, the Mississippi Territory, and as far away as Tennessee.

Because the fort was an obvious and unbearable challenge to white power and authority, as well as a constant testimony to the viability of black life outside of slavery, whites from the surrounding states and territories persistently demanded its destruction. Again, federal troops were available to crush an element of the black freedom struggle, and in the summer of 1816, after a siege of four days, a cannonball from a naval battery hit an ammunition magazine in the fort. The blinding explosion that followed took the lives of almost three hundred of the inhabitants, led to the surrender of the others, and marked the effective beginning of the First Seminole War. White Americans were determined that this dangerous mix of courageous black fugitives and Indian warriors should be rooted out of a place so deep in the heartland of slavery.

III

In a sense, the explosion at Fort Appalachiola was a symbol of the serious questions many black people were raising about the utility of a struggle for freedom in the midst of white America. They asked, how could black people remain on this continent and ever move beyond the range of federal cannon? It was a hard question, and because of it, the thought of emigration never left the black community.

For many men and women, emigration was not an escape. Rather it represented a recognition of the hard realities of America, and a determination to move forward, to go beyond the stunting barriers of life here, to create a new history. At its best, it was a movement of hope, reaching towards new life and independence; not an act of hopelessness and despair. (Many whites, for their own reasons, also favored black emigration, especially the emigration of the free black population; and at times, this white activity and interest led to confusion. But for the most part, black people understood why *they* wanted to leave America.)

Within the expanding emigrationist movement, Africa was considered the focal point of heritage and new beginnings. One of the persons who was offered an opportunity to return to the homeland was Denmark Vesey, the free, middle-aged black craftsman of Charleston, South Carolina. But this proud, impressive leader was bound to the enslaved black community by ties of blood, sentiment, and revolutionary commitment. He was determined to struggle for freedom in America or die. Beginning late in the second decade of the nineteenth century, moving out of a base of the African church in Charleston, Vesey built on a reservoir of long-standing black discontent and hope. After several years, he created what can only be termed an organization of tremendous revolutionary potential.

Through a widespread insurrectionary conspiracy, Vesey and his strong leadership cadre planned to seize power from the white rulers in Charleston and its environs, and somehow to establish freedom for the black people there. Like Gabriel's group, they invoked all the melded traditions of black struggle to encourage and strengthen their recruits. For instance, in his secret meetings Vesey promised the people that "Santo Domingo and Africa will assist us to get our liberty if we will only make the motion first."

At other times he read from the more sanguinary, messianic passages of the Old Testament, and reminded the Africans of Charleston that there was once a freedom struggle under God in which it was reported that "they utterly destroyed all that was in the city, both man and woman, young and old . . . with the edge of the sword." Out in the fields, leading what were supposed to be perfectly safe prayer and witnessing meetings, it is said that he moved the people to the creation of the spiritual "Go Down Moses," and prepared them for their role in the creation of their own freedom.

Suddenly, just when the plot was ready to unfold, Vesey's revolutionary conspiracy was betrayed—a not surprising development when one considers the hundreds of people who were involved over a considerable period of time. In June, 1822, Vesey and more than thirty other alleged leaders in the movement were executed. At the time, it was noted by many persons that neither Vesey nor any of his key lieutenants ever spoke a word that might identify any other persons who were involved. Men marveled at their large silence, and yet, according to black tradition, the essential message of Denmark Vesey broke through clearly to young black people like Nat Turner in Virginia and Frederick Augustus Washington Bailey on the Eastern Shore of Maryland.

Chapter 7

Freedom Struggle in the North: Intimations of Things to Come (1820 – 1830)

I

By the mid-1820s, the legal institution of slavery had been virtually abolished in the states above the Mason-Dixon Line. But this was no signal for the end of the freedom struggle in the North. Rather, the northern states became a stage on which men might catch some crucial intimations of what a postslavery America might be like. On that stage, the one hundred and thirty thousand black Northerners quickly found that the elimination of legal bondage did not seriously affect the continued presence of virulent white racism. It was expressed in a thousand forms of antiblack prejudice, proscription, discrimination, exploitation, and physical attack.

Representing only about 2.5 percent of the population of the northern states, blacks often found themselves in a beleaguered position. Wherever they turned, the marks of white oppression were present. When they looked for housing, they were usually allowed only the worst, most often at exorbitant prices. When they looked for jobs, the line of prejudice greatly limited their choice. In many cities they were liable to attack on public transportation vehicles. Throughout the North, most black people were deprived of the right to vote and to hold public offices. In addition to these acts of discrimination, blacks were often subjected to scurrilous barrages in the public press. There were many times when the action of northern mobs, or the slave-catching agents of southern slaveholders made it literally necessary for black people to fight for their lives and for the little property they may have amassed. By and large, such treatment was a vivid illustration of the fact that blacks had no intrinsic citizenship rights under the federal constitution—or in most state constitutions.

So, in their small enclaves (11,000 in New York City, 7,500 in Philadelphia, 1,600 in Boston, for instance), the struggle for black freedom was largely defined by these constrictions and attacks on their humanity. Fighting for freedom meant that they fought for jobs and housing; they petitioned, demonstrated, and campaigned for the franchise; they committed acts of civil disobedience on transportation facilities and in other public accommodations. They organized self-defense militia within the black community. By the end of the 1820s, they had founded the first newspapers to take up their cause.

In addition to these more obvious elements of the struggle for humane livelihood and for the right to participate actively in the life of their communities, blacks in the North were waging another more subtle kind of battle. Through a plethora of clubs, lyceums, debating societies, churches, and improvement societies, they were also attempting to prove to the white world (and to their doubting brethen) that they were worthy of all the things they fought for. So they sought to bind up the wounds of their own community, to improve the quality of its life, to serve its needy, to demonstrate their capacity for self-determination, self-improvement, and freedom. Although such things hardly seemed revolutionary, they were that part of the struggle that gave the lie to the white aspersions on black character, manhood, and capacity. Even more important, they built the black community from within, preparing it for the continuing stages of its struggle towards new humanity.

II

Beyond all these activities on their own behalf, this embattled black northern community was constantly engaged in action on behalf of that vast majority of their people who lived in the slave states. Some went so far as to enter (or, just as likely, reenter) the South on dangerous rescue missions on behalf of relatives and friends in slavery. Others made places of refuge available along the way for the fugitives. Many persons in churches, lodges, and societies, as well as in individual families, gave regular assistance when the escaped brothers and sisters finally made their way to the northern cities and towns. Besides, they signed hundreds of petitions, sent them to Congress, wrote to newspapers, supported and participated in the rising abolitionist movement—any and everything to bring about the downfall of slavery and the emancipation of their people.

Crucial to this northern activity was the rise of the black news-papers, the first of which was *Freedom's Journal*. It appeared in 1827, declaring that, "it shall ever be our duty to vindicate our brethren when oppressed, and to lay the cure before the publick *(sic)*." Of equal importance was the national black convention movement, which began to take hold at the end of the decade. Almost yearly calls went out from and to the black community, and especially its leadership, urging them to gather to discuss issues of mutual concern relating to the struggle for freedom. Such activity, of course, held radical potentials, challeng-ing the rights or abilities of whites—even white friends—to determine the best means of struggle and the best definitions of freedom for black people.

III

Both the development of the newspapers and the rise of the conven-tion movement placed great emphasis on the use of the written and spoken word as instruments in the fight for freedom. During that period, the critical potential of the word was seen most clearly in the life of the man who happened to be an agent for *Freedom's Journal* in Boston, David Walker. A native of Wilmington, North Carolina, Walker had traveled extensively in some of the more western states and territories before settling in Boston in 1827. During his travels he had caught a broad and unforgettable picture of the sufferings of his people. To make a living, Walker was a used clothing dealer. Actually, his life was consumed by the struggles of the black community toward freedom, in both the North and the South. Out of that driving com-mitment and concern, out of the anguished memories of his travels, and after a prodigious amount of work, he produced in 1829 one of the signal documents of the other American revolution, a seventy-six-page pamphlet, called *Walker's Appeal . . . to the Colored Citizens of the World But in Particular and very Expressly to those of the United States of America.*

As the title suggested, Walker's *Appeal* was the first Pan-African-oriented call to struggle published in America. Its pages sought to analyze the situation black people faced as a result of the racism and "avarice" of white America. Then, predicting divine assistance in the fight, the booklet urged all the children of Africa in this country to enter into a serious commitment to the active struggle for freedom,

whatever the cost. In his summons to revolution, Walker was insistent
that

> The man who would not fight under our Lord and Master Jesus Christ, in
> the glorious and heavenly cause of freedom and of God . . . ought to be
> kept with all of his children or family, in slavery, or in chains, to be
> butchered by his cruel enemies.

At the same time, in the manner of so many similar calls for black
struggle which would come after him, Walker's *Appeal* was also directed toward the white community. Interestingly enough, Walker re-
served the name "Americans" for the white people of the continent,
and said to them,

> I speak Americans for your good. We must and shall be free . . . in spite
> of you. You may do your best to keep us in wretchedness and misery, to
> enrich you and your children, but God will deliver us from under you.
> And wo, wo, *(sic)* will be to you if we have to obtain our freedom by
> fighting.

In that context, the *Appeal* put forth repeated calls to the "Americans"
for repentence and the changing of their rapacious ways.

Unfortunately, the "Americans" chose not to hear David Walker's
appeal to them for radical change, for faithfulness to their own revolutionary and religious traditions. Instead, as his pamphlet ran
quickly through three editions and found its way down into the South,
all the whites chose to hear were his insurrectionary calls to black
struggle for freedom. Threats against his life came from every direction, a price was placed on his head; and in June, 1830, less than a year
after the *Appeal* was first published, David Walker was found dead on
the streets of Boston. The black community was convinced that he had
been poisoned, but by then his *Appeal* had taken on a life of its own,
had become a milestone in the militant pamphleteering tradition of the
other American revolution.

Chapter 8

"Slay My Enemies with Their Own Weapons" — Nat Turner (1825 – 1835)

I

For almost a century and a half, beginning in 1831, there has been persistent speculation over the question of whether or not any copies of Walker's *Appeal* found their way into Southampton County, Virginia, where Nat Turner lived. The speculation is interesting, but essentially unimportant. For Nat Turner and David Walker were obviously in touch with the same voices, attuned to the same spirits, obsessed by the same messianic calls to struggle for black freedom. Thus, whether or not the *Appeal* reached Nat Turner was not the point, its basic message and assumptions had long possessed him.

Born in 1800 into Virginia's slavery, Nat Turner was a product of the deepest inner life of the black community. His earliest relationship to that community was through his immediate family: his mother, father, and grandmother—a family not far removed from Africa. There is every evidence that this family did not consider themselves simply as "slaves," for if they had, Nat's father would not have broken away to freedom and Turner himself would not likely have become a Messenger. Indeed, from the outset, the members of his household taught young Nat that he was meant for some special purpose in this world (and, therefore, so were they) and they guided him in that path.

For instance, the immediate family and the surrounding black community was convinced, with Nat, that he had learned to read without human instruction. Soon they were fascinated by his early experiments in the ancient crafts of Africa and Asia: pottery, papermaking, and the making of gunpowder. Perhaps they thought that such things were all

33

manifestations of the esoteric knowledge the community was convinced that he possessed, including, for instance, knowledge of events
and times before his own birth. Meanwhile, his grandmother, "a very
religious woman," instructed him in what she knew of the Christian
Bible and the traditions of Africa, and she taught him the songs that
came with nighttime and sleep to the black community.

We are not sure of all that Nat learned from his immediate family,
but it is clear that his father taught him at least one thing: slavery was
not meant to be endured. (Who can imagine the conversations in that
family before his father ran away into the shadows of history? How
much of their substance did Nat carry to his own death?) From the rest
of the community of captives, Nat learned the same lesson. He knew of
the myriad injustices suffered by his people. He learned their songs
and prayers, their stories and heroes—like Gabriel and Vesey. But Nat
claimed that his most profound lessons in struggle came from his own
lonely, personal wrestling with the spirit, whom he readily identified as
"the same spirit who spoke to the prophets." According to certain black
traditions, it was out of Nat's hard solitude in the forests that the song
"Steal Away to Jesus" first emerged.

II

By the time he was twenty-five, Turner had grappled many times in
the darkness of the woods and fields with the spirit of his God. He had
been driven into his own thirty-day wilderness experience, had seen
visions of black and white angels battling in the heavens, had read
messages in blood on the leaves of the trees, thereby catching up the
traditions of Africa and the Bible which had been so fully mixed in the
teachings of his grandmother. He was especially impressed by the
words he regularly heard in his solitude: "Seek ye first the kingdom of
God and all things shall be added unto you."

As the years went by, his visions led him to the conviction that the
kingdom he sought was a kingdom of justice and righteousness, a
kingdom of freedom for black people. Moreover, he was convinced that
all slaveholders, all supporters of slavery, were enemies of this divinely ordained kingdom, and that he, Nat Turner, was called to vindicate the righteousness of God. Indeed, he said that the spirit told him
he should simply wait for the proper sign, and when it came, "I should
arise and prepare myself, and slay my enemies with their own
weapons."

In February, 1831, the sign came in an eclipse of the sun. After one false start in July, 1831, Nat was prepared in August. His planning had obviously been far less extensive than that of Gabriel or Vesey. Perhaps he was far more convinced of direct, divine intervention than they. Whatever was involved, in the darkness of an early morning near the end of August, Nat began his work of judgment. He moved with a core cadre of four other men, and an initial fighting group of some fifteen to twenty others, expecting to build his army of messianic struggle as he went.

According to the teachings of the black community, Turner had no doubt about the context of black struggle in which he was operating. One oral tradition records in this way Nat's last words of instruction to his followers:

> Remember, we do not go forth for the sake of blood and carnage; but it is necessary that, in the commencement of this revolution, all the whites we meet should die, until we have an army strong enough to carry out the war on a Christian basis. Remember that ours is not a war for robbery, nor to satisfy our passions; it is a struggle for freedom.

Whatever the actual words, the definition was precise: it was a war for freedom, and the small band, armed with hatchets and axes, set out on its sanguinary way. In their movement towards freedom, as they marched down Barrow Road, heading towards Jerusalem (Virginia), planning to capture a cache of arms there, they took the lives of at least sixty to sixty-five white men, women, and children.

III

But they never reached Jerusalem. For they were poorly armed for a struggle that finally pitted them against the state of Virginia and the military forces of the United States. Thus, when the heavens did not break open on their behalf, "General" Nat and his men found themselves under the gun, scattered, killed, captured. For a time, Nat escaped capture; and while they searched for him, most of his men were executed and a wholesale slaughter of black people was unleashed in the area. Even as some of Nat's companions faced death, however, it was said that "in the aggonies *(sic)* of Death (they) declared that they was happy for that God had a hand in what they had been doing."

When Nat was finally captured in October, 1831, he told his counsel that he wanted to plead "not guilty," for he "did not feel" that he was a guilty person; he was simply following the commands of God. At that point, even a white Virginia lawyer caught something of the special character of this hero of black struggle. For at the end, he described Nat, and himself, in this way:

> clothed with rags and covered with chains, yet daring to raise his mana-
> cled hands to heaven, with a spirit soaring above the attributes of man; I
> looked on him and my blood curdled in my veins.

The lawyer was not alone. The essential tie between black religion and the struggle for black freedom had been written in much blood. Across the South and the nation men trembled at the thought of black preachers and their potential for transforming the religion of the slaveholders into the messianic, revolutionary calling of the captives.

Out of such fear and trembling, after Southhampton a congeries of new laws swept across the South seeking to stem the movement of black freedom. They were laws prohibiting the captives from being taught how to read and write, forbidding them to preach, laws insisting on increased white vigilance, laws interdicting independent black meetings. Essentially they were laws testifying that the earlier body of similar legislation simply had not worked; and yet men continued to try to legislate away the struggle for freedom.

For instance, shortly after Turner's insurrection, this statute was enacted in Mississippi:

> It is unlawful for any slave, free Negro, or mulatto to preach the gospel
> upon pain of receiving thirty-nine lashes upon the naked back of the . . .
> preacher.

But neither laws, lashes, nor death had yet been able to halt the movement towards freedom, and no one could predict where Nat Turner might arise in another form. Indeed, before long, there was a sense in which Turner did return among his people. For blacks responded to the new laws and lashes with an answer that whites could hear without really hearing. Like so many black-struggle answers, it was disguised in a song, and some of the words said,

> You might be Carroll from Carrollton
> Arrive here night afo' Lawd make creation
> But you can't keep the World from movering round
> And not turn her back from the gaining ground.

Only when that last ambiguous line was repeated again and again in the chorus might it become clear that "not turn her" was old Prophet Nat in disguise, alive on the lips of his people. Even in song, the struggle continued.

Chapter 9

Resistance, Rebellion, and Flight: The Unmaking of Slaves (1830 — 1840)

I

In the development of the pre-Civil War struggle for black freedom, Nat Turner's status was clear. His break with the slave system, his open challenge to its power, his audacious attempt to organize his fellow captives to seek a new kingdom of justice—these were all unambiguous elements of the other American revolution. At the same time, there were many aspects of the movement for black freedom which were far more subtle, much less easy to identify as serious attacks on the system of slavery or as challenges to the government that protected the system. Nevertheless, it is of utmost importance that we recognize the crucial role those more covert forces played in the defeat of slavery.

At this point, it would be wise to review Kenneth Stampp's helpful description of the slave system and its methodology for producing the ideal slaves (in *The Peculiar Institution*). Only as one ponders this is it possible to appreciate the varied ways in which black men and women resisted and eroded all mechanisms for the making of slaves. Using the documents of the nineteenth-century slave owners, Stampp noted a methodology for creating slaves out of free human beings, for developing servile mentalities from childhood, which could be broken into six related elements. They were:

1. The establishment of strict discipline over the captive African community in order to develop "unconditional submission" among them.

37

2. The development within black people of a sense of rank inferiority as individuals and as a group, especially in relation to their African ancestry.
3. The development of raw fear, "to awe them with a sense of their master's enormous power." (Of course, it was always to be understood that behind the power of the master stood the constitutional power of the local and federal governments.)
4. The establishment within the enslaved person of a sense that the master's welfare was really synonymous with his own, and therefore must be defended and forwarded at all cost.
5. The creation of a willingness within the African-American captives to accept the slaveholders' standards of conduct as their own.
6. The development within the captive people of "a habit of perfect dependence" upon those who claimed to be their masters.

II

When these elements of the slave-making process are properly assessed, then it is clear that there were many important, subtle aspects of black rebellion which resisted and subverted the process. Indeed, every enslaved black man, woman, and child who began to think his or her own thoughts about liberty, justice, and independence was a participant in the freedom struggle. Many of the purposely broken tools, the carefully stolen goods, the mysterious fires, the use of African herbal knowledge for poisons, the "accidental" deaths of overseers, the suicides and abortions, were all part of the black determination to break the slave-making system, to resist it, to assert some significant level of freedom and independence, often while remaining in the exterior coils of the South's peculiar institution.

Then, of course, it is necessary to measure properly those persons who decided to make the physical break, to flee toward freedom, to join the constantly moving stream of fugitives northward or to Mexico or to the Indians of the wilderness. Every decision to break the chain of fear and doubt, every final tearful parting with friends and family, every passage into the darkness of the future—every person who decided for freedom and moved to seize it presented an unmistakable challenge to that system that sought to create and maintain slaves.

III

Black people who made these internal and external breaks with the system paid a great cost, a fact that a young black captive named

Frederick Augustus Washington Bailey was to discover in the 1830s. Bailey, a tall, strong, and immensely creative young man, who grew up on the Eastern Shore of Maryland, was in his late teens when in 1833 his "owner" sent him to a slave breaker. It was the job of this white man to see to it that neither Bailey nor any other enslaved person ever developed the moral strength and physical courage to challenge the system of his bondage.

The goal was to break his natural will to be free, largely through the use of physical force. But young Bailey, though faltering, did not break. After several harsh beatings by Covey, he decided that he would take his stand. So, with the encouragement of an African medicine man, he challenged Covey. Bailey told the white man that "he had used me like a brute for six months, and that I was determined to be used so no longer." That day, they wrestled and fought for two hours in the barn where Bailey had been taken for a beating, and the black young man finally prevailed.

Later, when he had become Frederick Douglass, the barnyard fighter claimed that "this battle with Mr. Covey was the turning point of my career as a slave." According to Douglass, the fight "rekindled the few expiring embers of freedom, and revived within me a sense of my own manhood."

But the endurance of such physical abuses was only a part of the price that men and women had to pay for the freeing of their spirits, their bodies, and their minds. For instance, when Bailey-Douglass finally began to make serious plans with several of his friends for an escape from slavery, they found that some of the greatest obstacles they faced were within themselves. As they met to discuss the ways in which they would actually break free and make their way north, their vivid fears were described by Douglass in this way,

> At times we were almost disposed to give up, and try to content our-
> selves with our wretched lot. . . . Upon either side we saw grim death,
> assuming the most horrid shapes. Now it was starvation, causing us to
> eat our own flesh;—now we were contending with the waves and were
> drowned;—now we were overtaken, and torn to pieces by the fangs of
> the terrible bloodhound . . . (or) after swimming rivers, encountering
> wild beasts, sleeping in woods, suffering hunger and nakedness—we
> were overtaken by our pursuers, and, in our resistance, were shot dead
> upon the spot!

Such terrifying visions were not simply products of the wild imaginations of Douglass and his friends. They were based on the actual experiences of many black people who had set out on freedom road. They were part of the objective and subjective realities that they had to conquer. And yet they continued to move out of the South by the thousands, not simply from the Eastern Shore of Maryland, but from Texas and Louisiana, from Mississippi and Alabama, from Georgia and the coasts of South Carolina, sometimes covering more than a thousand miles in the quest for freedom.

Thus, there are three essential reasons why these lonely individuals, these families, these communities in flight, must be counted as a crucial part of the other American revolution. First, they had fought and won the inner struggles of the spirit which must precede all truly revolutionary movement. Second, they presented continuous challenges to the slave system, eroding its strength, testifying to its weaknesses, depriving it of valuable property. Finally, as their numbers increased in the 1830s and 1840s, these black fugitives became the source of increasingly acerbic confrontations between the forces of the white North and white South over the best way to protect the South's alleged economic and political rights to black lives. Eventually, the insistent presence of the fugitives would stir both white and black populations into a state of intense agitation, opening them to the coming of war.

IV

Before the major conflict came, these black runaways were involved in other battles, some directly against the armies of the federal government. For instance, in the 1830s, many persons in flight from slavery were still choosing Florida as their place of refuge and the Native Americans there as their allies. At the same time, they continued to attract other black fugitives from the farms and plantations of Florida, as well as from other states. By the middle of the decade, the white community of the South had determined that this combination of continuing Indian presence and of black-Indian alliance was absolutely intolerable.

At the end of 1835, as a part of the Indian removal policy of Andrew Jackson and his government, Federal military forces opened hostilities in Florida against the remaining Seminoles and their black allies. Once again, in this Second Seminole War, blacks were fighting for their freedom against the forces of the American government. Indeed, they were so deeply involved in the gruelling guerrilla warfare that a contemporary white historian offered this assessment of their role:

[He said,] The Negroes, from the commencement of the Florida war, have, for their numbers, been the most formidable foe, more blood-thirsty, active and revengeful than the Indian.

Only after several years of struggle did the combination of federal deceit and overwhelming firepower finally lead the majority of the Indians and blacks to end their resistance.

Then, when the Indians were forced to make the long, painful trek from their ancient burial places in the East to the strange land provided by the government across the Mississippi, hundreds of black people went with them.

V

As these children of Africa trekked westward towards an ambiguous future, the fight for black freedom continued in the places where it had begun, on the European slave ships. The best known of these nineteenth-century insurrections took place in 1839, on a Spanish ship, *L'Amistad*, off the coast of Cuba. Because Cinque, the leader of the African rebellion, and his men guided the ship to American waters after their victory, they joined the history of this ongoing struggle.

Two years later, a similar uprising took place in a setting more immediately connected to the American situation. In this case, 131 enslaved blacks were being transported from Richmond, Virginia, to New Orleans, Louisiana on the ship, *Creole*. The slave-trading journey was never completed. Instead, the black captives, led by men named Madison Washington and Ben Blacksmith, engineered a successful insurrection and made their way to the relative safety of the British colony of Nassau. With the assistance of their fellow Africans on that island, and in spite of many American protests, the temporary black masters of the *Creole* completed their own journey, and were never returned to slavery.

In Maryland barns, in the seemingly endless nights of escape, in the everglades of Florida, on the trail of tears to the west, aboard slave ships with strange names, the struggle continued; the other revolution took root.

Chapter 10

Vigilance and Disobedience:
The Northern Duties (1830 – 1840)

I

When black men, women, and children made the break out of slavery toward the North and Canada, they often found they were not alone. All along the way towards the destinations they had fashioned in their hopes and dreams there were places of haven, conveyances of hope, manned by other blacks and their white allies. Sometimes, these cities of refuge were no more than a clearing in the woods where food and clothing could be found. At times they were located in the upper level of an old barn, or in the dangerously cramped space of a steamer trunk. At times the place of safety was the false bottom of a wagon rolling by the unsuspecting glances of a score of hostile eyes. Or it was the hold of a ship (which now had black crewmen and was headed out of slavery, along the Mississippi or the Ohio).

All the black people who offered their food and clothing to the fugitives, their homes and wagons to the black folk in flight, their lies to the authorities, their unctuous, deceptive smiles to the search parties, and sometimes their lives to the cause—all these were engaged in serious civil disobedience against the laws of the United States. Often this informally organized system of disobedience which grew out of a commitment to black freedom was called the Underground Railroad. In its deepest reality, it was an underground element of the other American revolution.

Here, then, was one of the major effects of the unending stream of fugitives. The black people who streaked like shadows of judgment across the landscape of America were evoking new forms of struggle and conflict. For, as they moved towards the North, and as they sought refuge there, they elicited support from their brothers and sisters, which in many cases could only be expressed in civil disobedience to federal laws. As the size of the runaway movement increased, blacks in the North recognized the cost they were being called to pay. For instance, in 1835, delegates to the national black convention meeting in Philadelphia resolved that

> our duty to God, and to the principles of human rights, so far exceeds our allegiance to those laws that return the slave again to his master . . . that we recommend our people to peaceably bear the punishment those (laws) inflict, rather than aid in returning their brethen again to slavery.

In addition to the many individual acts of assistance, "Vigilance committees" to impede the slave catchers and aid the fugitives were formed in dozens of northern communities where black people lived. As with so many elements of the other American revolution, this black civil disobedience was impelled by positive, human impulses and desires. Duty to God, commitment to human rights, concern with the brethren were the decisive, impelling forces. Through these actions of aid and succor, the black community of the North was inextricably tied to the larger future of the masses of black people in the South, and was able to play a critical role in the struggle for their joint liberation.

II

In the course of this phase of the struggle, there were hundreds of occasions on which black people in the North physically intervened to rescue fugitives from the slave catchers and their legal aids. For instance, late in 1836, a black vigilance committee in Boston organized such a rescue and precipitated what became known there as the "Abolition Riot." Two black young women had been claimed as the fugitive property of a Baltimore man, and his attorney had brought the women into court to secure the right to return them to his client.

Just as the lawyer was addressing the federal official, we are told that

> someone in the spectator's section shouted "Go, go," whereupon some colored people rushed to the bench and bore the prisoners down the courthouse steps and shoved them into a waiting carriage.

In the course of reporting this well-planned and defiant action, a contemporary document referred to a participating black sister "of great size" who scrubbed floors for a living; the report said that she "threw her arms around the neck of one officer, immobilizing him," thus making it impossible for the man to give chase to the rescue party.

Although the sister "of great size" and great courage remains among the thousands of nameless participants of these northern rescue squads, it is important that the vigilance committees also proved a training ground for many well-known black leaders of the period. For instance, Henry Highland Garnet, David Walker, William Wells Brown, Charles S. Ray, Lewis Hayden, Jermain Loguen, and John Mercer Langston (Langston Hughes's maternal grandfather) were all developed—at least in part—through the mechanism of these local committees.

The spirit of the vigilance committees was typified in a young man named David Ruggles in New York City. A native of Connecticut, Ruggles had made his way to the big city in 1827, when he was seventeen years old. Although he wandered into many modes of earning a living—from selling butter to selling books, the center of his life, like that of David Walker, was service to black struggle. By 1835 Ruggles was a leading figure in the New York vigilance committee, and paid the price for his role when his bookstore was burned down, and when he was almost kidnapped.

None of this deterred him, and he continued the creative underground activities, engaging in rescues, providing hiding places, securing jobs for the continuing stream of black fugitives who made their way to his city. He was still on duty when Frederick Augustus Washington Bailey finally broke loose and moved stealthily into New York in 1838. Ruggles took him in. Later the vigilance leader brought his own brilliant friend, the clergyman, J. W. C. Pennington, to his home to perform a secret marriage ceremony for Bailey and the woman he later called "the wife of [my] youth." Then Ruggles quietly sent the couple off to New Bedford, Massachusetts. There Bailey became Frederick Douglass, practiced his trade as a caulker in the shipyards, and began to sense his own deepest vocation in the struggle.

III

Eventually, Frederick Douglass joined Ruggles and many of the other vigilance committee leaders as active participants and leaders in the white-controlled, organized abolitionist movement. But there were other paths of struggle leading from the vigilance groups. In Pittsburgh, Pennsylvania, Martin Delany, a young specialist in the common contemporary medical practices of "Cupping, Leeching, and Bleeding," as well as an aspiring doctor, was also a participant in these rescue operations. But he was not satisfied with the alternatives for black freedom which were proposed by the abolitionist movement. So, late in 1839, he set out for a journey through many parts of the southwestern states and territories (perhaps going as far south as Cuba) searching for a place where black people might establish an independent nation. After traveling for almost a year, Delany concluded that there were too many whites wherever he went in the continental area. So he bided his time and worked on that persistent question: what is the best situation for American blacks who seek self-determination and self-government? It was a question that would remain at the heart of the struggle for black freedom.

Chapter 11

Black Abolitionism — and Beyond (1830 — 1850)

I

While the black fugitives, insurrectionaries, outlyers, and quiet resistants provided a constant pressure against the system of slavery from the underside, while they exacerbated the tensions between the white North and South, another sort of pressure was being applied by their brethren in the Abolitionist movement. Without having formally used the term, black folk were, of course, the first abolitionists, the first to offer their lives in the struggle for the immediate end of the system of African bondage. Nor was this surprising; who knew the system more intimately than they? Who suffered more deeply from its crimes? Who had given the greatest number of familial hostages to its unpredictable perversities? Who therefore, could be more completely committed to its total abolition?

So, when the first white men submitted their petitions for the abolition of slavery during the colonial period, there had already been black precedents in protest—beginning with the oral tradition—aboard the ships and on the slave-bound American land. When larger local and national white organizations for abolition came into being, they often had to turn to black churches for meeting places. When the national white abolitionist periodicals began to develop in the nineteenth century, they depended largely upon the support of black subscribers for their existence. In black men and women like Charles Remond, J. W. C. Pennington, Robert Purvis, Sojourner Truth, and Frederick Douglass the organized, white-controlled antislavery movement found many of its most effective speakers and organizers. Indeed, by the 1830s, black people had provided both the base and the heart of the formal abolitionist movement.

When the American Anti-Slavery Society (AASS) was formed in the winter and spring of 1833–1834, there were three black men on its twelve-man executive committee. In a sense, the AASS provided the first organized experience of concrete black-white alliance in the history of the struggle for black freedom in America; and, not surprisingly, this initial experiment bore many of the seeds of the strengths and weaknesses of all such alliances.

II

In the course of the life of the American Anti-Slavery Society, three central issues and problems came into focus. First, blacks controlled neither the actual power nor the machinery of the organization (and others like it). Men like William Lloyd Garrison, Joshua Levitt, Lewis Tappan, and others, though often honorable, courageous, and untiring in their work, had no doubt that this was a white country and that the AASS was one of their organizations for the cleansing of the nation.

Second, considering the state of America, North and South, it should not have been surprising to find that there were many white participants who were adamantly against slavery, but who still fell far short of a commitment to black equality in all realms of the nation's life. Many abolitionists failed to work for that equality either in their organization, their businesses, or their personal lives.

Third, it was obvious that the basic driving forces of the black and white abolitionists were not always the same. By and large, as they crisscrossed the young nation, lecturing, agitating, petitioning, preaching, and organizing against the evils of the slave system, the white men and women were essentially seeking the vindication of the America their fathers had defined. The freedom of the slaves was a means to this end. Ultimately they worked to free the vision of their Pilgrim and revolutionary forefathers from the sinful institution of bondage. They searched for a kingdom that was largely an extrapolation of their own best hopes for America.

The blacks in contrast, were fighting for their lives, and for the lives of their mothers and children, their fathers and uncles and aunts. They were seeking to reunite lost families. They were attempting to release all the life and hope that lay cramped and bludgeoned in the South. On a certain level, for the black abolitionists, the end of slavery was an end in itself, for it carried with it a host of very human hopes and dreams.

At the same time, when they were most sober, the black abolitionists knew that the end of slavery would not mean the realization of a free and humane society. Their experience in the North had taught them that. Even when they were most sanguine about the coming of a society of justice and brotherhood in America, these black abolitionists knew that it would be neither a return to America's bloody Eden, nor an extrapolation on the white-controlled kingdom of God. Rather, the new society would have to be hewn out of the harsh and beautiful American experience, as a new creation, extending in depth and meaning beyond anything white men—or black men—had ever known. At its best, the other American revolution held that new creation as its ultimate goal.

III

In 1840, as a result of certain long-festering political and personal differences, there was a final split within the ranks of the American Anti-Slavery Society, and a new organization, the American and Foreign Anti-Slavery Society was created. Although some black abolitionists fell on both sides of the dispute, the most important effect of the split in the white ranks was to add impetus to the persistent call for independent black organizing in the freedom cause. The national black conventions, which had been neglected, were now revived. In them, blacks explored far more radical acts of struggle than they had been free to propose in the white-dominated antislavery societies.

For instance, at the black convention held in Buffalo, New York, in 1843, the popular young abolitionist preacher from Troy, Henry Highland Garnet, stirred the session to a fever pitch with his resounding—and somewhat theatrical—call for insurrection among the enslaved brethen in the South. After suggesting a wide-scale campaign of systematic noncooperation, Garnet said that it was necessary to face the fact that "there is not much hope of redemption without the shedding of blood." (This biblically based statement continued to find wide application throughout the history of the other American revolution.) So he offered his incendiary counsel to his brothers and sisters in slavery, saying

> Brethren, arise, arise! Strike for your lives and liberties. Now is the day and the hour. Let every slave throughout the land do this, and the days of slavery are numbered. You cannot be more oppressed than you have been . . . RATHER DIE FREEMEN THAN LIVE TO BE SLAVES. REMEMBER THAT YOU ARE FOUR MILLION! . . . Let your motto be resistance! *resistance!* RESISTANCE! No oppressed people have ever secured their liberty without resistance.

After a fierce debate, in which Frederick Douglass opposed Garnet's position, the convention decided by one vote that it would not be wise to send such a message to the exposed bondsmen in the South from the relative safety of Buffalo, New York. Later, many white abolitionists condemned Garnet's statements (as they had David Walker's), partly because they loved white America more than they hated the injustice of black slavery. But it was obvious that a new level of anger, rebellion, and resistance was rising in the black community.

IV

Indeed, certain black traditions claim that it was in those heightening days of the 1840s that a group of black young men in Saint Louis went further than Garnet, and actually formed the cadre of a secret black guerrilla army. Called the Knights of Liberty, it is said that they dedicated themselves to organizing and arming for the next ten years; then, if it proved necessary, they would lead a military movement against the slave system of the South. It is no longer possible to be certain about the nature of this liberation army—if, indeed, it did exist, but we do know that black men and women had such thoughts regularly on their minds as they lived through a period in which the power of slavery and its supporters seemed constantly on the rise.

It was in this kind of anxious setting that Martin Delany came to the National Convention of Colored Freemen in Cleveland, Ohio, in 1848 and proposed,

> Whereas we find ourselves far behind the military tactics of the civilized world, Resolved that this Convention recommend to the colored Freeman of North America to use every means in their power to obtain that science, so as to enable them to measure arms with assailants without and invaders within.

Although the resolution failed, the informal organizing of black armed groups went on apace in the North. For many black persons were fully serious when they spoke of "no redemption without the shedding of blood." They knew too much of their history, and had seen too much of America to expect anything else in the long struggle for their freedom.

Chapter 12

White Compromise, Black Struggle: The Search for "Our Country" (1850 — 1854)

I

By the middle of the nineteenth century, the hundreds of thousands of Africans who had survived the terrors of the middle passage had now become an unrealized nation of nearly four million persons within the United States. Almost 90 percent of that number, more than three million black folk, were in slavery, living in the South and Southwest. All together, both free and bond, black people represented some 16 percent of the entire population, nearly one out of every six persons.

By 1850, the implications of this major black presence for the total life of the nation were becoming more painfully clear with each passing day. Certain ironic lessons were being written in blood on the streets and fields and walls of America.

In the first place, in a society committed to white supremacy, any efforts by black people to struggle for life, liberty, and the pursuit of human dignity carried an intrinsic revolutionary character. Indeed, in a nation that was unabashedly described by its citizens as "a white man's country," the black presence itself was unbalancing, dangerous, potentially explosive. Moreover, when a large, enslaved population was massed at the base of a society supposedly committed to freedom and opportunity, no white movement towards this purported freedom could escape the heavy weight and the jagged edges of the chains that black folk wore.

Nowhere was this latter paradox more obvious than in the conflict between the "democratic" white movement for "free land for free men" in the new West, and the expanding system of slavery. Ever since the days of the Constitutional Convention, the issue of the black enslaved presence in the newly usurped western lands was an abrasive one. White leaders were constantly trying to work out compromises to determine how far toward the Pacific (and the Canadian border) could slavery and all its economic, cultural, and political baggage be allowed to go. In 1820, the Missouri Compromise set the slave/free line at the 36° 30' parallel in the territory of the Louisiana Purchase. But as white Americans took the land of the Mexicans and the Indians by conquest and deceit, as they pushed relentlessly west and north, the question of black slavery in this newly acquired land was raised again.

II

By the end of the decade of the 1840s, the American body politic was being ripped apart in the course of the arguments over this matter. In Congress, in town halls, on street corners and drawing rooms, in journals across the land, an acrimonious and sometimes deadly debate built up. And the black presence was at the heart of it. As white men looked at the new territories and planned for their settlement, three major points of view were pressed forward. One group, usually known as Free Soilers, wanted no slavery anywhere in the new lands (but most of them wanted no free blacks either). Another, a proslavery group, believed that slavery should be free to go wherever white men were free to go, and receive federal protection as well. A third group, advocating "popular sovereignty," claimed that the white settlers in each area should decide upon the slavery issue by majority vote. None of the groups had in mind any question of black freedom, equality, or democratic participation.

Then, in 1850, just as it appeared that the debates over the issue would tear the country apart, a new compromise plan was enacted by Congress which tried to give each of the three white camps something of what they desired. Most important for our purposes was the offering of a drastically strengthened fugitive slave law to the proslavery forces. Such a law placed all black people at the mercy of the slave catchers and gave them no recourse in the courts. Once more, it was obvious that white compromise had been achieved at the cost of black freedom.

The Fugitive Slave Act of 1850 served as a tremendous catalyst to the forces of resistance which were already at work in the black community. All across the North, wherever their numbers made it possible, black people gathered together to protest the law and to discuss their possible responses to its harsh and deadly provisions. Wherever they met, the underlying sentiments were the same as those recorded in a meeting in Elmira, New York, where the blacks "vowed they would defy the Fugitive Slave Law at the sacrifice of their lives." At an anti-Fugitive-Slave-Law rally in Allegheny, Pennsylvania, Martin Delany pointedly turned his glowing black face toward the white mayor of the city and said,

> If any man approaches [my] house in search of a slave—I care not who he may be, whether constable, or sheriff, magistrate or even judge of the Supreme Court—nay let it be [President Millard Fillmore] surrounded by his cabinet as his bodyguard, with the Declaration of Independence waving above his head as his banner, and the constitution of his country upon his breast as his shield—if he crosses the threshhold of my door, and I do not lay him a lifeless corpse at my feet, I hope the grave may refuse my body a resting place, and righteous Heaven my spirit a home. O, no! He cannot enter that house and we both live.

Nor were black people simply engaging in angry rhetoric. In city, town, and rural areas, they began to organize for mutual defense and civil disobedience at a level previously unknown. New, militant vigilance commitees were formed. In some places, like Chicago, armed, active, black patrols were commissioned to seek out slave hunters and see to it—by any means necessary—that they did not invade the black community.

III

Meanwhile, other blacks organized for another kind of action: exodus. During the decade of the 1850s, directly as a response to the stringencies of the Fugitive Slave Law and other similar developments, some twenty thousand persons fled the black communities of the North and made their way to Canada. This meant a movement of some 7 percent of the northern black population. Their flight was often highly organized. Sometimes a pastor and most of his congregation would fill the cars of a northbound train. Sometimes a local vigilance committee leader would transport a company of men, women, and children across the Canadian border. They were determined to live in freedom.

Of course, most blacks remained to stand their ground, to struggle as best they could in this strange native-exile land. Among them, the practice of civil disobedience continued and expanded. But it is likely that no example of black resistance so stirred the society in the early years of that decade as the events that transpired near a rural Pennsylvania community called Christiana.

There, in the fall of 1851, a local black vigilance committee took a bold, defiant stand against representatives of the forces of slavery and the federal government. Led by a former captive named Samuel Parker, an armed group of men and women barricaded themselves in Parker's house and refused to give up several runaways whose former "master" had come to claim them. In spite of the presence of two United States marshals (who threatened, in fine style, to burn the house down), Parker and black people of the local community defended their endangered brothers. In the course of the struggle, one in which black women played an active part, the white slave owner was killed, his son was seriously wounded, and the federal marshals beat a hasty retreat. When they returned, a company of United States Marines was with them, but by then Parker and other leaders of the resistance were on their way to Canada.

When word of the incident spread to the black community across the country, there was an overwhelming outpouring of sympathy and financial support for the men and women they called "the victorious heroes of the battle of Christiana." Obviously, the spirit of resistance was alive, and many African-Americans knew that in the struggle for freedom and humanity there were no other arms they could ultimately trust but their own.

IV

While events like Christiana stimulated an almost unanimous black opinion on the right and necessity of self-defense, there were deepening divisions within the black community concerning the positive, offensive steps they should take in their struggle for freedom. Two of the major opposing positions were represented by Frederick Douglass on the one hand, and by his friend, Martin Delany on the other. Raising his arguments from a black abolitionist position of protest and agitation Douglass assumed that blacks had no other essential destiny than the one bounded by America. So he placed great emphasis on the necessity of whites, especially white leaders, to act justly in relationship to black needs. Black protest and agitation served to pressure such white action.

For instance at mid-century Douglass was saying,

We deem it a settled point that the destiny of the colored man is bound up with that of the white people of this country . . . we are *here*; and . . . that is *our* country; . . . the question for the [white] philosophers and statesmen of the land ought to be, what principles should dictate the policy of the action towards us? We shall neither die out, nor be driven out; but shall go with this people, either as a testimony against them, or as an evidence in their favor throughout their generations. We are clearly on their hands and must remain there forever.

With those words in his *North Star* newspaper, Douglass identified one of the most vexing questions in the movement for black freedom in America: what does it mean to blacks for America to be "*our* country"? In statements like this one, Douglass himself assigned to blacks a passive sense of belonging and proposed that the major actions needed to come from whites. He defined the position of his fellow Africans as that of an unwanted but inescapable burden on the hands of the white majority.

By the 1850s, Martin Delany, one of the most black-conscious men of his time, had taken another, far more revolutionary position. He put it forward initially in 1852 in his landmark publication, *The Condition, Elevation, Emigration, and Destiny of the Colored People of the United States, Politically Considered*. The key word in that title was not "emigration," as so many persons have thought, but "elevation," and "destiny." For Delany, the crucial issue was not where black people were located, or what whites would do. Instead, his primary concern was for the "elevation" of the peoples of Africa to their rightful destiny in the struggle for a new humanity.

The redemption of Africans and Africa was his great vision. All his conclusions flowed from that point. Thus he called out,

The time has now fully arrived when the colored race is called upon by all the ties of common humanity, and all the claims of consummate justice, to go forward and take their position, and do battle in the struggle now being made for the redemption of the world. . . . But we must go from among our oppressors; it never can be done by staying among them.

Looking at the massive evil of the Fugitive Slave Law, Delany was forced to a very different conclusion from that of Douglass regarding the white leaders who shaped and maintained the law. He said, "A people capable of originating such a law as this are not the people to whom we are willing to entrust our liberty at discretion."

Black people had a key role to play in the development of mankind and of their own people. They could not play that role while cramped into the oppressive structures of a white racist society. Therefore, in faithfulness to their history and destiny, they must struggle to leave America to establish a new, self-determining existence. Whatever that struggle for a new beginning might cost, blacks must be ready to pay it. Those were the major themes being raised by Delany, and as the anguished decade developed he received an increasingly receptive hearing among key segments of the black community.

V

For an enslaved, embattled people to be called to fulfill a universal destiny was a revolutionary vocation. Then, when Delany and his allies (like the brilliant young native of Virginia, H. Ford Douglas) were asked to state the conditions under which black people could remain in America, they were not less revolutionary in their assessment of what was necessary. At an emigration convention they organized in Cleveland, Ohio, in 1854, Delany and his colleagues defined what they considered to be the only honorable terms for a continuing, free black presence in America. In words very different from Douglass's, they said,

> as men and equals, we demand every political right, privilege, and position to which the whites are eligible in the United States, and we will either attain to these, or accept nothing . . . as a people we will never be satisfied nor contented until we occupy a position where we are acknowledged a necessary *constituent* in the *ruling element* of the country in which we live.

No goals could have been more revolutionary at the time. If they were to remain in America, the children of the slave ships demanded equal rights with the children of the masters. But even more important, they were defining what America would have to be if it were ever to be truly their country. For them, the children and grandchildren of the masters could no longer be the privileged ones. The country could no longer "belong" to whites. Black people would have to move to master their own lives and to share in deciding the direction of the life of the nation at large. They would do this not simply as supplicants, or even as voters or minor office holders. Blacks would have to become participants in the positions and centers of power, responsibility, and control in the land. Only then could it truly be "our country," responding to black needs and to black visions of the best human good.

How would these things come to be? At that stage of history neither Delany nor his associates had any delusions about the harsh and costly nature of the struggle to transform their position in America—if they remained. It was, indeed, a struggle for the transformation of the entire society, its directions, and its goals. Thus they wisely said it is futile hope on our part to expect such results through the agency of moral goodness on the part of our white American oppressors. . . . if we desire liberty, it can only be obtained at the price which others have paid for it.

Moreover, whatever else happened in the struggle, they pledged never to lose a sense of their peoplehood, never to forget the shores from which they came, the blood in which they were baptized. So they said,

no people, as such, can ever attain to greatness who lose their identity . . . we shall ever cherish our identity of origin and race, as preferable, in our estimation, to any other people.

Such a vision and commitment, in all of its fullness, was radical and revolutionary in the America of the mid-1850s. It was still radical and revolutionary in America on the eve of its bicentennial. For many black persons, its goals continue to be just and proper ones for the other American revolution.

Chapter 13

Black Slavery and White Freedom: The Impossible Peace (1850 — 1861)

I

In spite of the struggle and debate that encompassed and often racked the black population of the North, in spite of that community's obvious radicalization under the brutal strokes of the white nation in the early 1850s, it is still necessary to remember that the seat of black power was in the South. Ultimately, it was the continuing, heaving, shaking movement there that would be most important in shaping the destiny of black America.

In the summer of 1852, a white Virginian declared,

> It is useless to disguise the fact, its truth is undeniable, that a greater degree of insubordination has been manifested by the negro population, within the last few months, than at any previous period in our history as a state.

Throughout the South, the same underlying sense of malaise was apparent everywhere, and regularly it broke out into action towards freedom.

Sometimes the action would be preceded by a letter from a black woman in the North which would travel devious routes to its recipients in slavery. The letter might say,

> tell my brothers to be always watching unto prayer, and when the good old ship of Zion comes along, to be ready to step forward.

Harriet Tubman was on her way down from Philadelphia, and soon, in the hushed arbors of the plantations, a song might go up, calling,

> Get on board, little children
> There's room for many a more.

Before daybreak, another company of fugitives had joined the "many thousands gone," breaking the chains of slavery.

In every form, the struggle continued. Hated overseers somehow stumbled and fell into cauldrons of boiling molasses. Others fell off of railroad flatcars. Attempts at poisoning were constantly reported (and many were not). The fire of black arsonists continued to burn as an act of struggle and protest. Everywhere, in swamps, in forests, in caves, there were outlyers, challenging the power of slavery, calling other black people to a precarious but independent life outside the law and order of bondage.

It was impossible for the nation to escape its history, to avoid the consequences of its decision to try to accommodate white freedom and black slavery within the same society. On the edges of the South, in the Kansas-Nebraska Territory, a democratic vote by whites was supposed to determine the future of the black enslaved presence. Instead, by the middle of the decade a guerrillalike civil warfare had erupted between the proslavery and free soil whites. Men were awakened in the stillness of the night and executed. The compromises simply would not work. The very existence of the captive black presence was both judgment and peril.

II

But blacks did not leave the fighting in the hands of whites. Eighteen hundred and fifty-six was an election year; and all the divisive elements of the society were bursting to the surface. The new North-dominated Republican party was sensing its strength, and the South was recoiling from the purported abolitionist connections of the new party. In that year, reports of black insurrectionary activity increased markedly. Black guerrillas struck in North Carolina. Black ironworkers organized for insurrection in Tennessee. In Kentucky, searchers found caches of arms and explosives in the black community. In Texas, blacks and Mexicans reportedly conspired for joint action against their common oppressors.

Then, in a situation where abolitionist activities, congressional compromises, popular sovereignty, guerrilla warfare and many forms of black struggle had failed to resolve the explosive issues rending the nation, the Supreme Court assumed that it would succeed at the task. In 1857, Roger Taney's court announced its Dred Scott decision, putting forth two essential messages. The first was that blacks had only such rights in America as whites deigned to give them, that they were invested with no intrinsic, inalienable citizenship rights of their own. The second message from the court was that Congress had had no authority to set the original 36°30′ slave/free line in the Missouri Compromise, and that legislation was declared unconstitutional.

While whites were primarily concerned about the court's attack on the long-nurtured compromise, black people were far more troubled about the court's attack on them. For many blacks it was the last straw, the final evidence that the American government meant them no good. Indeed, some faced for the first time the harsh and terrifying possibility that the American government was not only a protector of slavery but was an outright enemy to all the hopes of the free black community as well.

The rage and fear went beyond even the levels of 1850. Respectable black moderates like Robert Purvis of Philadelphia were now saying that

We owe no allegiance to a country which grinds us under its iron hoof and treats us like dogs. The time has gone by for colored people to talk of patriotism.

This theme was repeated wherever the black community gathered in the hundreds of meetings that were held after the announcement of the court's decision. Indeed, not only did blacks talk openly of nonallegiance to America, some spoke of revolution. Purvis himself was one of these who asked, albeit tentatively, "Why not . . . welcome the overthrow of 'this atrocious government' and construct a better one in its place?" In one of the meetings following the decision, Charles Remond, abolitionist stalwart, called for a Garnetlike insurrectionary address to the blacks in the South, and said, "He knew his resolution was in one sense revolutionary, and in another treasonable, but so he meant it."

III

A tremendous sense of agitation, movement, and urgency coursed through the black community and built to almost unbearable heights. All the defiant civil disobedience of the vigilance committees and slave rescue groups was markedly increased. While some black people spoke of revolution, others hastened their moves to Canada and Mexico. Martin Delany made plans for an expedition to Africa in search of the place of new beginnings. Still other black men made plans for an expedition to Harpers Ferry, Virginia, and they were there in 1859 when

John Brown led his abortive revolutionary thrust against the system of slavery and the government that protected it.

One of the black young men who joined Brown was John Copeland, an Oberlin College student who had been born in North Carolina. Still in his early twenties when he joined Brown, Copeland was among those captured and sent to the gallows. Shortly before his death, he wrote these words to his family in Oberlin,

> I am not terrified by the gallows, which I see staring me in the face, and upon which I am soon to stand and suffer death for doing what George Washington was made a hero for doing. . . . could I die in a more noble cause?

For hundreds of thousands of black people, Copeland's question had a sure answer. Perhaps even more important for the history of black struggle was his conscious joining of his life with that of the American revolution. In a sense, he was dying in an attempt to fulfill the American revolution, for he knew there could be no peace in America until the two revolutions were joined.

Still, there was always that overwhelming majority of men and women who loved peace, reconciliation, and order among whites more than revolutionary justice and a fulfilled humanity for blacks (and for America). At every level of society, they attempted to find new compromises that would provide some way to avoid the fiery conflict that John Brown's raid promised. So, in 1861, even after the secession of most southern states had become a reality, the new Republican president, Abraham Lincoln, still vowed to the rebels that his administration had no intention of interfering with their "peculiar institution" of inhumanity, so long as it did not seek to expand its sway. For Lincoln, the unity of the white North and the white South was like a mystical vision that seemed to blot out those earlier visions of judgment, redemption, and righteousness that had possessed Nat Turner and David Walker. But the black visions would not die.

Chapter 14

Civil War and the Surge toward Freedom: What Did the Handwriting Say? (1861 – 1865)

Although the destruction of the oppressors God may not effect by the oppressed, yet the Lord our God will surely bring other destructions upon them—for not infrequently will he cause them to rise up against one another, to be split and divided, and to oppress each other, and sometimes to open hostilities with sword in hand.

David Walker's *Appeal*, 1829

I

There was no peace for America while slavery existed, while black men were determined to be free, while the contradictions of the democratic republic ran like an immense moral fault through the center of its life. And when the war finally came, it gathered up all the ironies of the black and white struggles in America. For while the bloody Civil War surely cleared the way for the final smashing of slavery's chains, it also had profound, detrimental effects on the radical movements that had been building in the black community since David Walker's *Appeal*. Certainly, it diverted much of the raging, cascading power that was surging through black America in the 1850s.

Part of the paradox lay in the fact that the roaring of the guns in Charleston Harbor seemed to announce the beginning of three separate wars. At least, there were three dominant sets of interpretations, three different fueling forces behind the men who directed the conflict, behind many of those who fought and died.

Throughout the black community, there was a sweeping conviction that God was at work in the war, that he was moving as David Walker had predicted, chastising the white oppressors and opening the gates of freedom. All over the country, that was the substance of the conventional black wisdom (not all agreed, though). The influential *Anglo-African* announced that

> circumstances have been so arranged by the decrees of Providence, that in struggling for their own nationality (the whites of the North) are forced to defend our rights.

Stirring black orators, like the popular Dr. John Rock, told cheering crowds of his people,

> I think I see the finger of God in all this. Yes, there is the hand-writing on the wall: . . . *I have heard the groans of my people, and am come down to deliver them.*

Repeating the essential Anglo-African analysis, Rock said that the federal government had not intended to be an agent of God, but "While fighting for its own existence, the government had been obliged to take slavery by the throat, and sooner or later *must* choke her to death." Many black people saw the war as a fulfillment of the American Revolution, a divinely ordained means of completing the revolution's most important unfinished business.

The only problem with this black interpretation was that at the outset of the war, no one in the leadership of the white North, and very few persons among the masses of their people, had seen the same vision. Neither Lincoln, his generals, nor the vast majority of their soldiers was committed to a war for black freedom. Such a revolutionary mission did not possess them. At times they admitted that they also saw divine handwriting on walls, but the message was very different from the one that blacks had read. For instance, Lincoln made it absolutely clear that his first and overriding objective was to *preserve* the Union, to bring white North and South back together so that this white man's country might continue to work out its Divine destiny. For him, that was a destiny in which blacks counted for little.

Therefore, when the black men crowded to the recruiters, they were rudely repulsed, and told that there was no room for black fighters in the United States military—although thousands of black laborers were working for the Union forces. When their militia companies marched on the streets, in many places they were jeered and harassed by the white populace and sometimes they were physically attacked. Again and again, the white soldiers made clear the fact that they were not fighting "a nigger war." They were fighting for the Union, fighting for the government, fighting to show those Southerners who was in charge of America.

Of course, among the southern whites there was a third interpretation of the war. It was for the vindication of states' rights, for the
preservation of their "peculiar institution," for the establishment of
their right to secede, to live free from the domination of the North.
And, of course, it was for pride, honor, and many other things wars are
fought for. (But for our purposes, that third set of reasons is far less
important than those that animated the black and white sectors of the
North.)

III

In the long run of the war, none of the three views of its nature and
its goals ultimately prevailed. Nevertheless, in the fall of 1862, when
men cared not so much about long views as about finding some way to
bring the unexpectedly lengthy and sanguinary conflict to an end, it
appeared as if the black vision would triumph. For in September of
that year, Lincoln announced his plan for an Emancipation Proclamation. As he readily admitted, it was a war measure. Lincoln sought to
win back the seceded states with the ambiguous threat of emancipation
for their enslaved African people. The proclamation attempted to create confusion behind their lines. It made no promise of emancipation to
the blacks who were in bondage in the "loyal" border states, although
these were the only slave states over which Lincoln's government had
any effective control. Still, the word of its promulgation was like the
coming of the Lord.

Blacks in the North were caught up in a paroxysm of celebration and
thanksgiving, which was climaxed in the nationwide gatherings on
January 1, 1863, the day of the official proclamation. Now they believed that they had solid, substantial proof that the hand of God was at
work. In the midst of the war, emancipation had been pronounced.
Even though it was pronounced more to the winds than to any real
bondsmen, the document was there. The nation was committed to this
pathway. How, asked the black community, could such a revolutionary
direction be thwarted?

Not long before the official proclamation was made, the attorney
general announced, in essence, that the Dred Scott decision had been
annulled. In an official advisement, he declared that, "Free men of
color, if born in the United States, are citizens of the United States."
For the black community this was simply another evidence that the
war had been wrenched out of the conservative white channels and
transformed into a crusade for their freedom. For the federal government, both the Emancipation Proclamation and the attorney general's

advisement were part of a preparatory prelude to the recruitment of black fighting men for the military forces of the Union.

In the brutally lengthened war, with white men resisting military service, it was finally decided that this untapped black strength and eagerness would have to be used. Lincoln and his advisors also concluded that there now needed to be more honorable official reasons for the war, reasons to which blacks could relate. Finally, it was also obvious that the nation would have to recognize the citizenship rights of the men it recruited to fight for its life.

So, shortly after the Emancipation Proclamation was released, official, intensive recruitment of black soldiers for the Union armies began. A "Black Committee" of recruiters was organized. What did this mean for the movement of black struggle in America? Perhaps its effects in the North are best suggested through the lives of three men. H. Ford Douglas, one of the youngest and most dynamic of Martin Delany's colleagues in the emigrationist movement of the 1850s, had publicly advocated black treason during that period. He had announced that he was prepared to join "an invading army" against the oppressive government of the United States. Now, less than a decade later, Douglass somehow managed to enlist in a white regiment, and in 1862 he was one of the first black leaders to enter the furnaces of the war.

Delany, for his part, had made all preparations to emigrate to Africa, and was stopped almost literally at the water's edge by the outbreak of the Civil War. In 1863, he became a most active member of the "Black Committee," which the government had organized under the direction of an old-line white abolitionist. Delany had not yet become a part of the "ruling element" of America but he was working assiduously to recruit black troops for its army. Indeed he did so well that his own 17-year-old son insisted on volunteering, and just before the war ended, the father received a commission to form a *Corps d'Afrique* for the Union side.

Frederick Douglass also became a part of this recruiting committee, and he made hundreds of speeches to blacks across the country, urging them to forget the cruel history of the federal government, pressing them to believe that a new day had dawned.

These three lives symbolized what had happened to the furious cresting of the movement for black freedom in the North. In the course of the Civil War, it became totally intertwined with the cause of the federal government and its armies. In turn, this relationship meant that the freedom movement was also allied to the Republican party, which controlled the government, and to the often rapacious industrialists of the Northeast, who wielded great power in the party and who had their own visions of the nation's postwar future. Indeed, among this strange set of allies, there was almost no one who agreed with the best black interpretations of the war, none who saw it as a completion of the unfinished business of the American revolution. Still, this was the camp that the northern black freedom movement had joined.

IV

In the South, the initial reactions of the masses of black people to the war were somewhat different, but their consequences turned out to be the same. When the war began, many outside observers had looked for the coming of some massive, bloody uprising among the enslaved population across the South. But there is every evidence that a solid folk wisdom (and the reticence all people experience in the face of great danger) told the black people of the South that any revolutionary move of that nature would probably serve to unite the white forces. For no image could possibly strike a more mutually responsive chord of fear in the hearts of white people everywhere than the specter of an armed black uprising spreading across the South.

There were, of course, expanding opportunities for the outlyer bands, and some of them became part of the guerrilla supporters of the Union forces. Small-scale uprisings continued to take place; and arson was widely used. Moreover, blacks found many ways to cooperate with Union forces whenever they were nearby. The major open response to the war which emerged from the black freedom struggle in the South, however, was a tremendous, bursting expansion of the familiar fugitive activities.

We are told that even before the guns went off at Charleston, there were thousands of blacks poised and ready to break for freedom with the first sounds of war. Then, when the conflict actually began, a new phase of the self-liberating black movement out of slavery began. As W. E. B. Du Bois described the steadily increasing thousands of men and women who left plantations, farms, homes, and factories in those days of war, he said, "it was like the great unbroken swell of the ocean before it dashes on the reefs."

They stormed into the northern army camps and other military installations, every age, every condition, at every hour of the day and night. They headed North or South, whichever direction brought them into earliest contact with the military forces of the Union. From Port Royal in South Carolina, one military commander reported,

> Everywhere I find the same state of things existing; everywhere the blacks hurry in droves to our lines; they crowd in small boats around our

> ships; they swarm upon our decks; they hurry to our officers from the
> cotton houses of their masters, in an hour or two after our guns are fired.

Then the Union official added, "I mean each statement I make to be
taken literally; it is not garnished for rhetorical effect."

There was no rhetoric about the black action either. Men and women
were in search of freedom. Most never heard of an Emancipation Proclamation and it had no effect on them. Instead, they were determined
to take their own initiative, to seek it out, to seize it as best they could,
to thrust their children before them into the promise of a new life. For
them, this vast churning of humanity towards the Union camps was as
much a part of their struggle for freedom as the work of Vesey, Gabriel, Turner, and a thousand nameless outlyers in the swamps and
everglades. And everywhere the roaming army of people went in
search of freedom, wherever they stopped to rest and wait and hope,
they sent up the songs of their foreparents, and wrested others from
their own experiences. With tremendous power and anticipation, they
sang words like,

> Slavery chain done broke at last,
>   broke at last, broke at last.
> Slavery chain done broke at last,
> Going to praise God till I die.

In the course of the four years of the war, at least half a million
blacks participated in this self-liberating movement out of slavery. In
their actions they were saying that they too believed that this was a
war of deliverance, but they knew that the time must be seized, that
the deliverance must be shaped by their own courage, strength, and
endurance. If God was moving in the war, then he was only opening
the door, and they had to decide to go through.

V

Nevertheless, even these courageous black men and women of the
South could not escape the ironies and paradoxes of the war. For they,
too, eventually found themselves allied with the forces of the same
federal government that so short a time ago had guaranteed the
South's right to control their lives. Now they were in the camps of the
armies of this government seeking its aid and protection. Soon,
thousands of former bondsmen were fighting in the armies that had
once been used to put down their struggles for freedom.

What happened in the course of the war, then, was that the major elements of the struggle for black freedom in both the North and the South were drawn by the tremendous power of the conflict into a forced and fateful alliance with the federal government and its Republican leadership. These two unevenly matched allies had visions of the nation's future which were just as contradictory as their visions of the war, especially where the future involved black freedom and equality in America. For a time, that inherent conflict between blacks and their Republican "allies" was covered over by the death of Lincoln and the rise of his myth, and then by the struggles between Congress and the new president. But myths do not create freedom, and white conflicts cannot be counted on as a permanent substitute for the self-sustaining black struggle toward liberation.

Chapter 15
Reconstruction: Struggle, Hope, and Betrayal (1865 – 1877)

I

It should not have been surprising. The differing black and white visions concerning the nature of the war could not ultimately be denied, and the temporary, crisis-created illusion of unity of purpose could not last. Thus, as the Civil War ground to its close, several profoundly conflicting views concerning the nature of the peace and the shape of the postwar American society pressed their way into the open.

Within the white community, the struggles tended to focus largely on the politics and mechanics of putting the rent republic back together again. Who should lead in the process of reconstruction, president or Congress? What should be the North's posture towards the rebellious South and its leaders? What were the best mechanisms available for reinstating the seceded states? Always, these questions were accompanied by a persistent, burning issue: how should the northern Republicans maneuver to retain the unquestioned control of the government which they had gained during the crisis of secession and war? (Back of that concern, of course, was the determination of the northern commercial-industrialist-white racist interests, which the Republicans represented, to dominate the future shape of America.)

Behind and beneath all these white questions and concerns, looming as an all-pervading but largely unwelcome issue, was the question of the future of black people in America. By and large, even though the war had forced them into certain acts that recognized and legitimized a minimal level of black freedom (like the Thirteenth Amendment to the Constitution, which was the real emancipation proclamation), as the war ended, whites were looking for ways to fit the black population

71

into their own plans for America's continued development as a white man's country.

II

Of course, the view from the black side was very different. The black community counted and mourned the thousands of their soldiers who had died in battle or succumbed to the ravages of war-connected diseases. They considered these lives legitimate arguments for their right to participate fully in the new, postwar America. As they moved across the battle-scarred countryside, as they gathered in the cities, as they lingered in the army camps, many black people sensed the power of their own presence and knew that a special moment was at hand. In spite of all its ambiguities, they were still convinced that the war was part of God's action in history on behalf of their freedom.

So, even before the conflict formally ended, the newly freed blacks began pressing demands that, under the circumstances, were nothing less than revolutionary. Hundreds of thousands of them had seized their own freedom, thus affirming their right to be free. Then, in conferences, conventions, church meetings, and gatherings of every sort in North and South, the former slaves expressed their ideas about the nature of this new freedom. Above all, they insisted on a right to vote, untrammeled by any hindrances. In many places, they asserted their right and their readiness to participate in the functions of government itself, both in the North and South. Consistently, they demanded land, to provide an economic and political base, to free them from the old structures of dependency which so many white men and women were eager to reinstate in new forms.

In effect, the war had set an unintentional revolution in motion in regard to the status of blacks in America. Many of them recognized this, and sought instinctively to consolidate, legitimize, and develop the new situation as quickly as possible. Under the circumstances of the postslavery, postwar period, it appeared that the federal government must play the central, guaranteeing role in the situation. Only their legal, economic, and military powers were adequate to the situation. So, there was wide agreement with the black-owned New Orleans *Tribune* when it said to the government,

It is folly now to deny the [Southern] Rebellion and not accept all its logical results. Revolutions never go backward.

During Reconstruction, the major concern of the black struggle for freedom was to take the accidental revolution set in motion by the war and to legitimize, protect, and develop it.

III

To develop the other American revolution, black people often had to fight both northern white "allies" and southern white enemies, neither of whom desired any revolution that would place the former enslaved people into a central, self-determining role in the political, social, and economic life of the nation. For instance, Lincoln before his death had done very little planning about the possible future of a large, newly freed black population in the South or the rest of America. For a long time he continued to toy with the fantasy of exporting the large majority of the black population to some other part of the world. So, neither he nor his administration saw the possibilities that the Freedman's Bureau had for becoming an agent of forwarding the revolutionary transformation of the South. For them, it was largely another war-inspired measure to be done away with as soon as possible after the war.

Then, when Lincoln died, it was obvious that his successor, the "loyal" Tennessee Democrat, Andrew Johnson, had no stomach for any changes that would radically alter the position of blacks in America. Indeed, under Johnson, blacks found themselves faced with a series of so-called Black Codes, which were essentially an attempt in every southern state to reinstate the white controls of slavery without reinstating the institution itself. Harsh restrictions on legal rights, personal movement, labor rights, as well as various strategies for making the prison system a substitute for slavery's forced labor were only a part of the repressive codes. Johnson had every intention of bringing the South back into the Union with these codes in force. (Meanwhile, in his native state of Tennessee, a white terroristic organization known as the Ku Klux Klan was formed to provide extralegal sanctions for the maintenance of white supremacy.)

As blacks fought this early postwar reaction, they found white allies again, this time in Congress. The Republican leadership there, especially in the House, demanded the right to shape the Reconstruction process and to place their stamp, rather than the president's, on the development of the postwar nation. In the course of this campaign, a few of the so-called Radical Republicans were sincerely concerned about the establishment of black rights and black equality. Most were not. Their primary concern was to bring the strength of the new black voters to the side of the Republican party. With that in mind, and in many cases with a determination to punish the South, they pressed the legislative action to support the black demands for votes and representation. But they did not work for implementation of the black demand for land. That would have required confiscation and government action more radical than any they were prepared to see. Revolution was not really their goal.

Nevertheless, as a result of the limited moves of the radical Republicans in Congress a new set of openings was created for the ferment and movement of the black struggle for freedom in the South. In the winter of 1866–1867, Congress demanded that the southern states that Johnson had recognized hold new Constitutional conventions. They insisted that these southern conventions ratify the Fourteenth Amendment to the Constitution, which conferred all citizenship rights to black people and supposedly guaranteed those rights. In addition, Congress demanded that black people participate fully in the new state conventions.

IV

This was the institutional starting point of the brief experiment in new democracy which was called Reconstruction. Its revolutionary nature was clear. The children of the slaves were being mandated to play a central role in shaping a new government, which would include both them and their former slave masters. The outlyers, the arsonists, the returning fugitives, the men, women, and children whose best skills and gifts had been denied for so long were now called to play a part in creating a new society.

Southern blacks recognized the meaning of the time. They gave themselves fully to the tasks. They eagerly attended all the political conventions and turned them into mass religious meetings and great love feasts. They crowded around the halls where the conventions were meeting. They watched their black representatives with pride. Children sang in the streets,

> We are rising
> We are rising
> We are rising
> as a people.

Old black preachers who had nurtured the strength and courage of the congregations for so long, while waiting for such a time, now preached from such a text as this:

> He hath put down the mighty
> From their seats
> And hath exalted them
> Of low degree!

In New Orleans, some blacks dared to demand for the black community "an effective share of the power of the convention, from the president down to the doorkeeper, and from the clerk and the chief reporter down to the printer." In Louisiana and in Alabama there were harsh fights, in some cases resulting in armed confrontations, over the rights of blacks to participate fully and to provide leadership for this new period.

In most places, however, the black demands were comparatively modest. Most often, relatively conservative white allies served to moderate the black thrusts towards the future. So after the conventions were over and the new legislatures were formed, only in South Carolina was there a black majority (in the lower house). Even there, blacks still deferred to their white Republican allies, believing that such deference was necessary if they were to gain the support of the federal government in guiding these new state governments through the difficult process of a constitutional revolution. As a result, none of the state legislatures enacted the highly controversial, but sorely needed, revolutionary policy of land confiscation. And when the United States Congress also failed to act on this issue, blacks were left in a dangerously exposed position.

V

Nevertheless, it was a time of tremendous hope and excitement. As the new southern state legislatures met in the 1867–1868 period, the essence of black struggle was to support and maintain these revolutionary governments. (They were revolutionary precisely because blacks were participating.) Not only were blacks present in legislatures, but they moved into elective offices at every level of southern life. Among other things, they became sheriffs, justices of the peace, county commissioners, and professors at formerly white state universities. They knew such a transformation of the role of black people represented the first bold steps toward the creation of a new society in America, and as the opposition built up, they fought a courageous but doomed battle to hold their ground, to support these governments.

Some opponents were easily predictable. The white forces of the South—both those who had long held power, and many new aspirants—did not intend merely to sit by and watch their former bondsmen become an integral part of the government. Instead, by every possible legal and extralegal means, they organized to oppose the new developments. Ultimately, the most effective weapon in this southern white counterthrust was paramilitary force, symbolized most fully in the rise and glorification of the Ku Klux Klan and other similar terrorist organizations. Arson, rape, assassination, and mass murder were all among the tools of these armies of reaction. But they could not have succeeded if the federal government and the Republican party had been determined to protect the fragile democratic experiments of the postwar period.

Early in Reconstruction, as early as 1868 and 1869 in some cases, it became obvious that blacks were again losing their white allies. For a democratic, revolutionary Reconstruction to succeed in the South, for blacks to seize and maintain a role as an integral part of the politics and society of the section, northern whites would have to be ready to pay a significant cost. That cost would likely have included prolonged military struggle against the forces of reaction as well as a commitment to long-range economic and political support of the freedom.

Only through a committed federal presence and an encouragement to black self-defense and self-development could such gains as had initially been made be consolidated and expanded. But for all that to happen, whites in the North would have had to be committed to black equality. Unfortunately, they were not even committed to full citizenship rights for the small black minority who lived in the northern states with them. Thus they were in no way prepared to face the long, hard costs of a struggle seriously to reconstruct the South. Reconstruction in the South required reconstruction in the nation where blacks were concerned, and the nation did not want it.

As time went on, it was clear that there was no leadership among the white majority capable of pressing them beyond their limitations towards this fulfillment of their own revolution. White racism and fear were too strong. White leaders were too weak. The desire to put aside moral reform and move on to the business of exploiting the continent and the world predominated. Part of the irony, of course, was that there were no persons more committed to this capitalist exploitation than the white Republican leadership, the former allies of black freedom. Was this what the handwriting on the wall was all about?

VI

Meanwhile, left with only a token federal military presence, constantly discouraged by local white allies from moving in active, aggressive self-defense, blacks in the South carried on the struggle as best they could. Thousands of them lost their lives in this courageous attempt to create a new meaning for the American revolution. Many were cut down right at the polling places. By the beginning of the 1870s several states had already fallen into the hands of the white "Redeemers" who represented the reactionary forces of the society.

Still, even at the end, in places like Louisiana and Alabama, blacks were fighting not only for the survival of Reconstruction governments but for what must be called proportionate black power and leadership in those governments. Finally, in another series of compromises and bargains following the election of 1876, the last, token federal support for and protection of the black struggle for a new South was abandoned. The attempt to legitimize and consolidate the quest for black freedom through constitutional southern governments had failed. Perhaps the black folks in New Orleans had been wrong; perhaps some revolutions did go backward.

Chapter 16

Beyond the "New South": Searching for a Way (1875 – 1900)

I

For a brief time, Reconstruction had provided the nineteenth century's most complete opportunity for the federal government and the nation at large to forge a binding chain between the best possibilities of the white American revolution and the deep and pulsing movement of the black struggle for freedom. It was a magnificent chance for the two revolutions to become one in the creation of a new society, a society in which blacks would become in the words of Delany's Cleveland convention, "a necessary *constituent* in the *ruling element* of the country." It was an opening for the two people to find an authentic ground of common humanity.

Instead, America chose a "New South." This meant the betrayal of both revolutions and the abandonment of any search for true reconciliation between the former master class and the former slaves. It meant a white-controlled South was as legitimate as a white-controlled North, in spite of the ineradicable black presence.

The New South also meant that for the first time since the end of the eighteenth century, the political, religious, and intellectual leaders of the North were prepared to acquiesce in the old southern bromide about knowing "their Negroes" best. The constant irritant and threat of northern white scrutiny, protest, and rhetorical attack were now removed, and the white South was by and large left to work out its own best means of subduing the spirit of black freedom and repressing the thrust of its movement.

Although it was the source of a tremendous wave of disappointment and temporary despair, this abandonment to the mercies of the New

South neither crushed black people's spirit nor destroyed the movement of their struggle towards freedom. They continued to build structures of strength and endurance within the black community. Schools,
churches, clubs, associations, fraternal orders, and businesses all increased in number and scope during the post-Reconstruction period.
And beneath all the others stood the beleaguered but powerful force of
the black family.

At the same time, the political struggle also continued. For instance,
blacks did not give up their attempts to wrest at least some local
political control so that they might protect and sustain their people.
They continued to attempt, sometimes successfully, to elect individuals to state legislatures, and on rare occasions to the national Congress.
But the surging, revolutionary force of black participation in the electoral and representative processes had been broken. So it was not
surprising that many black persons began to seek out other alternatives in the struggle for freedom.

II

For those blacks who were convinced that freedom was not possible
in the South, and yet who considered this freedom as necessary to their
lives as food and water, the thought of emigration reemerged as a
major alternative. As early as 1870, a group of black "laboring men,"
many of them Civil War veterans, began organizing in this direction. Based in Louisiana, they first sent a series of scouts out into
the southland, "to see whether there was any state in the South where
we could get a living and enjoy our rights." Over a period of years it
was finally decided that the rapidly deteriorating situation offered
hope for neither economic nor political rights. Then this determined
group reshaped themselves into a "colonization council," and with
many others, they began turning their thoughts towards the West.

Before the decade of the 1870s was over, tens of thousands of black
people had broken with the patterns of white domination in the South,
gathered their families and what little possessions they could carry,
and headed west. Often they went towards Kansas. In 1879 alone some
forty thousand black folk left the southern states for that general
destination. When large numbers of the group became temporarily
stalled in Saint Louis (because of a lack of funds and transportation),
blacks in that city urged them to return to the South. In response these
new pilgrims insisted that "they would rather go into the open prairie
and starve there than go [back] to the South to stand the impositions
that were put on them there." They had been told that they could be

"independent forever" in the West and they were not about to turn around.

As in the days of slavery, these decisions to turn away from and defy white power, these long and painful journeys into the wilderness, were all costly matters. But men and women thought they were a reasonable price for freedom. Indeed, in this period, there were some black people who were again willing to go as far as their homeland of Africa if they could find opportunities for self-determination there.

III

Obviously, for most blacks exodus was no real alternative. They had to stay where they were, and other means of struggle had to be found. With the federal government lost as an ally, other alliances seemed necessary. From the North, one of the most gifted and provocative of the younger journalists, T. Thomas Fortune, predicted the coming of a set of class alliances that would finally transcend race. In his work, *Black and White: Land, Labor, and Politics in the South,* the southern-born Fortune said,

> The hour is approaching when the laboring classes of our country . . .
> will recognize that they have a *common cause, a common humanity* and
> a common enemy; and that . . . if they would triumph over wrong . . .
> they must unite! . . . When the issue is properly joined, the rich, be they
> black or be they white, will be found upon the same side; and the poor, be
> they black or be they white, will be found on the same side.

In the midst of the 1880s, this did not appear to be an idle hope. The rapacious industrial expansion that had grown out of the Civil War was crushing hundreds of thousands of working people. As new forms of labor organizing developed, the voices and ideologies of socialist thinkers began to be heard. Fortune was reflecting this ferment, and although he never turned seriously towards this alternative himself, many black men and women did experiment with alliances based on common class grievances as a means of forwarding the struggle for black freedom.

There were many variations on this theme. Peter S. Clarke, the stalwart educational leader from Cincinnati who had been deeply involved with Frederick Douglass and the black abolitionists in the prewar period, now turned towards the Marxist-oriented Workingmen's party and became one of the first blacks to attain a position of leadership in the socialist camp. Taking a far less doctrinaire position, many thousands of black people were drawn to the Knights of Labor, the most exciting workers' movement of the 1880s. Although they were not Marxist in their orientation, the Knights came to public attention through a series of well-organized boycotts and strikes that temporarily challenged the domination of the new tycoons of American industry. For a time they were an exciting, militant, all-inclusive labor union, and blacks as well as women were readily included in their ranks. At their height, the knights claimed a membership of some seven hundred thousand workers, and about ninety thousand of these were said to be black.

Where black struggle was concerned, the Knights were most impressive (though not most numerous) in the South. There they often worked secretly to organize both black and white workers, and their organizers sent back reports of meetings, boycotts, and strikes in which "harmony prevails between white and black workingmen." Then, just as it seemed as if Fortune's prediction might be realized in the Knights, they began to buckle under the increasing and vicious opposition from the white capitalists and their minions of the North and the South. When white and black organizers were killed in the South, the wavering national leadership proved unprepared for the challenge, and in the long run the Knights turned out to be more promise than a reality.

IV

Even in the midst of fierce repression, black people continued the search for allies in their struggle. In the South, during the 1890s they tried another union alternative, the United Mine Workers (UMW). Again, this was not an ideologically oriented organization, but its major challenge to the New South (and to the nation) was that it attempted to bring black and white workers together to oppose exploitation. According to Richard L. Davis, the best-known black organizer of the union, such solidarity was necessary to

> solve the race problem, better the condition of the toiling millions, and also make our country what it should be, a government of the people, for the people, and by the people.

Obviously, in a racist and exploitative society, such goals were revolutionary. Unfortunately, the struggle for black freedom could not be linked to objectives like these over any long period of time. For, here again the combination of an increasingly fearful national leadership and a harrowing local opposition in the South drained the UMW movement of its force for radical change. When Richard Davis died in 1900 the UMW had no real replacement for his leadership and concerns among black people.

Nevertheless, the search for allies continued. Considering the beleaguered state of the black community, especially in the South, this was not surprising. It was in the South that the broadest-based—but least politically focused—attempt at alliance with white forces was attempted in the farmers' alliances and the Populist movement. There is evidence that hundreds of thousands of black people who were based on the land became part of the colored farmers' alliance movement, and they continually sought grounds for solidarity with the parallel white farmers' groupings.

This attempt at class-based cooperation was focused in the South and in the West, and in both places it occasionally produced startling intimations of the possibilities for black/white solidarity. Through the ranks of the Populist parties, blacks and whites met and planned together in the West. In the South, while there was less joint organizational work, there were instances of blacks and whites facing white mobs together in a united front, of black and white votes deciding elections against the white status quo. Here, again, though, a combination of misguided leadership at the top and a susceptibility to racist fears and physical attacks on the local level finally destroyed this alliance-in-the-making. Whites were still not ready for the revolutionary changes that any serious class alliance with blacks would force upon them.

V

At the same time that these experiments with black/white solidarity were being carried on, there was no diminution of the independent black thrusts toward freedom and the assertion of their full humanity. Throughout the South, evidence abounded of men and women taking courageous risks to keep the light of liberty and hope alive within the black community during these extremely perilous times.

Under the continued murderous pressure of white terror and exploitation, men like the Reverend M. Edward Bryant, an African Methodist Episcopal (A.M.E.) leader in Alabama, urged the people to continue a relentless fight. Speaking to a group of black people in Selma, in 1888, Bryant declared that they must "swear never to rest contented night or day until the tyrannical spirit of oppression . . . shall be plucked up root and branch, and a man and a woman shall be known by the way they conduct themselves, without regard to color." (Martin King's dream had been dreamed many times before him, even in the heart of Alabama.)

But Bryant, who was deeply involved with the struggles of the black community, knew that mere words would not accomplish what needed to be done. So he urged blacks, whenever possible, to ally themselves with progressive white forces like the Knights of Labor, and carry on a joint struggle for a new society where justice would prevail. He also knew, however, that black people would always have to be prepared to bear the major weight of the struggle for their freedom, and he exhorted his people to "Let the world know that we prefer death . . . to such liberty as we have today." Trying to avoid any unnecessary provocation in such an explosive setting, knowing that his words would be reported to powerful, hostile white authorities, Bryant said that he was not advocating "war or resort to force." At the same time he would not back down from his conviction that it was necessary for blacks to move into the storm of white oppression with "a fixed, unyielding unalterable determination to defend ourselves when attacked, and to petition, persuade, and demand our rights whatever may be the consequences."

In Bryant's case, the consequences were soon clear: he was faced with threats of immediate assassination which he knew he could not ignore. Leaving all his personal belongings behind, he narrowly escaped to an exile in the North. Similarly in Memphis, Tennessee, the gifted and intrepid Ida B. Wells, first female editor of a broadly circulated black newspaper, refused to be silent. In words and in defiant deeds she boldly advocated the rights of the black community and sought to organize her people to take decisive steps towards their own independence—including the step of westward migration. Carrying a gun against the threats of an angered white community, she continued her campaign of publishing truth until her press was destroyed and her partner intimidated. Finally she was forced to choose between exile and allowing the black men of the community to keep their vow to defend her to the death. Knowing that such a defense would provide the excuse for a widespread white slaughter of an outmanned and outgunned black community, in a hard decision, she chose exile.

Among black people of the North, there was a constant support for many determined efforts at resistance and for the practice of armed self-defense. Although it was admittedly easier to offer this encouragement from the North, the black community there recognized that they were really encouraging a tradition of struggle that had a long history in the South. Then, when persons like the Reverend Bryant and Ida B. Wells were forced into northern exile, black folks readily took them in, thereby continuing the fugitive link between the northern and southern struggles.

VI

In addition to the fields of energies that swirled about such courageous individuals, the attempt to build black protest organizations was also a part of the independent thrust for freedom. In 1890, under the energetic guidance of Thomas Fortune, the Afro-American League was formed, one of the first post-Reconstruction attempts to create a national organization in the black abolitionist tradition. But the league never attracted the mass support to which it aspired.

Instead, large numbers of ordinary black people responded to the terrors of America in a traditional manner. In the early years of the 1890s there was extensive talk of "Africa Fever" throughout the black community. Thousands of Afro-Americans were seriously considering African emigration as the only real alternative in their search for freedom. Partly they were inspired by the speeches and lectures of men like Bishop Henry McNeil Turner of the A.M.E. church and Edward Wilmont Blyden, the Pan-African publicist. But much of the response came out of their own pondering of the situation in America.

The search for independence in Africa was a notion that was especially popular among the masses of the people, both the unlettered and others. Much of the spirit of this surging towards the homeland was represented in a letter from an anonymous brother in Arkansas who wrote to ask about Liberia, saying

> Are tha any White People over in Libery if there is none ar tha going there . . . if it is a Negro country and we can be free and speak our own mind & make our own laws then we are redy to come at once *(sic)*.

Once again, emigration meant self-determination, self-government, freedom. And thousands were ready to go at once. Of course, there were no transportation facilities for thousands, but that did not deter some of these would-be pilgrims. Indeed, one black group, whose forebears had originally left Florida earlier with the Indians, spent several years wending their way back from Oklahoma to the port of New York, and finally to the docks of Savannah, traveling more than three thousand miles before they were finally able to board a ship for Africa. That was the quality of the hope that was invested in the search for "a Negro country (where) we can be free." In many cases, Liberia and other West African destinations produced something less than the black pilgrims had hoped for, but that does not diminish the meaning or the quality of their struggle.

Even those black persons who could not seriously entertain emigration as an alternative for their own lives nevertheless understood the concerns of their brothers and sisters. For there was no denying the antiblack reality of America. By the late 1890s, its signs were everywhere. In 1896, in the *Plessy* v. *Ferguson* decision the Supreme Court made official the attempts to segregate the black community out of the structures of power and authority and to make their subjugation more easily accomplished. The number of brutal, savage lynchings were sometimes more than two hundred each year, and thousands of blacks were unofficial victims of white violence. Adding insult to injury, black Americans had to endure these things while listening to the justifications of white northern apologists and the literary vilifications of the southern white leaders.

Against this background of experience, it should not have been surprising that many blacks immediately questioned and condemned American intervention in the Spanish-Cuban war. Indeed, as a part of their ongoing critique of American society (a necessary element of any freedom struggle), black people offered some of the most important and most prophetic analyses of the significance of the newest phase of American imperialism. They also saw, as one black socialist said, that "the American Negro cannot become the ally of Imperialism without enslaving his own race." Thus it was only fitting that in the course of the three-year American military action against the Philippine independence fighters, a significant number of the black American soldiers went over to the other side, following the movement of their own people's freedom struggle to its logical end.

Chapter 17

Towards a New Century: "To Protest Forever" or "To Possess this Land"? (1900 – 1914)

I

Although their calendars announced the beginning of a new century, although the din of church bells and the rhetoric of a thousand editorials and sermons confirmed the fact, the dominant realities in the lives of America's nine million black people were still harshly familiar and reminiscent of old ways.

In the South, where almost 90 percent of the black population still lived in 1900, the idea of a new year and a new time seemed especially ironic. Sharecropping and other forms of peonage tied hundreds of thousands of families to other men's land and other men's control. Black participation in the electoral process was smashed or subverted through mob action, economic blackmail and a series of legal ruses like the grandfather clause, the white primary, and the purging of voting lists. While the federal government stood by, organized, extralegal vigilante groups like the Ku Klux Klan provided much of the force and terror behind this exploitation and repression. Over it all, like a grim backdrop, hung the pall of acrid smoke from burning black bodies, and the sounds of dying men and women swaying from the trees along many roads, and the raucous yells of savage white crowds, gouging out eyes and flesh, cutting off sexual organs.

Meanwhile, in the North, much of the old also remained. The discrimination and segregation in many areas of public and private life, the diseases, despair, and crime that so often grew out of these conditions, the hypocrisy of a "progressive" America, pretending that all was well—these persisted. Still, in the South and in the North, black people refused to give up their freedoms without struggle, even against the harshest odds, and in both North and South they continued to seek for ways to advance the positive struggle for freedom and dignity.

Those men and women who were determined to press the other American revolution into the twentieth century found that one of the major obstacles in their way was the philosophy and leadership of Booker T. Washington. As the first southern-based, national black spokesman to be projected and accepted by many elements of the nation's white leadership, Washington generally assumed that this was indeed a white man's country and that it would always be so. His strategy was based on those assumptions.

Taking his cue from his own situation at Tuskegee, in the heart of Alabama, he urged black people to do whatever was necessary to survive, to learn whatever would help them to fit into the scheme of things whites had devised. He told them to "let down your buckets" in the midst of a racist white society and to try to live with whatever was placed within them. (Some buckets brought up nothing but blood.) From this position, he discouraged black political participation and backed away from the open struggle against disfranchisement. He stood against any black alliances with forces that challenged the basic assumptions of the white, capitalist, industrialist leaders who had become his patrons and protectors. For Washington, there was no revolutionary struggle, no movement for self-determination, no thrust to become "an essential part of the *ruling element*" of America, only the fight for survival. Within this constricted arena, the "Wizard of Tuskegee" sought to build his own empire of power and influence.

II

From the point in the last years of the nineteenth century when he moved to ascendancy to the time of his death two decades later, it was almost impossible to participate in the struggle for black freedom in America without relating in one way or another to Booker T. Washington. In spite of some of Washington's positive contributions to black development, many persons who took active leadership in the black freedom movement eventually felt they must challenge Washington, his servile philosophy, and his underhanded tactics of manipulation and control. Certainly this was the context for the rousing challenge that was presented to the black community by John Hope, the brilliant young black scholar, when near the turn of the century, he called out,

Rise, Brothers! Come let us possess this land. Never say: "Let well enough alone." Cease to console yourselves with adages that numb the moral sense. Be discontented. Be dissatisfied. "Sweat and grunt" under the present conditions. Be restless as the tempestuous billows on the boundless sea. Let your discontent break mountain-high against the walls of prejudice, and swamp it to the very foundation. Then we shall not have to plead for justice nor on bended knee crave mercy; for we shall be men. Then and not until then will liberty in its highest sense be the boast of our Republic.

This multiple challenge to possess the land, to claim the Republic by forcing it to do justice and, by implication, to deny Washington's leadership became a major theme in the first decade of the twentieth century. Those elements of the freedom movement which were identified with the tradition of black protest were especially bold in setting it forth.

Still there were other forms and manifestations of struggle as the century began. Blacks refused to cease experimenting. For instance, in the spring of 1900, a call went out for the formation of an independent black political party, one that would be socialist and anti-imperialist in its orientation. Those black leaders who signed the appeal said they realized that such a proposal was "revolutionary in character," but they felt justified "because of the ruthless betrayal of popular government by both the two great political parties."

In another part of the struggle, the indefatigable, flamboyant Bishop Henry McNeil Turner, with his continuing access to the grass roots of the southern black community, still pressed forward the idea of African emigration. Having visited Africa several times, Turner claimed there was no other pathway to true black self-development and self-determination. Thus he urged hundreds of thousands of blacks to sign petitions calling for the federal government to provide reparation payments that would pay for the cost of transportation and settlement in the motherland. The petitions arrived in large batches, but they suffered the fate of most black requests to the Congress. Meanwhile, thousands of blacks continued searching for a more proximate place of independence, and made their way to Oklahoma, hoping to develop black control in at least several sectors of that state.

Still, the vision of Africa would not die. A group of middle-class American blacks, most notably W. E. B. Du Bois, were present when the first formal Pan-African Congress was convened in London in 1900. With only a few African countries represented, it was a small beginning, but it provided a critical continuity with many pan-African experiences of the past, and it anticipated one of the important elements that would soon be added to the combustible mixture of black struggle in America.

III

While the full significance of pan-Africanism was still hidden in the past and the future, it was the black protest position that began to attract new attention in the first years of the twentieth century. No one represented that position more fully than William Monroe Trotter of Boston. Trotter, an honor graduate of Harvard, and a member of one of the city's best known black middle class families, had decided to set aside a financially and socially successful career in real estate to devote his life to the struggle for black freedom. With an equally brilliant (but eventually less courageous) friend named George Forbes, Trotter organized a new black newspaper, the Boston *Guardian*. Its first issue announced the credo of both the paper and its senior editor. It said,

> We have come to protest forever against being proscribed or shut off in any caste from equal rights with other citizens, and shall remain forever on the firing line at any and all times in defense of such rights.

Although the language was more vivid, the *Guardian*'s position was largely the same one taken by *Freedom's Journal* more than seven decades earlier. The focus was not on black control, hegemony, or becoming a part of the "ruling element" of the society. It did not catch John Hope's vision of a movement "to possess this land." Rather, its emphasis was on protest and exposure, seeking for rights that would be granted by the white leaders of America. Of course, in a racist society, such a position faithfully carried forward eventually meant confrontation and a struggle for the right to define the nature of the society itself.

From his Boston base, Trotter also went to war against Booker T. Washington in a fashion at once more open and more brutal than anything yet experienced. Then, when Washington ventured into Trotter's city, the visit produced an uproarious melee in a church auditorium and provided a short visit to the local jail for Trotter and some of his associates. Partly as a result of the sense of injustice that Trotter's jailing aroused in him, partly as a result of his own experiences with the savagery of the New South, W. E. B. Du Bois soon joined hands with Trotter. Together, they were the critical, moving forces in the organizing of the Niagara Movement, the twentieth century's prototypical black protest organization.

Niagara was almost as much a movement against Washington's dominance as it was for black freedom. It attracted a largely middle-class and articulate group of editors, teachers, clergymen, and other black professionals whose major strengths were in the independence of their organization and in the forthrightness of the protest they raised. They were heirs of the black abolitionist tradition, offering a twentieth-century response to Frederick Douglass's call to "agitate, agitate, agitate!" They took their name from their first meeting place, a hotel on the Canadian side of Niagara Falls. At their next annual session they walked barefooted over the "sacred ground" where John Brown had walked at Harpers Ferry. In both places, they raised stirring cries of protest, anguish, and hope. On another occasion they urged black people to forge alliances with Socialist forces rather than continue dependent on the two major parties.

Ultimately, though, they failed as an organization. They failed because Du Bois and Trotter could not work together, because neither they nor any of the others were skilled at the kind of large-scale organizing they hoped to do. They failed because they lacked money. They failed because they did not speak to many of the critical economic issues facing the black community, especially in the South. They failed because they seemed fearful to deal with the harsh realities of the raging white mobs. But they also failed because the times were not yet quite right for the success of such an outspoken, black-shaped and black-controlled organization.

IV

Instead, the National Association for the Advancement of Colored People (NAACP) was formed, organized largely by white men and women who were both intellectual and biological heirs of the antebellum white abolitionists. Beginning in 1910, Du Bois gave more than twenty of the most productive years of his life to the NAACP, as editor of its organ, *Crisis*, and as a member of the board. Although he worked with the predominantly white-directed association in an autonomous and independent style, Du Bois had made a choice that many of his colleagues rejected. Trotter, for instance, had left Niagara earlier to organize the Negro-American Political League, and he continued to insist on black control of all organizations in the struggle for black freedom. Ida B. Wells-Barnett, who had been involved in the conferences that preceded the formation of the NAACP, chose a more local base for her continuing struggles. In Chicago, she formed the Negro

Fellowship League, and persisted in her lucid investigatory reports on the uses of white mob action against the life of the black community.

While Du Bois moved into an alliance with the white liberal forces of the NAACP, other colleagues tried to shape new black organizations for the struggle. Still others, like Hubert H. Harrison, sought out more radical white alliances, with the Socialist party and with the Industrial Workers of the World, the most radical mass labor organization yet produced by America. Though they likely saw a different vision than John Hope, they, too, sought ultimately to possess the land.

Meanwhile, deep in the heart of the black community, a certain continuity prevailed, a heaving base of blackness remained, and the old land could not be denied. Out of the empty lots and basements of Newark, New Jersey, a black native of North Carolina named Timothy Drew came preaching a new identity for black people in America, and was transformed himself to Noble Drew Ali, leader of the Moors in America. In Dayton, Ohio, a group of blacks banded together under the name of The Hand of Ethiopia, and pressed forward programs of black consciousness and solidarity, including the use of black teachers to teach black children.

And out in Oklahoma, in the spring of 1913, it appeared as if Africa had indeed stretched forth its hand to the beleaguered black community of that new state. For in response to a call from some of Oklahoma's black settlers, one "Chief Sam" from the Gold Coast had appeared there, bringing word of a black-owned trading and shipping company that would make available a way back home, a way to the future. Just before World War I began, a group of black pilgrims sailed with Chief Sam in search of freedom. Most did not find it, but their readiness, and the readiness of the thousands who signed up for the next ships (which never came) testified that the struggle towards hope had in no way relented. Men and women seemed too determined: they would possess one land or another.

Chapter 18

World War I and the Exploding Revolutions (1914 —1918)

I

By now, it is generally assumed that wars tend to exert profound effects on revolutionary movements. Nevertheless it is still impossible to overstate the tremendous impact of World War I on the development of the movement for black freedom in America.

In the first place, it must be noted that the brutal, bloody war was a terrible trauma in the heart of the European experience, one from which that continent never really recovered. The war jolted Europe out of the false complacencies and certainties of the nineteenth century and finally announced the beginning of the twentieth century in the West. Coming as it did at the height of Europe's conventional colonial exploitation of the non-Western world, the conflict shook the foundations of that system of domination, and the damage proved irreparable.

Black Americans watched the war and saw the white powers call their nonwhite oppressed colonial people into the fray. Then, when America eventually did the same, the action affirmed in many black minds the basic unity there was between their situation in America and the oppression of nonwhite peoples in Africa and the rest of the world. That was only one of the ways in which the war provided a clearer international context and focus to the struggle for black freedom in America; but it had even more immediate and clearly measurable effects on black struggle. Paramount among these was the stimulus that it provided for a stunning movement of black people out of the South. The war came in a time of depression for the southern farm laborers. A disastrous plague of boll weevils had destroyed many cotton crops, floods had despoiled vast sections of the earth, black sharecroppers felt themselves pressed more desperately against the wall than ever before. The war came in the midst of the unrelenting white savagery called lynching.

At the same difficult time, the needs of war were placing sharply increased demands on the productive capacities of the northern industries; but the fighting had also cut the supply of European immigrants who provided the base of the working force for the factories. So the time was ripe for black people of the South. Soon the northern manufacturers, aided and abetted by black newspapers and recruiters, began an all-out campaign to suck this new source of labor into the machines of war. Black people were ready, and they began to flood out of the South.

They came from places called Groveton and Shaw, Shreveport and Americus. They came from Jackson and Birmingham, from Sylvester and Byhalia. They carried their boxes and bags and suitcases out of Cedar Keys and Valdosta and Estill Springs, sometimes moving by night. They left in the darkness at times because the white South knew that this newest black exodus was a form of a struggle, a declaration of independence from the ancient tyrannies, and they tried to stop it. So they arrested labor recruiters; they imprisoned local black people on false charges when they appeared at the railway and bus stations. They used many weapons in their arsenal of intimidation—including murder.

But the movement did not stop. The people traveled by train and by riverboat. They went alone, and in families, and in supportive companies, and congregations more than a hundred strong. They left by the tens of thousands during those war years, and their movement bore the rhythm and the content of those earlier times when black pilgrims made their way to freedom land. Yet there was something distinctively new. Perhaps black people sensed that their movement for justice and self-determination was taking a new direction. For we are told of one group of nearly one hundred and fifty persons from Hattiesburg, Mississippi, who "held solemn ceremonies while crossing the Ohio River." Indeed, it was reported that "They knelt down and prayed; and men stopped their watches and, amid tears of joy, sang the familiar songs of deliverance."

II

They sang the old songs, but they had begun a new time. There had never been an exodus like this in the old days before the Civil War.

This time some half a million black folk left the South within a decade. This time, they moved into the heart of the urban centers of America. This time, blacks were pressed into the basic industries of the society, becoming the newest proletariat. Perhaps most important of all the differences was that this time the migration took significant numbers of blacks to many more parts of America. Now the struggle was everywhere. Although they might deny it, the other revolution was at everyone's door.

This was also a period when black people from outside the continental United States, especially from the Caribbean Islands, came in larger numbers than ever. This migration, when combined with the upheavals within the American black community, and with the powerful dislocations of the war, would produce a most explosive product. But no one had clearly seen that when one Marcus M. Garvey of Jamaica landed in America in 1916.

World War I stimulated movement on other levels as well, involving feelings and ideas, emotions and analysis. For instance, the early black responses to the war took many forms. Some were simply affirmations of the ancient idea that white men's wars should not concern black folks. Others spoke from a more sophisticated political position, pointing out that the control of African colonies was a crucial issue in the war, and they urged blacks to see the significance of such questions beyond all patriotic and democratic rhetoric. Still other critiques went even deeper into the heart of the affair, into the meaning of the twentieth century.

For instance, Hubert H. Harrison, the most important and influential radical black intellectual teacher of the period, stood on the sidewalks of Harlem and told the cheering crowds:

> As representatives of one of the races constituting the colored majority of the world, we deplore the agony and bloodshed (of the war); but we find consolation in the hope that when the white world shall have been washed clean by its baptism of blood, the white race will be less able to thrust the strong hand of its sovereign will down the throats of other races.

Working from that set of hopes and assumptions, Harrison declared that as a result of the war he looked for

> a free India and an independent Egypt; *for nationalities in Africa flying their own flags and dictating their own internal and foreign policies.*

During the first phases of the war black radicals and intellectuals, and others, regularly raised such prophetic critiques. (Indeed, the struggle for black freedom in America was never without its incisive, analytical, and radical critiques of American foreign policy.) For black men and women wanted to know why this nation seemed so eager to support its allies in a war for the freedom of other peoples, when so much of its own black population was still subject to injustice, exploitation, and death at the hands of their white neighbors. When President Woodrow Wilson first raised the banner of a war "to make the world safe for democracy" black leaders launched slashing attacks against this southern-born defender of segregation.

III

But war is war, and after America officially entered World War I, black people had to face the harsh realities of the government's power to conscript their sons and fathers, to imprison dissenters, to harass all opposition (and to offer rewards bathed in the perfume of patriotism to all who conformed their words and actions to the needs of "the white world"). Soon the soft-pedaling of black struggle concerns was being justified, and criticism of America was discouraged. Leaders like Du Bois proposed that blacks temporarily "forget our special grievances and close our ranks shoulder to shoulder with our own white citizens and the allied nations that are fighting for democracy."

It was a shameful proposal, to transmute all the great concerns of the historic black struggle for freedom and justice into "special grievances." But the brutal reality, as Du Bois put it, was "the choice between conscription and rebellion," and neither he nor most black leaders was ready for rebellion. But there was a seething, explosive element at work which could not be denied by calls to "close ranks." Some blacks actually chose to engage in subversive activities on behalf of the Germans. More important for these purposes was the fact that some of the very white Americans who were supposedly fighting for democracy overseas took time during the war to continue their brutal murders of black people at home.

Just before July 4, 1917, whites in East Saint Louis, Illinois, unleashed a vicious pogrom upon the black community. With the aid of militia and police forces, they managed to kill scores of black men, women, and children and to injure hundreds of others. Closing white ranks, they burned black homes, picked off black targets with rifles and pistols, threw black children into bonfires, and smashed babies' skulls against the ground. When word got out, cries of anger, outrage, and anguish swept the black community. Men and women made promises of revenge; many made even more important rededications to struggle for the total transformation of America. In many cases, at least in words, this black response to events in the southern Illinois town suggestively exposed the revolutionary potential of the Afro-American community.

IV

One black leader in Frederick Douglass's old home city of Rochester, New York, addressed a rally of black people there, recalled the events that had transpired in East Saint Louis, and said,

> It is a man's duty to be loyal to his country and his flag, but when his country becomes a land of oppression and his flag an emblem of injustice and wrong, it becomes as much his duty to attack the enemies within the nation as to resist the foreign invader. Tyrants and tyranny everywhere should be attacked and overthrown.

Similar responses came from many parts of black America, and in such a setting of outrage and determination, one may justly ask, was there a connection between the massacre of blacks in Illinois and the decision made by a number of black men in Kansas? Shortly after East Saint Louis, they participated in short-lived, predominantly white revolutionary movement in Kansas, one that vowed to march on Washington and take over the government of the United States. The Green Corn Rebellion, as it was called, was undisciplined and poorly led; nevertheless it marked the first time in the century when blacks (including a group of brothers who had maintained their African names) consciously chose to join their own radical concerns to those of white revolutionaries. But the direct connection to East Saint Louis may only be surmised.

In the same way, we may ask how deeply were the bloody images of East Saint Louis lodged in the minds of the black men of the supremely "loyal" Twenty-fourth Infantry Regiment when they took up arms against the white community of Houston later that summer. Responding to repeated injustices in their own situation, taking both military and civil law into their hands, these trusted mercenaries startled the white nation as they marched with their guns on the city, and killed fourteen persons, including one policeman.

The black community's strong and positive response to this unexpected "attack [on] the enemies within the nation" was reminiscent of the reaction to the fight near Christiana, Pennsylvania, almost seven decades earlier. Indeed, it was so widespread and staunchly supportive of the soldiers that the leaders of white America realized they had a very dangerous situation on their hands. The government immediately placed the Houston soldiers in secret confinement. Then, later that year a totally secret trial was held, and thirteen of the men were executed in the chilly darkness of a December morning. When the execution was finally announced publicly, the place of burial remained a secret, as if the white powers were hoping that they could contain the contagion of those thirteen black lives.

Nor were the dangers confined to America. In many places where blacks and whites seemed to "close ranks," there were harsh and abrasive experiences. Over in France on the fields of death, blacks found much of America's racism dogging their steps in their relationships with their fellow servicemen. There, they chose a less dangerous path than that of Houston, and, like so many black generations before them, poured their feelings into songs like,

> The cracker marines went over the top,
> parlay voo;
> the cracker marines went over the top,
> parlay voo;
> the cracker marines went over the top
> because at them us black boys shot,
> inky, dinky, parlay voo.

(Were the songs based on any realities at all?)

V

Meanwhile, recognizing the powerful transformative potentials of this time, other black men and women were working out the hard, theoretical questions that must finally undergird each new stage of struggle. For instance, Hubert H. Harrison, having left the Socialist party, was now putting forth the dictum of "race first." Replacing the Socialist shibboleth of organization and struggle on the basis of class alliances, Harrison declared that race must be the first consideration in all new strategies of struggle. Black solidarity thus became a mandate. Along with this solidarity, Harrison taught the need for a new black internationalism, a kind of revolutionary Pan-Africanism that joined all the children of Africa in opposition to European domination. In these views he was joined by other important publicists and teachers like John E. Bruce and William Bridges. Ultimately, none of these men took the concepts of black solidarity and internationalism to the masses of black people in a way that would match the power, range, and tremendous potential of Marcus Garvey. As for that wartime visitor to America, he was still watching, learning, moving among the other teachers, just beginning to organize.

At the same time, a counterforce of sorts was at work, challenging the "race first" position. In 1917, the weak Socialist links to the black community were given some new strength and life when A. Phillip Randolph and Chandler Owen, two young, articulate, recent converts to the Socialist party, began to proselytize for the party in Harlem and transformed an older publication into *The Messenger* magazine. They called their journal "the only Magazine of Scientific Radicalism in the world published by Negroes," and the description told something of their problematical attitudes towards themselves and other black folk.

For a time, though, they did produce one of the most exciting and aggressive radical journals in America, one that was subsidized by Socialist party sources, insisted on the Socialist position of "class first" organizing, harshly attacked all other views (especially black ones), and eagerly heralded the coming of the Socialist revolution in America. Only as blacks entered the struggle for *that* revolution, said *The Messenger*, would any real level of black freedom ever be realized. For them, the Socialist revolution (which they said was imminent) was the only *other* American revolution that counted.

When revolution did come, it was not in America. Before the European War was over, its dislocative movements helped to precipitate the most important revolution of the century. As word of the Russian revolution reached here, both the advocates of "class first" and of "race first" were quick to hail its importance. None of them could possibly know then, however, that the movement of Lenin's Bolsheviks to power was one of the single most important contributions of World War I to the development of the black freedom struggle in America. Nor could they know that the influence of the "Red" revolution on the black, other, American revolution, would eventually turn out to be at least as paradoxical as the gifts that Patrick Henry, Thomas Jefferson, and company had bequeathed.

Chapter 19

After Three Hundred Years: "If We Must Die . . ." (1919)

I

In the middle of the year 1919, remembering the official anniversary of the coming of the first Africans to the Virginia colony, W. E. B. Du Bois wrote these words in the *Crisis:*

> In sackcloth and ashes . . . we commemorate this [year], lest we forget; lest a single drop of blood, a single moan of pain, a single bead of sweat, in all these three, long, endless centuries should drop into oblivion.
>
> Why must we remember? Is this but a counsel of Vengeance and Hate? God forbid! We must remember because if once the world forgets evil, evil is reborn; because if the suffering of the American Negro is once forgotten, then there is no [guarantee], down to the last pulse of time that Devils will not again enslave and murder and oppress the weak and unfortunate.

No one reading those words in August, 1919, would have considered them overblown, for the events in the summer of that tricentennial year had already become the occasion for much sackcloth and ashes, much deep reflection on the meaning of the black experience in this strange land.

The most important developments of the memorial year were the release of a new flood of black internationalism and the explosion of a powerful, previously unmatched force of radical black urban resistance into the mainstream of the other American revolution. Considering the international scope of the war, and the stark transformation it had already wrought in black and white America, these radicalizing developments were to be expected.

101

Earlier, as the year began and much world attention was focused on the Peace Conference in Paris, men like Hubert Harrison and John E. Bruce followed intently the discussions concerning a projected League of Nations. As a result, they called again for the children of Africa everywhere to organize on an international scale or face the prospect of new defeats under the power of the coming "white international." For instance, Bruce said,

> Whether we be in Africa, or Asia, or Europe, America, and the Islands of the seas, our destiny is one; we are facing the same conditions, wrestling with the same obstacles, fighting the same unrelenting foe.

So he concluded, "Unless we organize the world over we must continue to fight and never triumph, wrestle and never overcome."

II

In a sense, when Du Bois arrived in Paris early in the year, he was following the mandates of that black internationalist thought, even though his own vision was not as radical or militant as that of men like Harrison and Bruce. Still, Du Bois's work in organizing the second Pan-African Congress made a significant contribution to the ongoing development of an international African context for the black struggle for freedom in America.

Monroe Trotter was also in Paris that winter. While Du Bois had gone in some style, his irrepressible former associate had been refused travel documents and instead decided to take a job as a cook on a small European-bound freighter. When the *S.S. Yarmouth* (later part of Garvey's Black Star Line) arrived at Le Havre, its Harvard-educated second cook jumped ship and somehow made his way to Paris. There, acting as a representative of a coalition of black groups in America, he insisted on raising the issue of the protection of the rights of black people as a part of the peace treaty. (The same issue was being raised in a slightly different form by the Japanese representatives.) Of course, Trotter had to carry on his fiery advocacy on the outside, sending in statements, petitions, and broadsides at regular intervals, for he was not allowed anywhere near the conference. At the same time, his fearless embodiment of the black protest tradition attracted the attention of many persons in this country as well as in France—but no guarantee of black rights in America ever appeared in the Treaty of Versailles.

In his single-handed attempt to pierce the overwhelmingly white, international peace conference with black concerns, Trotter represented a historic black tradition, and his activities in Paris suggested ways in which that protest stream would move in the future. Du Bois, in contrast, sought to organize an international black counterbase for dealing with the white organization. Still, his mode of operation was unquestionably shaped by the perspectives of the American protest tradition. For he nourished the somewhat naive hope that his Pan-African Congress might be called upon by the Peace Conference as an advisory group, especially with regard to the future of the African colonies.

There were, however, other international approaches. By this time in America, one of the most talented of the black publicists and organizers, Cyril Briggs, a native West Indian, had begun to develop the African Blood Brotherhood (ABB). The ABB was the first American-based black organization that sought to develop a firm connection between the struggle for black freedom in America and the revolutionary movements of Africans in the homeland and elsewhere. (The younger Martin Delany had seen a vision like this, but he had not been able to organize such a group.) After developing a membership of several thousand persons, the ABB eventually lost its way between the whirlwind that was Garvey and the rise of the Communist party; but in 1919, the ABB represented a most significant promise, one whose intrinsic, theoretical validity has never been denied.

III

It is likely that the largest and most important single force of Afro-American men who had caught some new international vision were to be found among the thousands of servicemen who were members of the American Expeditionary Forces in Europe. Many of the dilemmas of the new age were caught up in them. They had seen both the shame and grandeur of modern European civilization. They had experienced all the racism and fear that the war had not dislodged from the lives of their fellow military men and American civilians overseas. They knew they had been used in a cause that was not ultimately theirs. They realized that their own first and last battlefield was in America. On their return, many of them joined the African Blood Brotherhood.

While in Europe, Du Bois had spent several weeks among the black armed forces as they prepared to embark for the United States. In

May, 1919, he attempted to speak for this contingent of black men. He put forth a litany of indictments against America for the lynching, disfranchisement, exploitation, and humiliation to which the soldiers now returned. Then he added, "But by the God of Heaven, we are cowards and jackasses if now that the war is over, we do not fight a sterner, longer, more unbending battle against the forces of hell in our own land." Later, in a more reflective moment, Du Bois said, "A new radical Negro spirit has been born in France, which leaves us older radicals far behind."

This was no secret knowledge. A new, more experienced, more fiercely determined and potentially radical element had been added to the arena of black struggle in America. White people in America knew it, and they looked to the discharge of the hundreds of thousands of black servicemen with a mixture of deep apprehension and bitter resolve. By 1919, the Ku Klux Klan had moved to the apex of its revival, and more than one hundred thousand white men were members. They were preparing to do whatever was necessary to keep America a white man's country. They were digging in against the tides.

Meanwhile, the flooding black movement into the northern cities had continued at a rapid pace, sometimes multiplying their black populations by several hundred percent, creating explosive bulges in the taut and searing edges of the ghettos. All this added to the fears and anger of men and women caught in the trap of their own unexamined history. So these white men and women unfurled a banner and hung it across the width of South Parkway in Chicago. (Did they ever dream that "their" street would one day be renamed for a leader of the other American revolution and become Martin Luther King, Jr. Drive?) Its words expressed their defiance, hatred, and terror, and offered their response to the "New Negro" who seemed to have sprung up everywhere. Appropriately enough, the wording on the banner was taken from the allied slogan at the World War's crucial Battle of Verdun: "They Shall Not Pass."

IV

Although it was originally hurled at oncoming German troops, the use of the slogan at South Parkway and Forty-third Street was appropriate, for America had never come so close to general racial warfare as it did in that late spring and summer of 1919. From Charleston, South Carolina, to Longview, Texas, from Washington, D.C., to Chicago, Illinois, black and white people went to war on the streets. There were various specific occasions: the taunting attacks of arrogant white servicemen; the movement of white mobs against black people; the violent reaction of whites to the continuing black search for a place to live and breathe. Most often the initial intention of the whites was the same: to invade the black community, to attempt another slaughter, another scorched earth. But in 1919, the outcome was different, a new stage in history had been reached.

Throughout the nation that spring and summer, thousands of black people decided to fight back, to move out into the streets against the white aggressors. Often they pressed on to carry the offense to their historic oppressors. Especially in Washington and Chicago, the fighting was fierce and extensive. Black men set up roadblocks of wood, bricks, and concrete on the streets of their communities. Both blacks and whites used cars of armed men to roar like armored military vehicles through the opposite communities. Black snipers operated from the windows of houses. Bands of attackers swooped down on persons of the opposite race who happened into their territory. Everywhere, black veterans played a central role in the fighting, often using weapons they had managed to smuggle back into the black community, weapons as large as machine guns. In Washington, the battle went on for several days. In Chicago, it lasted for almost a week, spreading over much of that sprawling city.

In these conflicts, almost without exception, blacks had to fight against both white civilians and various forces of white law and order. Nevertheless the struggle continued. All classes and persuasions of black folks found ways of helping, serving, supporting. On one level, it was largely a set of self-defense operations, and much of that spirit was expressed in the poem Claude McKay produced out of the maelstrom of that summer:

> If We must die—let it not be like hogs
> Hunted and penned in an inglorious spot,
> While round us bark the mad and hungry dogs,
> Making their mock at our accursed lot.
> If we must die—oh, let us nobly die,
> . . .
> Like men we'll face the murderous, cowardly pack,
> Pressed to the wall, dying, but fighting back!

But even at this level, there had never before been such widespread urban action of armed black self-defense. Never had there been such national black participation and approval. The nation learned a lesson. Nineteen-nineteen was one of the last times that white civilians attempted any significant invasion of the black communities of the urban North. (Their police and military forces were now handed the task alone.)

V

For an oppressed people to take up arms against the depredations of their historic oppressors was an essentially revolutionary development. For that people to be scattered across the breadth of America and working at the base of the nation's industries was no less revolutionary in potential.

Some black people saw this, and went beyond the valorous sonnet of McKay to assess the larger, political meaning. In a popular, somewhat flamboyant tone, two former servicemen who were participants in the Washington, D.C., warfare put it this way:

> This is the second emancipation of the Negro.
> It has taught the Negro to arm himself to the
> teeth and stay armed.
> It has taught the Negro that in forty-eight
> hours of hard fighting for himself at home
> he will get more recognition than a year of
> fighting overseas.
> It has taught the Negro that it means nothing
> to be patriotic and fight with and for the
> American white man . . .
> It has taught the white man that he cannot
> train Negroes to fight and then tell them
> whom, when, and where to fight.

At the end of their pamphlet the young writers concluded,

> On with the dance,
> Keep time with the music.

The tricentennial had been celebrated with strange music and dances; but it was clear that after 1919, the struggle for black freedom in America was never the same again. All the movements and tendencies that had been created or heightened by the war had been emblazoned on the streets of cities embroiled in racial warfare. A ferment unlike anything since the decade prior to the Civil War was at work. It was into this setting that Marcus Garvey brought his own explosion.

Chapter 20

Look for Me in the Whirlwind: The Rise and Fall – and Rise – of Marcus Garvey (1919 –1925)

I

Paraphrasing Marxist thought, C. L. R. James, the great Pan-African revolutionary scholar once said, "Men make history, but only so much history as they are able to make." Such a deceptively simple statement must surely apply to Marcus Garvey. Before World War I, as a result of his internal and external pilgrimage in Jamaica, other parts of the Caribbean, Central America, and England, Garvey had shaped many of his own hopes and visions for the future of African peoples. But it was the overwhelming catalytic power of the war, the radical angry ferment of the black community in America, and the revolutionary explosions all over the world which ultimately formed the nexus for the rise of Garvey and Garveyism. Then it was the bloody summer of 1919, embodying so many of these world-shaking forces, which finally capapulted him and his movement to a center of prominence and power in America and beyond.

Ever since his arrival in the United States at the age of twenty-eight, Garvey had been sizing up the situation, sensing the mood, absorbing every possible element of black life in America. At the end of 1917 he had begun formal organizing for the Universal Negro Improvement Association (UNIA). On a certain level "improvement" seemed such a mild, unradical idea. But it had many of the same connotations as the nineteenth-century concept of the "elevation" of African peoples which Delany had put forward; and Garvey, like Delany, tied the concept to the larger thrust of the "redemption" of Africa. In a racist society, in a white-dominated imperialist world,

107

wherever black men and women took those things seriously, and tried to organize and act on them, they were on a revolutionary path.

Garvey was calling upon an oppressed and downtrodden set of peoples to "improve" themselves, to "elevate" themselves, to redeem their colonized homeland. Black people heard the message, and many sensed the call to struggle which was implied. They did not need to see the uniformed companies of the African Legion to recognize that they were being challenged to tasks that might involve serious struggle against those who had exploited and murdered them. Garvey was calling on them to love themselves first, to value themselves first, to fight for themselves first, and above all, through black international action, to free themselves and their homeland.

II

Obviously, none of these teachings was new in the development of the other American revolution. All had their precedents in the recent or more distant past, through men like John Bruce, Hubert Harrison, Bishop Turner, Martin Delany, or David Walker. What was new was the twentieth century. New were the confusing, exhilarating forces that were abroad, the new movements that deeply affected black people and their oppressors. New was Marcus Garvey and his extraordinary power as a publicist and an exhorter, and the availability of a mass print medium, *The Negro World*. New were the many signs Garvey had given that he might indeed be able to organize the children of Africa as no one had ever done before. By 1919, there were reports of dozens of branches of the UNIA, not only in the United States but in many other parts of the black world as well—including Africa. In addition to *The Negro World*, other UNIA businesses and subsidiaries began to be established, but none so electrified the black world as the organization of the Black Star Line.

This putative international shipping line was proof that Garvey meant business, and each person tended to interpret for himself the fullest significance of the business at hand. For some, the ships (far more attractive in hopes and dreams than in their weatherbeaten and unseaworthy reality) were the long-awaited means to return to Africa to begin a new, independent life. Others took seriously the rumors that there were secret levels on these vessels which would hide the invasion force of armed black troops who would drive the white colonizers from the African mainland. One of Garvey's own stated purposes was to create significant commercial ties among the scattered peoples of the African diaspora.

Significantly enough, it was in the summer of explosion and armed racial struggle that Garvey made the first public announcement of the development of the Black Star Line. As a matter of fact, that meeting at New York City's Carnegie Hall in August, 1919, seemed to embody all the most radical, revolutionary hopes that men and women held for Garvey and his movement. He seemed to leave no doubt in people's minds that he intended to build firmly on the militancy and sense of grim determination that then gripped the black community. What else could the excited audience believe when he shouted from the stage,

> we say to the white man who now dominates Africa, that it is to his interest to clear out of Africa now, because we are coming . . . 400,-000,000 strong; and we mean to retake every square inch of the 12,000,000 square miles of African territory belonging to us by right divine.

Continuing that challenging theme, he placed the struggle for Africa in the context of world revolution and said,

> Every American Negro and every West Indian Negro must understand now that there is but one fatherland for the Negro, and that is Africa. . . . as the Irishman is struggling and fighting for the fatherland of Ireland, so must the new Negro of the world fight for the fatherland of Africa.

III

And what did all of this have to do with the daily oppression and death faced by black people in America? To that question Garvey offered a strange answer, a bizarre set of connections between the struggle for Africa and the struggle for freedom in America. He solemnly promised the Carnegie Hall gathering that

> in the next few months we will be so organized that when they lynch a negro below the Mason and Dixon Line, if we can not lynch a white man there, and since it is not safe to lynch a white man in any part of America, we shall press the button and lynch him in the great continent of Africa.

Waves of applause and tremendous feelings of excited anticipation swept through the black crowd at those words. Indeed, throughout the entire meeting, Garvey and his colleagues kept the audience in a constant state of high emotion and agitation. It was the same at meetings across the nation; but it was perhaps even more important that black people in other parts of the world were now looking to the black community of America with messianic hopes, telling stories of the invincible black soldiers who would one day appear to liberate them. Nothing symbolizes this ecstatic longing more than the lonely fires that some men and women kept burning along the Gold Coast of West Africa during those days, fires that they said were meant to serve as a guide to Marcus Garvey's ships of redemption and return.

But men can make only so much history as they are able to make, and although Marcus Garvey's movement went on to reach its apex in 1920–1921, it never kept its promises to the waiting black world, never fulfilled the magnificent revolutionary potential that had kindled fires of hope across the globe. A major element of the historical limitations lay directly within Marcus Garvey himself. It was not long before some persons began to recognize his lack of real strategy; Garvey had not even any set of organizing principles to discipline his great visions to the hard struggles that must precede their realization.

Indeed, there was every evidence that he had no real stomach for the dark, uncertain night of the soul to which he seemed to be inviting the black peoples of the world, no real desire for a revolutionary, anticolonial struggle that was more than rhetorical. As a matter of fact, he had suggested this problem when he proposed the search for a "safe" place to lynch a white man. For he thereby revealed his failure to understand that there was no safe place in the world for black resistance, and certainly no safe route to the redemption of all of Africa. Beyond the stirring dream, the impassioned speeches, the reams of petitions and documents, there was a disquieting emptiness, a failure of nerve, a soft underside of self-indulgence and fantasy.

IV

As his comments about lynching white men had indicated, Garvey's difficulties were thrown into flagrant relief when the question of black struggle in America had to be faced. Somehow, he thought he could use America as a launching base for a drive against Africa, without really addressing the nature of the other American revolution. Indeed, for him, there was no other American revolution. Though he put the idea in different ways, Garvey was at one with Booker T. Washington in the belief that this was a white man's country, and that the real energies of black struggle ought not to be wasted here. Ultimately, of course, this was a betrayal of all the men, women, and children who had sacrificed their lives in the historic struggle for black freedom in America.

This set of Garvey's internal limitations was tied to other limitations within his movement organization. Evidently there were critical elements of Garvey's style and personality which made it almost impossible for men and women of equal stature to work over long periods with him. Moreover, his distaste for detail and organizational strategies, combined with his problems with outstanding co-workers often made for serious difficulties within the organization.

There was, of course, a large complement of persons who were cooperative and loyal enough, but who brought no real gifts and skills comparable to the immense organizational reality that Garvey had created. Yet there were many competent, single-minded men and women who spotted the empty spaces at the center of Garvey's analysis and strategy; and their attempts to fill that space with their own ideas led to harsh internecine conflicts. Finally, there were considerable persons in the organization who were there as agents of Garvey's enemies.

Among his many external enemies, ranging at times from the Communist party to the government of the United States, none were more implacable than the governments of the various colonizing powers of the West. Moving in their separate spheres of imperialist influence and control, they mounted a careful attack against Garvey, seeking to undercut his movement at every point, often taking his promises of confrontation and challenge far more seriously than he seemed able to take them himself. But they were taking no chances with anyone who threatened to use military force to "redeem" Africa for black people, and who seemed to draw so many black people as devoted followers. So they schemed to undercut his negotiations for a Liberian base of operations. They blunted his attempts to deal with the League of Nations.

It was the American government, however, acting with the aid and cooperation of various black allies, which brought the most direct and vivid pressure to bear. Though Garvey's focus was on Africa, he had created a powerful dynamic in the black community in America; he was building on a long-existent, deeply felt rage. There was no way of predicting where all this might take a people whose very presence was a revolutionary potential. They, too, were taking no chances.

In keeping with its historic response to the other American revolution, the federal government brought to bear the mechanics of its legal system against Garvey (in addition to other more subtle approaches). When that happened, he immediately began to wilt. Over a period of several years, as he was indicted, tried, and finally jailed on a set of flimsy charges and highly suspect evidence, Garvey organized no serious black resistance, and discouraged his UNIA from doing so. Instead, for reasons too numerous to mention here, he meekly submitted himself to the American system of white justice.

So, in 1925 when he wrote his first letter from the federal prison in Atlanta, he could offer his followers nothing more immediately operative than the messianic hope of his return, saying

> in death I shall be a terror to the foes of Negro liberty. . . . If I die in Atlanta my work shall then only begin, but I shall live, in the physical or spiritual to see the day of Africa's glory. When I am dead wrap the mantle of the Red, Black, and Green around me, for in the new life I shall rise . . . to lead the millions up the heights of triumph with the colors that you well know. Look for me in the whirlwind or the storm. . . . I shall come and bring with me countless millions of black slaves who have died in America and the West Indies and the millions in Africa to aid you in the fight for Liberty, Freedom, and Life.

V

In a sense, then, Garvey was saying from Atlanta that it was only through his death and departure that he could be freed to enter into the terrible furnaces of the black struggle for life and liberty in America. Perhaps he was right. He had lifted men and women to a world of hope, affirmation, and determination they had only dreamed before. He had voiced their own greatest commitment and defiance to the white world. He had opened up the floodgates for the great rivers of pride, resistance, and rebellion that would ultimately sweep beyond him.

Perhaps he was right, "I shall live . . ." For even before his death the great influence of the man and his movement was seen roaring through the other American revolution. He was the model for the black Abyssinians who battled the police in the streets of Chicago. He provided new inspiration for Noble Drew Ali. He drew into his circle of influence the quiet part-time preacher, Elijah Poole, from Georgia, who would one day meet Allah on the streets of Detroit. He numbered among his most devoted disciples the Reverend Earl Little of Omaha, who had a son named Malcolm.

These were only a few indicators of Garvey's continuing power. More important was that no one after him could organize among the masses of black people without establishing some position on Garvey and Garveyism. For in the long run the entire black community was deeply affected by his vision and his call. And among many blacks there was a profound, not always articulated, recognition that while men make only so much history as they can, they bequeath even more than they make. (But they have no control over what they bequeath: for in the early 1970s, both Stokely Carmichael and Roy Innis called themselves Neo-Garveyites, and a group of Black Panthers published a testimony of their struggle, using the title, *Look for Me in the Whirlwind.*)

Chapter 21

Black and Red Together: The Broken Hope of the Communist Party (1919 –1936)

I

The UNIA has justly been referred to as the black international, for at its best it was an attempt to use the seething base of black life and struggle in America to shape a worldwide organization for the redemption of Africa and the spiritual transformation of her peoples. From the period during the war when Garvey began serious organization to the time of his incarceration in Atlanta, no other vision of international struggle and movement could take hold in the black community, at least not without coming to terms with the UNIA.

This was certainly true for the Communist, or "red," international. From the outset, as the Communists organized here in America, there were many formidable obstacles in the way of black people choosing this Marxist, "class first," revolutionary international as a vehicle for their own freedom struggle. First of all, of course, there was the powerful gospel of racial solidarity which permeated the black community, with Garvey as its major prophet. The "red" international was, unmistakably, also a *white* international, and black people were highly sensitive to that fact.

Besides, the American Communist movement had very few blacks involved in its earliest development; and to make matters worse, much of that development was necessarily being carried on underground in the midst of bitter, often unnecessary, obscure doctrinal and personal battles. Another important problem was that the Communist party in

America, unlike many of the white organizations with which blacks had chosen to work in other times, was ultimately directed from Moscow, thousands of miles away. The closest analogy blacks could find to such an arrangement did not strike them positively, nor was it entirely inaccurate. They thought of Rome and its Catholic church.

Nevertheless, there were a small number of Socialist-oriented blacks who recognized that there were some significant differences between Rome and Moscow. Among them were a handful of men who had been far more radicalized by their European war service than Du Bois had dreamed. Some of the group, especially after they perceived the gaping political and strategic holes at the heart of Garveyism, turned towards the red international. These early converts to the Communist party were people like Grace Campbell, a brilliant, inde-fatigable organizer: Lovett Fort-Whitman, a former theater editor for *The Messenger;* Cyril Briggs; Haywood and Otto Hall, two army vete-rans and former Garveyites; and several other leaders of the African Blood Brotherhood.

Their motives were various and mixed, but a central hope grasped them all—that the long struggle for black freedom in America might be caught up in a truly universal revolution for the rights of all the oppressed. In theory, here was another resemblance between Rome and Moscow: both lifted the personal and the national concerns of their believers to universal levels and pressed them into the vanguard of history. (But the Communists predicted that the revolution was com-ing before the Day of Judgment. Indeed, they said there would be no other Day of Judgment. Perhaps this expectation of imminent revolu-tion, of an early solution to the centuries-long problem, was part of what attracted these first black members.)

II

Claude McKay was one of the black persons who was drawn to the Communist movement in those days (but who evidently never formally became a member of a party), and he corresponded with Leon Trotsky about the role that black people in America might play in the coming world revolution. A response from Trotsky in the mid-1920s sum-marized a great deal of Communist thinking on this matter, and it focused the problem of black struggle in the red international. Trotsky wrote to McKay,

> it is of the utmost importance today, immediately, to have a number of enlightened, young self-sacrificing Negroes, however small their

number, filled with enthusiasm for the raising of the material and moral
level of the great mass of Negroes, and at the same time mentally capable of grasping the identity of interests and destiny of the Negro masses
with those of the masses of the whole world, and *in the first place with
the destiny of the European working class* (my italics).

Then, in a pointed and significant addition, Trotsky noted that the
work of this committed black cadre

is not to be carried on in a spirit of Negro chauvinism, which would then
merely form a counterpart of white chauvinism—but in a spirit of solidarity of all exploited without consideration of color.

Although the faces and the voices changed, although the message
itself would vary from time to time, Trotsky's position remained the
essential viewpoint of the red international, the one to which it continually returned through decades of struggle. It was, of course, a
position on the place of blacks in world struggle which was hammered
out by whites. It subordinated the black freedom movement in
America to the mass movements of the "whole world," and it pro-
claimed confidently that the leadership of the peoples' movements of the
world was in the hands of "the European working class." It was a
dangerous formulation for black people and their struggle, especially
when the proponents of this line tended, as Trotsky did, to equate
black nationalism and solidarity with the murderous racism of white
America.

All of these elements of the comintern's position were fed directly
into the stance of the American Communist party, and they were rein-
forced and distorted by the unmistakable racism and prejudice that
existed within the ranks of the American unit itself. Obviously, these
were formidable obstacles to recruitment among the Garvey-conscious
black masses, but, with significant stimulation from Moscow, the party
carried on an ever-widening attempt at expanding its minuscule black
membership.

The Communists attempted to bore into the UNIA while Garvey
was under indictment, but failed after a rather amateurish set of mea-
sures. Then, shortly after the black leader was sent to Atlanta, they
established their own American Negro Labor Congress (ANLC) under
a black cadre recently trained in Moscow. But the ANLC failed to
attract any significant body of the black working class. Towards the
end of the 1920s, a League of Struggle for Negro Rights engaged the
energies and talents of men like Langston Hughes and some of the
leadership of the by-then defunct African Blood Brotherhood, but that
turned out to be only slightly more successful than the ANLC.

III

Ironically enough, the turning point in the relationship of black people to the Communist party came not from the American party itself, but from a concatenation of events in Moscow and on Wall Street. In Moscow, as the Russian leadership watched the world near the end of the 1920s and predicted an imminent breakdown of capitalism and the coming of world revolution, a new approach to the black struggle in America was developed. Whether consciously or not, it was based primarily on elements long familiar to the other American revolution. Among the most important was an emphasis on the right of black people in America to self-determination and nationhood, especially in the black belt of the South. The second emphasis was on the crucial role of the black proletariat in America in the leadership of the revolutionary struggle among all nonwhite peoples, especially the peoples of Africa.

This focus on black self-determination opened up new avenues of organizing, particularly among the large majority of black people still in the South, and made allowances for certain expressions of black solidarity that had earlier been discouraged. It also lifted the hope and expectation of many persons to an almost messianic level as they anticipated both the transformation of America and the new role that blacks might play in the coming world revolution.

Then the stock market crashed and the miasmic cloud of depression began to spread over the land, carrying heavy burdens of despair, confusion, and fear into every corner of the society. It appeared as if the comintern predictions had been right. Now, in the midst of the deep perplexity that faced the nation, there were times when the Communists seemed to be the only ones who had answers, who displayed discipline, who knew where they were going—towards world revolution.

They were organizing the unemployed. They were leading marches on the city halls and welfare offices seeking economic benefits for all. They were breaking down the racial barriers within their own organization and at times flaunting their celebrated interracial sexual liaisons. They were leading the "flying squads" in Chicago and New York and other cities, confronting federal marshals, moving poor people's furniture back into the little cold-water flats after it had been put out on the sidewalks.

In the rural areas of the South, especially in Alabama, they took courageous—sometimes foolhardy—leadership in organizing largely black sharecroppers' unions to challenge the power of the white land-holders, storeowners, and authorities. They formed their own Communist unions to compete with "reactionary" American Federation of Labor unions for the loyalties of desperate men and women. After 1931, they scored a major propaganda victory on the issue of black freedom in America when they transformed an all-too-common attempt at legal lynching in Alabama to the level of an international cause célèbre called The Scottsboro Affair. At times, during the depths of the depression it seemed as if they were everywhere, calling men and women towards new possibilities, towards revolutionary change, for society and for themselves.

IV

Some black people, like many others, believed that the time had finally come, that this was the revolution that would finally fulfill and complete their own long struggle. (Unfortunately, there were many black persons who were ignorant concerning how long and how persistent their people's struggle had been, and how many sacrifices had been made for freedom. Such ignorance led them to believe that the Communists had come to bring something that blacks had never known before.) Young black people like teen-aged Angelo Herndon in Birmingham, Alabama, met the Communists after having lived a short but brutalized life. Later Herndon described the meeting in this way: "It was like all of a sudden turning a corner on a dirty old street and finding yourself facing a broad, shining highway."

On Chicago's South Side, a cautious, prematurely cynical young artist like Richard Wright felt the power of the Communist promise and began to drop his Mississippi-shaped guard. At one point, after having met the literature of the movement for the first time, after reading all night and into the cold dawn, he leaped up from his bed and wrote,

> I am black and I have seen black hands
> Raised in fists of revolt, side by side with the white
>   fists of white workers.
> And some day—and it is only this which sustains me—
> Some day there shall be millions of them,
> On some red day in a burst of fists on a new horizon!

It was in such a time that Langston Hughes became (at least for a brief, exciting time) a believer too, casting aside the past of his Christian faith, the past of his people's humiliation, casting aside more than

he knew, he called for the coming of the revolution, and said to black
people,

> Revolt! Arise!
>   The Black and Red World
>   Now are one!
> The past is done!
>   The Red Flag
>   Flies against the
>   Sun!

There were many persons, however, who were not sure that the
black past, with all its misery, anguish, grandeur, and struggle, was
meant to be cast aside. They questioned whether a really new day
should find them marching under the red flag of the white international. Still, the Communists came on strong in the black community.
In 1932, at a revivallike black and white national convention, they
became the first major political party to nominate a black man—James
Ford—for the office of vice president. In 1936 he was put forward
again. But in between those two elections, the Communist appeal for
blacks began to fall apart.

It was not simply that Ford himself was little more than an obedient,
unimaginative functionary, carrying no solid black concerns, exercising
no real power, based in no live constituency. Nor was it only a matter
of the subtle racism and paternalism that continued to exist in the
ranks of the party. Rather, what went wrong was deeper, indigenous
to the very nature of the party and to the nature of the black community.

Back in 1925, in a letter to a friend, Claude McKay had accurately
anticipated the problem when he said,

> I think the headquarters of the (Communist) International should be
> removed from Russia . . . I feel . . . that Russia has already had her
> Revolution—and that because so many of the Russian leaders of the
> International are connected with the Russian government, the Interna-
> tional will always consciously or unconsciously be influenced by Russian
> governmental politics internal and external—to the detriment of the
> proletarian movement.

Had McKay substituted the word "black" for "proletarian," he could
not have been more precise about the events that finally broke the
power of the Communist movement in the black community. Out of the
maelstrom of the worldwide depression, fascist governments rose to
power in Italy and Germany, posing obvious military threats to Com-

munist Russia. From that point on, the comintern became, more bla-
tantly than ever before, primarily an instrument for the protection of
the interests of the "mother country" of world communism. Everything
else was secondary—including the struggle for black freedom in
America.

In this context, especially beginning in 1934–1935, Russia and the
comintern repeatedly betrayed the black freedom movement here and
undermined the struggle of Ethiopia against Mussolini's Italian aggressors. Seeking America's friendship and support against the threat
of Adolf Hitler's Germany, the comintern began to back away from the
support of any conflicts, confrontations, and radical struggles that
might embarrass Russia's new friends in the "democratic" American
government. That meant backing away from the black struggle. Then
in the midst of Italy's invasion of Ethiopia in 1936, word leaked out that
Russia, for its own economic welfare, was selling crucial supplies to
Mussolini's government.

For many participants in the other American revolution, the message was clear. Neither the white American revolution of the "founding fathers," nor the red revolution of the "mother country" could be
the primary source of hope, support, and direction that they needed.
Ultimately, only black people committed to the vindication of their
fathers and mothers and the freedom of their children could create the
power that was needed for the continuing black struggle. All authentic
hope and strength would have to come first from within.

Chapter 22

Depression and Struggle: Towards "The Last Great Battle of the West" (1929 – 1939)

I

Even at the height of the Communist party's activity in the black community during the depression, the staccato, drumfire sounds of its messages never drowned out the pulsating, surging, deeper resonances of the movement towards black solidarity, nationality, and independence. Indeed, the continuing presence of this insistent, black-affirming movement was a major contributing factor to the ultimate failure of the party in black America.

The powerful wellsprings that Garvey had tapped would not be denied. They took many forms, and knew many manifestations. Noble Drew Ali reached the peak of his power just before the Wall Street debacle. At the time, some of his transformed, self-affirming Moors were so certain of their status as chosen people that they were boldly accosting whites on the streets of the North, calling them "Europeans," and warning them that their days were numbered. Not long afterwards, following a brief period in jail, Noble Drew Ali died under mysterious circumstances. There were unconfirmed suspicions that his death may have been the result of police beatings while in prison.

Whatever the cause of the prophet's death, his departure stimulated bitter infighting that had already begun among the leadership. Then, out of the struggles among his believers a new element in the search for identity emerged when a mysterious figure, W. D. Fard, began to be seen on the streets of Detroit. From his first appearance in the summer of 1930 to his disappearance four years later, Mr. Fard gathered several thousand followers, teaching doctrines that were an amalgam of the ideas of Timothy Drew, Marcus Garvey, and the Koran. Soon after his departure, he was declared to have been Allah in human form, and one of his closest followers, Elijah Kerriem (formerly Poole), became Elijah Muhammad, his true apostle.

For several years, in the midst of bitter—and sometimes bloody—internecine warfare among Mr. Fard's followers, the Temple People, or Muslims, gathered several thousand blacks into the fold, but remained essentially a phenomenon of the black community. Occasionally, through battles with the police, or as a result of reports of esoteric sacrifical practices among them, they came to more public attention, but in the 1930s they were essentially an underground presence.

During that period, there was a very public testimony to the continuing power of the spirit that Garvey represented: the black response to the Italian invasion of Ethiopia. When the war broke out, many black people predicted—rightly—that it was the real opening of the Second World War. All over America they called meetings of protest and outrage. They attacked Italians on the streets and destroyed their property in the black community. They raised funds, sent relief packages, and attempted to develop a black expeditionary force to go to fight at the side of the beleaguered Ethiopian forces. For millions of blacks, Ethiopia represented the hope of Africa's future as well as the grandeur of its past. Thus they made its struggle a part of their own. At the same time, the call for black emigration to other parts of Africa (as well as to a separate state in America) never ceased. All these were means towards independence, freedom, and black self-determination. All were part of the other American revolution.

II

As Garvey, the Moors, the Temple People, the Ethiopian campaign, and the Communist party links indicated, black struggle in America was profoundly attuned to the developments that were shaking international life and politics in the post World War I world. Perhaps one of the most fascinating aspects of this attempt by black people to connect their struggle to the development of race-conscious world politics involved Japan. Although much is still unclear, it is obvious that there were serious negotiations going on in the 1930s between black groups and individuals on the one hand, and representatives of the Japanese government on the other. During a period when Japan was rising to challenge this country's imperialism in the Pacific, such links were watched closely by the American government. So, when war broke out with the Japanese, a series of sweeping government raids brought in scores of black people who had evidently allied themselves with the Japanese aspirations for a new nonwhite hegemony in the world.

Such connections, while fascinating in their implications, were not central to the developing patterns of black struggle in the 1930s. Instead, the critical reality remained the nationwide depression, and blacks shared the desperate spirit that led men to try many avenues of struggle for life, dignity, and livelihood. During these years, one of the most important black movements was focused in the various direct action campaigns that were carried out against white merchants in the black communities of the North, especially in Chicago and Harlem. The goal was more jobs for black people. The action was usually boycotts, picketing, leafleting, harassment, and then negotiations.

Sometimes these campaigns were abetted by the inexhaustible energies of the Communist party, but more often they were the product of independent black organizing. Usually, they were led by black religious leaders and professionals including one of the most colorful figures of the period, Sufi Abdul Hamid, who in his turban, cape, and high Russian boots struck an imposing figure on the streets and at the negotiating tables. But the real power was with the poor, out-of-work people who manned the picket lines day after day in all weather. Through their strength and persistence, these campaigns developed into the first examples of extensive mobilization for direct action and unarmed struggle and confrontation in the twentieth-century black struggle. Black people were out on the streets, constantly in motion, challenging first merchants, then city employment policies, then telephone and other public utility companies (led in Harlem by a young preacher named Adam Clayton Powell).

The momentum of this determined street action and the black defiance it released formed a volatile mix with the continuing pressures of desperate poverty, the humiliation and injustice of oppression, and the constant presence of police brutality. In Harlem, in 1935, all these factors, and more, helped to spark the first black urban uprising of the other revolution. As he watched Harlem break loose, the ubiquitous Claude McKay reported on the rage of the black community, turning itself against the most obvious and most vulnerable symbols of exploitation, the stores of the white merchants. McKay said,

> The storm broke in the afternoon and lasted all night long. . . . The Black Belt ran amok along Fifth, Lenox, Seventh, and Eighth Avenues, from 116th to 145th Street, and smashed and looted the stores. . . . It

was a spontaneous community protest against social and legal injustice. . . . Those who were angry vented their wrath by smashing the stores; those who were hungry looted them.

Only after seven hundred and fifty policemen had been called out, after three black persons were dead, and after hundreds of thousands of dollars of damage had been done—did the storm abate.

But it never really went away. All through those depression years there were signs of an acutely experienced subterranean movement of black anger and anguish that might at any moment erupt into other spontaneous explosions, or be turned to purposeful, radical action. Millions sensed this pent-up power, for instance, each time the young Brown Bomber, Joe Louis, smashed his way to victory over a white opponent, and black people all over the nation—and as far away as South Africa—poured into the streets, challenging every white they saw. (By diverting traffic from the black communities on those nights, the police made sure that there weren't too many white faces to be seen.)

III

Nor should it be thought that this seething black rage, this potential revolutionary fervor, was simply a response to the new experiences of the depression and the exploitation of the urban North. For at every moment of their lives, black people, North and South, were constantly reminded that the ancient, savage cruelties of the South had not disappeared. What more cause for struggle and resistance could be needed than such stories as the one that came out of Greenwood, Florida in 1934, telling of a twenty-three-year-old black man named Claude Neal who had been dragged out of an Alabama jail and taken to Florida for a highly publicized lynching? What were men and women to say, to feel, to do, when they got these details of Neal's execution:

> First they cut off his penis. He was made to eat it. Then they cut off his testicles and made him eat them and say he like it. Then they sliced his sides and stomach with knives and every now and then somebody would cut off a finger or a toe. Red hot irons were used on the nigger to burn him from top to bottom. From time to time during the torture a rope would be tied around Neal's neck and he was pulled up over a limb and held there until he almost choked to death, when he would be let down and the torture begun all over again. After several hours of this punishment, they decided just to kill him.

In the face of such ritualistic brutality, black people chose many forms of response. Some in the South decided to resist. Like their fathers and grandfathers, they armed themselves for self-defense, declaring their refusal to be slaves. Others turned to the voices of the organizers who promised a new power for the poor and black through the Sharecroppers Union, or in the ranks of the biracial Southern Tenant Farmers Union. Some determined, courageous, and visionary black men and women refused to give up the fight for political rights and political power, and even against tremendous odds, they waged small but important campaigns to recruit black men and women who would dare to go to register to vote. Repeatedly they were driven out of their communities for such activities, but the attempts were never fully stopped.

Many persons, of course, went North. In those cities it soon became clear that one of their reasons for moving was to secure the right of political expression. For surveys continually found that black voters took part in electoral political activities in the northern cities in impressively larger proportions than whites. Men and women were seeking an honorable way out. Often they were trying to find, in Lerone Bennett's words, a revolution that white people would not realize was a revolution. Many of them were on the streets of Harlem, Detroit, and Chicago when the explosions came.

IV

In another area, a group of black intellectuals and professionals formed the National Negro Conference (NNC) in 1936, hoping that it would provide a new, broad base for organization and action that would take the mainstream struggle beyond the legalistic tactics of the NAACP. After a short period of great hope, serious political mistakes and tragic left-wing betrayals permanently crippled the conference as a medium of black struggle.

One of the disruptive elements in the life of the NNC was the tendency of its national secretary, John P. Davis, to equate the struggle for black freedom with the success of the new Congress of Industrial Organizations (CIO). Thus he made the work of independent black organizing secondary to assisting the CIO in recruiting black members. Such a tendency, though ultimately destructive, was not surprising, for in the 1935–1940 period, the CIO exhibited much of the radical power and genuine inclusiveness some blacks had seen in the Industrial Workers of the World and in the Communist party. Moreover, the new union seemed seriously to encourage black participation in its struggles for the rights of workers and in its challenges to the older, racist American Federation of Labor.

For a time, many of the most courageous and progressive participants in the struggle for black freedom were deeply involved in the
dangerous, exciting work of CIO organizing. As blacks joined with
whites and carried on their sit-down strikes, as they shut down plants,
battled against brutal Pinkerton guards, and often risked their lives on
the picket lines, they were seeking again to forge that "class first"
alliance that has often seemed so logical in the history of black struggle, but has proved so hard to maintain. (Eventually, as the CIO
backed away from its serious confrontations with the recovering powers of the capitalist system, the force of its radicalism was eventually
dissipated into conventional union concerns. By then, its significant,
politically conscious black cadre was either absorbed into the white-
dominated structures or out of the organization.)

V

While the black and white forces of the CIO carried on their battles
against management, other black people turned away from unions and
eschewed all secular warfare to follow a short, bald-headed black god
into the kingdom of black and white unity. In the urban areas of the
Northeast, thousands of Afro-Americans were surrendering their lives
and their property to Father Divine, who claimed to be God, and who
had many white "angels" among the black majority. As a result, in the
midst of the depression, his followers were guaranteed food and shel-
ter in his earthly kingdom. Even more, he claimed to guarantee them
peace of mind, the experience of black-white unity and eternal fulfillment. It was a chaotic time, and men and women sought to work their
way towards freedom in many ways, some stranger than others. Was
there a revolutionary meaning to the presence of a touchable black god
and an interracial, well-fed, peaceable kingdom in the midst of a hungry America, torn by racial and class conflict? Was it escape or fulfillment?

Regardless of the answers to such questions, it was still obvious that
most persons would never make it into Father Divine's kingdom.
Meanwhile, outside the gates, by the beginning of 1939 the depression
was still hard, especially for black people. Shortly before the European
war began (or as it expanded, the Ethiopian supporters would have
said) some of the black men and women who had suffered most cruelly
in the depression and before it, and who would never make it into
Father Divine's kingdom, offered their own statement of struggle,
sought their own kingdom. Hundreds of Missouri sharecroppers, led

by a charismatic black preacher-organizer, decided to make a desperate attempt to resist the forces that had been grinding their faces into the dirt, breaking them off from any secure relationship to the land, evicting their families from even the meanest hovels. In the midst of the winter of 1938–1939, the predominantly black group took all their worldly possessions and began a pathetic but courageous demonstration along two major Missouri highways, hoping to call the "liberal" federal government to their aid.

The government did not come to the rescue of the sharecroppers before the forces of Missouri's law and order clubbed them off the road and put them into places that were good imitations of concentration camps. There finally was some federal assistance, but most of it was too late and too ineffectual to deal with the needs the black farmers (and their white allies) were raising. More important here, however, was that even the most exploited and powerless men and women were desperately seeking a way to struggle, to seize the time, to wrest some modicum of justice and humanity out of the hands of their oppressors. In the 1930s, wherever black people were in trouble they were experimenting, searching for a way. The pressures were extreme, the risks great, but millions of men, women, and children refused to despair— partly because extreme pressures and high risks were not new to them.

In those days, as he looked at the total situation from his dark tower, W. E. B. Du Bois called upon black people to turn towards self-reliance, self-determination, and solidarity far more fully than they had ever done before. Partly because he insisted on thrusting his new position into the pages of the *Crisis*, setting himself openly against the official, assimilationist position of the NAACP, Du Bois lost his job as editor. That did not deter him from seeing or knowing what was crucial, however, and in the closing pages of his impressive work, *Black Reconstruction*, he turned from that nineteenth-century experience to his own moment and summed up many of the issues that were at stake at that depression stage of the other American revolution. He said,

> This the American black man knows: his fight here is a fight to the finish. Either he dies or he wins. If he wins it will be by no subterfuge or evasion of amalgamation. He will enter modern civilization here in America as a black man on terms of perfect and unlimited equality with any white man, or he will enter not at all. Either extermination root and branch or absolute equality. There can be no compromise. This is the last great battle of the West.

Chapter 23
World War, World Revolution, and Black Struggle (1939 – 1945)

I

As the flames of war spread over Europe and licked out at many other parts of the world, their effect on black struggle in America was no less significant than the impact of the 1914–1918 conflict. The war wrenched individual lives as well as that of the larger community. It forced Paul Robeson to come home from his self-exile in England and Europe. Thus it brought back to America this supremely gifted, black giant of a man who had already become the most radically conscious and politically articulate performing artist to emerge from the Afro-American community. Deeply sympathetic to the Russian people, committed to revolutionary changes throughout the world, Robeson carried a special burden for the freedom of the African continent. For more than twenty years after his wartime return to his native land, he publicly pressed those issues, even when they placed him implacably against the policies of America, even when they cost him his career and his health.

When Robeson returned to America he found a friend who was in another kind of exile, C. L. R. James, the brilliant Trinidadian revolutionary scholar and writer. James had come to America in 1938 on business of the Trotskyite movement, and the combination of the war and a break in his health opened the way for him to extend his original six-month stay to fifteen years. During his period in America, although he was not widely known, James became one of the most important—if not the most important—theorists of the black struggle for freedom in America.

Operating largely underground as an independent Marxist and as a leader of various socialist splinter groups and organizations, James made highly significant contributions to the analysis of the role of black struggle in America in the context of the world revolutionary movements. Like Robeson he was utterly devoted to the success of the African revolutions and he was instrumental in the political development of Kwame Nkrumah, as well as in the creation of the ideology behind the crucial Pan-African Conference of 1945. Together with W. E. B. Du Bois, Paul Robeson and C. L. R. James were likely the most important bridges between the radical traditions of the 1920s and 1930s and the rise of the new black movements of the 1950s and 1960s.

II

Of course, the effects of the war on the black struggle reached far beyond such crucial, individual lives. When the war began, many persons viewed it with much of the same cynicism and detachment that had marked their response to the earlier years of the first World War. Some were convinced that the war was an act of God's judgment on the colonizing white nations, a judgment that could only benefit the children of Africa. In Harlem the president of a schismatic Garvey organization looked at the situation and said,

> Some Negroes are crying for peace. Peace, hell! Let [the whites] kill each other as long as they want to. The longer they do that the better off the Negro will be.

In Chicago, a black woman missionary spoke the mind of many persons when she affirmed the position of the Garveyite and added,

> No, we don' want no peace. God's punishin' the white folks by lettin' 'em kill each other off. Look at ol' Leopol' and' his Beljuns now! Look what ol' Mussaleeny did to Ethiopia! My God! Naw, don't vote for no peace. God don' want no peace.

Prior to Pearl Harbor, many forms of pro-Japanese sentiment began to surface. In 1940, A. Phillip Randolph, who had become a paragon of loyalty to the war aims of the capitalist, Allied powers, was forced to admit that,

> Among a considerable section of the Negro people, there is a belief that Negroes should look to Japan for leadership, based largely upon the fact that Japan is one of the darker races.

In the search for black freedom, the issue of race simply would not dissolve. In the light of the racism of America, it could not. Nevertheless, the Japanese attack on Pearl Harbor did lead to an abatement of much of the open, pro-Japanese sentiment. Government repression, intensive propaganda campaigns, and the creation of large numbers of wartime jobs, tended to reinforce the theme of loyalty to America. Still, there was a deep, sullen, seething undercurrent of black discontent and resistance. For instance, even after Pearl Harbor, when God's judgment became a more moot question, blacks were still organizing underground attempts at draft resistance, based on the need for freedom in America, based on the racism of the American Army itself.

There were too many contradictions at work in America. Again the nation was supposedly one of the leaders in a struggle for democracy, for the achievement of freedom for mankind. Yet its black people still found suffocating, terrifying oppression in the South, and were pressed into cities filled with racism and segregation in the North. Barriers against their employment were thrown up in the very war industries that were supposed to be the heart of the American "arsenal of democracy." But nothing seemed to outrage the black community so much as the treatment its servicemen were receiving. In training camps all over the nation, there were scores of incidents setting black men against white, especially against white military policemen. Many conflicts had led to bloodshed and death, and there was a constant roar of protest from black people against this treatment of their men.

III

Some black leaders of the mainstream protest tradition were deeply troubled by the rage they saw in the black community. They recognized how much potential there was for black radical action, action that the government might easily term seditious. Walter White, then executive director of the NAACP, looked back on the period and recalled,

> Discontent and bitterness were growing like wildfire among Negroes all over the country. Communists were trying as usual to capitalize on this.

According to White's account, it was out of their fear that the black rage might either be uncontrollable, or come under Communist control, that Randolph, White and others conceived the March on Washington movement in 1941.

It was a marching movement that never marched. Its purpose was twofold: to use the explosive threat of black direct action to gain concessions from the federal government in the treatment of black troops, in employment and in other areas of discrimination, as well as to find some nonradical channel for the unpredictable rising pressures of black rage. On a certain level, the movement succeeded in accomplishing both purposes—and it also failed. Some concessions on fair employment for black people were obtained from Franklin Roosevelt's administration, but many others, like the treatment of black troops, were given up without any real attempt at a march. Of course, the black community was not completely quieted down. In 1943, when it was patently clear that the March on Washington movement would never march, outbreaks took place in various parts of the country.

Racial battles were fought in many of the places to which black families were moving in those days of renewed migration: places like Mobile, Alabama; Los Angeles, California; Marianna, Florida; Newark, New Jersey; Detroit, Michigan; and Beaumont, Texas. During the conflicts in these cities scores of persons were killed, hundreds more were wounded, and millions of dollars worth of property was destroyed. Ironically, many of the white attacks against black people that started these struggles were launched over the issue of the right of black people to jobs, adequate pay, and status in the war industries.

Perhaps it was fitting that Detroit, symbolic center of America's democratic arsenal, provided the prototypical experience in the racial warfare of 1943. Since 1940, the black population of the city had expanded by more than 20 percent, and all the old struggles over housing, recreation areas, jobs, unions, and the upgrading of black workers were exacerbated. Finally, one evening towards the end of June, the built-up feelings and seething hostility exploded near an amusement park; and for more than thirty hours Detroit was engulfed in the nation's worst racial warfare since 1919. Only the arrival of some six thousand federal and state troops brought the hostilities to an end. But the end had not really come, and many black folks knew it. As a matter of fact, the black response to the warfare and explosions of that summer was similar to much that had been said and felt in the bloody summer of 1919. For instance, near the end of August, 1943, one Harlemite pondered his own community's recent uprising and said, "I'm in favor of it—hope it happens again. Let my people go."

IV

Not only did some blacks recognize the relationship of their actions on the streets of Harlem and Detroit to the experience of the outlyers and the Denmark Veseys and the David Walkers, but many persons also realized that they were part of an even larger struggle. For as the war moved towards its terrible ending, each day made it more apparent that the international visions of Hubert H. Harrison, Du Bois, Robeson, and many others were to be realized, at least in part. New forces of revolution were being released all over the nonwhite world. In China, Southeast Asia, India, Africa, wherever the victims of European colonization were, they had determined to be victims no longer. They were seizing the initiative, attempting to return their lives into the full stream of human history.

Many Afro-Americans sensed their ultimate unity with this resurrected, nonwhite, revolutionary world. They understood their common struggle against the cruel colonial heritage of the white West. Few persons expressed this sense of solidarity, common destiny, and common struggle more eloquently than did Adam Clayton Powell. From his pulpit in Harlem's popular Abysinnia Baptist Church and on the many platforms that he had across the country, he preached the word of the new time, of the larger meaning of the continuing black struggle in America, a struggle that he called "Civil War II." Concerning the postwar future of the white Western world, Powell asked rhetorically,

> What will the 'white man's world' do? Continue on its suicidal way to end ingloriously in a form of mass harakari? Try to stand outnumbered and ethically rotten against the 'fresh might' of a billion and a half non-Western people? If it does the . . . old white man . . . is finished. A surging rebellion is on its way to which Civil War II is only the prelude.

Whatever the decisions of the white world, Powell said he knew the black struggle for freedom in America would continue, like a mighty river, linking up with the other great movements of mankind toward freedom. Thus he predicted,

> The black man continues on his way. He plods wearily no longer—he is striding freedom road with the knowledge that if he hasn't got the world in a jug, at least he has the stopper in his hand. . . . He is ready to throw himself into the struggle to make the dream of America become flesh and blood, bread and butter, freedom and equality. He walks conscious of the fact that he is no longer alone—no longer a minority.

Powell knew that the struggle for black freedom in America was at once part of the best hopes of the American revolution, and—even more important—an integral part of the world revolution for freedom, justice, and humanity. In a sense, it was his way of saying that this was indeed, "the last great battle of the West." By the time the war was over, many black people in America agreed with him.

Chapter 24

Cold War and Black Freedom: A Time For Paradox (1945 — 1954)

I

At the close of World War I, the year 1919 had marked an explosive point of departure in the development of the other American revolution. Interestingly enough, 1946, the first full year after World War II, was also a turning point; not so spectacular nor outwardly arresting, to be sure, but critical as a year of transformation nevertheless.

Some of the changes were subtle. For instance, 1946 marked the resurgence of the recording industry, and for the first time a widespread audience was able to hear the new black music that had been crashing up out of the war years. Its harsh, strident, defiant beats, its fantastic improvisations on anguish and hope, its unmistakable strains of African and Afro-Cuban music all testified to a new sense, a new time in black America. "Bop" pressed beyond the courageous, defensive resistance of the Blues. The music presaged a new level of northern, urban-shaped struggle (including all the memories of southern experiences).

In 1946, the black servicemen returned as they had before, but they did not move into the massive confrontations of 1919. The depression had softened some of the hardest white edges and the New Deal had begun to change the atmosphere in America. Besides, the conflicts that had taken place during the war were reminders to the white world of the black determination to resist. At the same time, more beachheads had been opened in housing, and the GI Bill created new possibilities for both black and white veterans, removing many of them from the arena of job competition.

137

Nevertheless the black veterans still found America to be a battleground, with the confrontations more open in the South than elsewhere.
In Georgia, black men who came home from fighting for freedom were
still killed on lonely country roads when they dared to try to register to
vote in their home towns. In South Carolina a white policeman could
gouge out a black soldier's eyes while the young man still wore his
army uniform. In Tennessee, a veteran's defense of his mother against
a white man sparked a significant black-white confrontation, and led to
the jailing of dozens of black men. Still the returning servicemen,
joined by other courageous black folk, continued their stubborn
movement against the walls of white control. That they turned increasingly towards legal weapons in this unrelenting battle was another
intimation of things to come, another suggestion of the transformation
that the war had helped to bring about.

In 1946, there were also intimations of the ways in which black
people might use the prison system, as well as the courts, in the
struggle for their freedom. In this year, on a cold day in February, a
thief and hustler named Malcolm Little (better known on the streets of
Boston and Harlem as "Detroit Red") walked into a state penitentiary
in Massachusetts. Later in the same year, after having served a four-
year term for counseling draft evasion, the Messenger of Allah, Elijah
Muhammad, walked out of a federal prison in Michigan. What did this
concatenation of events mean? Perhaps at least this: On the prison
ships of the slave trade, black men had literally seized their chains and
transformed them into weapons in the struggle for liberation. In 1946,
as Malcolm and Elijah passed without knowing each other, they
seemed to mark the new point at which more black men than ever
before would seize the experience of their American imprisonment and
use it to liberate their minds and spirits for the struggles outside the
gates.

II

But at the time, those were simply harbingers of things to come, and
in the postwar years they were often embedded in hidden, solitary
lives. Meanwhile, on the larger scale of history, other, far more public
events were affecting the other American revolution. Perhaps of utmost importance were the liberation struggles going on in every part
of the formerly colonized world. Clearly, the control that Europe
had once exercised in that world was again being fundamentally
threatened, from Indochina to the Gold Coast of Africa. Now, to the

horror of the former white rulers, they were also faced with the specter of Soviet Russia, pressing not only for spheres of influence and defense in Europe, but continuing to claim hegemony over the direction of the revolutionary world.

The long-nurtured fears of communism (which had only been temporarily put aside in the Atlantic world by the exigencies of the war) now found reinforcement on three fronts. As a result of the movements of the war, Russian troops were a real presence further west in Europe than they had ever been before. At the same time, there was a tremendous fear for the revived power of the Communist parties within the Western capitalist countries, and a firm belief on the part of many persons in these countries that the Communist parties acting in concert with the Russian military forces would soon create revolutionary subversion. Finally, all this was tied to the unyielding conviction that Russia's hand was involved in every movement among the colonial peoples to obtain their freedom and independence from some of these same European countries.

It was largely the Western European attempt to deal with this (partly imaginary) triple threat of Russian communism, and America's decision to take a leading role in the struggle, which created the period of crisis and confrontation known as the cold war. By and large, it was a struggle for power, influence, and control in Europe and in the former colonies, carried out primarily between the white forces of capitalism and communism. Partly as a result of its own new economic penetration into Africa and its continued imperialistic relationship to many parts of Latin America and the Orient, partly because of its deeply entrenched heritage of racism and capitalism, partly because of its new military power born out of the war and its possession of the atomic bomb, America emerged as the anti-Communist champion of the cold war era.

In relation to the post-World War II struggles of the nonwhite world, what this meant effectively was that America consistently took positions that were counter to the liberation aspirations of the formerly colonized peoples. Usually, the alleged threat of Communist subversion or of the spread of Russian domination was the reason given. Whatever the reasons, its votes in the newly formed United Nations organization provided unimpeachable testimony to America's anti-liberationist role.

At the same time, to support its claims to be "the leader of the Free World," to prove that it really believed in the freedom of nonwhite peoples, the American nation had to find some way to deal with the liberation aspirations of its own major internal colony—the children of Africa in America. This paradox, involving the entire world of international political struggle, became the major public setting for the freedom movement of black people in America for almost fifteen years after the end of the war.

III

At the outset of the cold war period, there was loud, regular, and accurate black criticism of the American role in creating the Euro-American climate of the period, and especially in its new leadership of the white imperialist world. Black newspapers and journals, and many black intellectual leaders consistently agreed with such commentators as J. A. Rogers, dean of the self-trained black historians, who judged Winston Churchill and the American side of the cold war in this way:

> though (Churchill) spouts democracy, he is a fascist at heart. Imperialism and jim crow are fascism.

They understood and joined with P. L. Prattis of the *Pittsburgh Courier* when he looked at the role America was taking in the world and said,

> the strong wine of world leadership . . . will go to the head of America and it will discover that instead of fighting for the world it is fighting against it.

And by "the world," all of them meant, more than anything else, the nonwhite world, especially the world of Africa.

So, for a time, it appeared to be obvious that a faithful pursuit of the struggle for black freedom in America and in Africa demanded opposition to America's foreign policy and its role in the cold war. But in this, as in all wars, the pressures for conformity began to build, and the American government increased its legal and propaganda pressures against those persons and groups who publicly challenged the nation's foreign policy positions. In the face of this pressure black critics of America's foreign policy, like so many of their white counterparts, began to be quieted, to become less public. Nevertheless, in spite of the growing pressures and the continued withdrawal of black voices, certain courageous persons continued to follow their consciences and the logic of the struggle. Sometimes, such a position led to strange alliances.

For instance, in this period, stalwarts of the struggle like Paul Robeson, W. E. B. Du Bois, and Shirley Graham, the gifted novelist, and performing artists like Lena Horne and Canada Lee decided to align themselves with the Progressive party of Henry Wallace. At least some of their decisions were made because Wallace was at the time the only nationally known political leader who was opposing the American cold war stance, supporting the independence movements of the colonized world, and calling for the banning of the atom bomb. At the high point of their fervor, the participants in the Progressive party were convinced that their movement was that fulfillment of the American revolution of which men and women had long dreamed.

Before long, however, especially after a devastating electoral defeat in 1948, it became clear that the odd amalgam of overwhelmingly white liberal and radical forces behind Wallace had no real understanding of the dynamics of the black struggle for freedom. Yet, it was also true that for those persons who sought an organized national vehicle in their fight for black freedom and against American imperialism, there were few alternatives to the Progressive party.

Of course, the Communist party presented another option, but it was still reeling from a series of internal imbroglios brought on largely by its need to adapt its line to the changes in Russian foreign policy. And many black people remembered only too well the deep betrayals of their hope which they had experienced with the Communists since the mid-1930s. Still, the party was another of the few nationally organized voices in America calling for a foreign policy that would at least theoretically support the liberation movements of the nonwhite peoples, and which would stand with the struggles of African freedom.

IV

Among the persons who never caved in to the pressures of the cold war, Paul Robeson and W. E. B. Du Bois presented two of the most dramatic instances of courage, wisdom, and defiance. Both men were totally convinced of the essential unity of the cause of black freedom in America and the struggles for liberation that were going on throughout the world, especially in Africa. By the end of the 1940s, they were also convinced that most of the struggles towards economic and political independence among the nonwhite peoples had to evolve into some form of socialism, rather than commitment to the Western capitalism that had oppressed them. Whenever they turned, they found the

American government in league with the forces of reaction and colonization rather than the movements for liberation. They saw atomic
power being used as a threat rather than a promise of new energy and
prosperity. In their minds, there was no way in which they could be
faithful to the black struggle in America and not speak the truth concerning this antiliberation role of their nation in the world. At the same
time, they shared an admiration for the Soviet Union which often
tended to be naive.

In the spring of 1949, both men were present at a world conference
held by the left-wing international peace movement in Paris. In a
public address, Du Bois predicted the spread of socialism across the
world, and attacked America for being in the vanguard of the dehumanizing antisocialist forces. In his carefully impassioned language,
he said,

> Leading this new colonial imperialism comes my own native land, built
> by my father's toil and blood, the United States. . . . Drunk with power
> we are leading the world to hell in a new colonialism with the same old
> human slavery which once ruined us; and to a Third World War which
> will ruin the world.

Robeson repeated that theme, but in those days when American and
Russian forces were facing each other in threatening stances across the
zones of Europe, the black artist cut even deeper. For he told the
group that he did not believe black men in America would take up arms
against Russia "on behalf of those who have oppressed us for generations." Later he claimed that he had been even more specific, stating
that black soldiers would never fight in the name of a white racist like
Senator James Eastland of Mississippi.

This was dangerous language; these were dangerous ideas. Some
called it treason. Others called it communism. A few said it was
revolutionary, and they were closer to the truth. Whatever it was,
America would have none of it. In the fiercely rising tide of anti-
Communist hysteria that was sweeping through the nation in the late
1940s and early 1950s, men like Robeson and Du Bois were fair game.
For the repression sought out not only Communists, but it labeled as
Communist sympathizers all those persons who dared to speak publicly
against the American position in the world.

Du Bois and Robeson were especially anathema, because they were
black, articulate, and highly visible. They were, therefore, dangerous
unless they could be isolated and discredited. The attacks, especially
on the better-known Robeson, were fierce. He was accused of being a
secret Communist and was subjected to a severe white-listing cam-

paign, eventually choking off almost all of an income that had once exceeded one hundred thousand dollars per year. Then his passport rights were revoked, cutting him off from his vast European and African audiences. Du Bois suffered the pain of ostracism and indictment, also losing his passport. Others, including black Communist party leaders like Benjamin Davis, were sent to jail as political prisoners. Still, they never relented.

V

This kind of resistance was not the pattern for the mainstream of the black protest tradition during the cold war period. The mainstream leaders represented most clearly by an organization like the NAACP, took another tack. They backed off from the traditional black criticism of American foreign policy. (Indeed, some of them went before congressional committees and became shameful public accusers of men like Robeson and Du Bois.) Instead they used the international and domestic conflicts and tensions of the cold war as levers for obtaining certain crucial concessions in the legal battles against segregation and discrimination.

These courtroom-oriented forces knew that America was highly sensitive of its image as "the leader of the free world"; they knew there was great concern for its credibility in the freedom-minded nonwhite "Third World," a world that represented sources of economic and cultural exploitation as well as a sphere of struggle with the forces of world communism. They also knew that there was a reservoir of courage and defiance in the black community, North and South, which would regularly produce plaintiffs who would test the laws in court, often even at the risk of their own lives and the safety of their families. So, taking advantage first of World War II and then of the cold war, constantly citing international opinion, the protest wing of the black freedom movement entered into a series of challenges to the outward, legal bases of America's endemic, structural racism.

From 1941, when Roosevelt was pressured into his executive order on fair employment,through the wartime period and the postwar decade of the cold war, there was no single year that did not produce at least one new reaction on the part of the executive or judicial branches in response to black movement. For instance, in the years from 1944 to 1950, the white primaries were struck down in the courts, President Truman formed the first presidential civil rights commission, segregation in interstate bus travel was legally denied, segregation in the

Army was attacked, literacy tests for voting were declared unconstitutional, and the border states began token desegregation of the
graduate schools of their universities.

Then, in 1950, as the international power struggle developed into its
first major armed conflict in Korea, the courts seemed to open like a
dam. In separate decisions, cases involving five state universities were
decided in favor of the token black petitioners. Railroad dining car
segregation was struck down. Finally, with a group of courageous
black families as plaintiffs, the NAACP decided to make a frontal
attack on the basic principle of separate but equal education.

Every concession on the part of the government was a reaction to
black initiatives and to new black political power. In addition to the
resourcefulness of the lawyers and the great bravery of the plaintiffs, it
is also important to recognize that the decades of migration into the
North had developed new constituencies and new strength that could
not be ignored. What this series of legal victories meant, then, was
this: At the very time that the nation was moving to expand its own
overseas exploitation and to support the other white, colonial powers,
its own internal black colony was seizing the time, taking advantage of
the international crisis, consolidating the political and economic gains
of the last four decades, and pressing forward its own claims.

The price was great. At worst, it included both spoken and unspoken
agreements to support America's new colonialism. At best it required
silence on the subject. Most often it meant a refusal to stand with those
relatively few black people who insisted that the cause of freedom in
the nonwhite world was indivisible. To pay the cost meant repressing
the words spoken by the black prophet at the end of the nineteenth
century: "The American Negro cannot become an ally of imperialism
without enslaving his own race." It was a paradox.

VI

In spite of the paradoxical price, on a certain level the tactic worked.
Its success was epitomized in the *Brown* v. *Topeka* Supreme Court
decision of 1954, which seemed to vindicate the NAACP's decision to
tackle school segregation head on. In the light of the prevailing internal and international situation, however, it should be noted that the
Supreme Court made the minimum concession possible. Its hesitancy
to strike in radical justice at the fabric of segregation in the South and
North left the way open for long years of obstinate delay and great
suffering. But the door was also opened to great hope.

For black people, this announcement that all segregated schools are inherently unequal was a second emancipation proclamation (and it bore all the ambiguities of that first document). Beyond its cramped words they saw a victory for their own persistent, relentless crashing against the gates of segregation. Beyond the legal documents, they saw visions like those men had seen during the Civil War, handwriting on the wall, declaring that this was indeed the beginning of a new time in America. Much of that black jubilation was caught up in the words of a young man who was in the Marine Corps at the time of the court's decision. Writing later about his memories of the moment on May 17, 1954, when the announcement came, Robert F. Williams said,

> my inner emotions must have been approximate to the Negro slaves' when they first heard about the Emancipation Proclamation. Elation took hold of me so strongly that I found it very difficult to refrain from yielding to an urge of jubilation. . . . On this momentous night of May 17, 1954, I felt that at last the government was willing to assert itself on behalf of first-class citizenship, even for Negroes. I experienced a sense of loyalty that I had never felt before. I was sure that this was the beginning of a new era of American democracy.

Within a little more than half a decade from that joyous day, the government of the United States had declared Robert F. Williams a revolutionary outlaw; and in the years that followed, his voice was raised from Cuba and China on behalf of armed black insurrection in his native land. To understand the development of such paradoxes and ironies is to understand much of the nature of the other American revolution.

Chapter 25

Beginning in Montgomery: The Rise of the Southern Movement (1954 – 1960)

I

The comparisons that were made between the court decision of 1954 and the Emancipation Proclamation of 1863 were at once apt and ironic. As had the earlier edict from the federal government, this one had come out of the pressures of the black community and the exigencies of war. In the context of the changes sweeping the world, and in the light of the racism embedded in the structures of American life, the court's decision was a minimal, conservative one, ambiguous both in scope and implementation.

Here again, as with the proclamation, while the federal government made a halting beginning, it was black people who had to seize the time and create their own new openings. It was black people who surged forward, moving far beyond the original intentions of the tribunal, using the court's decision to continue the drive towards justice and black freedom.

Because of the broad interpretation that Afro-Americans chose to give to the court's actions, the schools became only one element of a far larger struggle. In Robert Williams' words, it now seemed as if "the government was willing to assert itself on behalf of first-class citizenship, even for Negroes." Therefore, black people could do no less than assert themselves, not only in schools, but in many other arenas as well.

The South was the central arena, the heart of the post-1954 struggle. Why? Partly because the outward signs and symbols of discrimination and segregation were most prominent there, and the courts' decisions seemed to give priority to an attack on those elements of the system of racism. Admittedly, they were more readily attacked than the problems of the North.

Moreover, the cold war period, with its anti-Communist repression and betrayals, was having a distinctly deleterious effect on the leadership of black movement in the North. The hysteria of the time (which was labeled as McCarthyism, but which ranged far beyond the man) had shaken many persons, cowed others, silenced large numbers, and broken the radical impetus that might have been expected to follow the ferment and agitation of the 1930s and 1940s. (Perhaps, too, the black community of the North had not yet found its real sense of place and power after the periods of great migrations. Perhaps there was too much physical and spiritual dislocatedness to make it possible for that community to produce the leadership and the mass commitment that could deal with struggles that would last five, ten, and fifteen years.) As a result, the next stage of the other American revolution developed out of the black community of the Deep South.

II

By the end of 1955, Montgomery, Alabama had become a symbol of this new black thrust. There, one of the South's many segregated urban bus systems became the focus of black struggle, and a quiet-spoken bespectacled black seamstress served as the prime mover. At the outset, as at so many times and places in the other American revolution, this move seemed to be of the mildest, most unassuming variety. Rosa Parks refused to give up her seat to a white man as the law required, and she was arrested. Because of much history that had preceded this act, an aroused black community decided on a brief protest. Then it determined that more was necessary. Out of their determination came the form of a bus boycott, one far more successful than they had dreamed. Into the leadership of that boycott they thrust a somewhat reluctant twenty-six year-old Baptist preacher with a doctorate in philosophy, Martin Luther King, Jr.

King, a short, dark, solidly built young man, was an unmistakable product of the comfortable, black middle-class community of Atlanta, Georgia. After graduating from Morehouse College, he had gone on to Crozier Theological Seminary and then to Boston University. From all appearances, he seemed prepared to settle into the relatively easy, rather protected life of a popular black Baptist preacher, perhaps combining that vocation with college teaching. Montgomery soon shattered both appearances and expectations.

There were, of course, some familiar ingredients to all this. There had been bus boycotts in the South before. Black religious leaders had played prominent roles in the struggle for black freedom ever since the slave ship days. The black churches had continually served as staging grounds for resistance, rebellion, and the movement towards new independence. (Even the name of the leadership organization, the Montgomery Improvement Association, had a familiar ring. Did its antecedents go back to the Universal Negro Improvement Association?)

But this was a new time. The black men and women of Montgomery had much history of struggle behind them, and they chose to believe that the Supreme Court had moved the federal government to their side. They began their boycott in the same year that hundreds of representatives of the colonized peoples of the world had gathered in Bandung, Indonesia to affirm the age of anticolonial struggle. Meanwhile, the relatively new medium of television was transporting Montgomery's movement around the world. So the people there were not only able to see themselves in a heroic mold on the evening news, but they could see and hear the responses of mankind to their battle. What it all meant was that black folk in Montgomery were now free to make far more history than they had ever been able to make before.

III

The bus boycott became the matrix for a mass movement, the first serious sustained campaign of that kind in the bitter history of the southern struggle. Eventually some forty thousand persons found themselves engaged in the movement, from those who planned, and organized, and operated car pools, to those who walked in dignity and hope, doing it, in the words of one sister, "for my grandchildren." The regular church gatherings evolved into a new struggle form, and these mass meetings, filled with praying and singing, inspirational sermons and testimonies, and movement news, became an established element of the southern struggle.

Still, it was not simply the meetings and the astoundingly rich rituals that thrust the people forward. Deeper than all this, encompassing it all, was a tremendous faith in the God of their fathers. Again and again, the people were taught in the mass meetings,

We must love [the white antagonists] for God said that we must love our
enemies as ourselves. Let's not hate them for with love in our hearts and
God on our side, there are no forces in hell or on earth that can mow us
down.

Within their own lives, thousands of black people were convinced of
these two things: that God willed their movement to overcome, and
that some kind of love of enemies was also the will of God. So they
picked up the idea of loving the white enemies and were greatly drawn
to a black Christianized version of nonviolence, not primarily because
they believed in white folks' consciences, or because they saw this as a
tactic in the struggle. Rather, they simply believed such a way to be
the will of God, and they were convinced that they must fight the battle
within the orbit of His will.

Within this context, the religious leaders were pressed towards even
higher levels of consciousness and action. The movement constantly
demanded that they transcend their own history, moving with black
people toward a force of assertion and hope which could be nothing
less than revolutionary in Montgomery, Alabama. In this situation,
King tested and expanded his natural, great gifts of oratory, brought
to bear his capacity to understand and sensitively to express human
suffering and rebellion. But now he could place these gifts at the service of a congregation far larger than any preacher had ever known,
and he was challenged to decide what would be the course of his own
increasingly uncertain life.

Early in the struggle, it was obvious that Martin King grasped
something of the special history he and his black people were being
called upon to make at that stage of the other American revolution. So,
at the close of one of his mass meeting sermon-speeches he wound up
with this peroration,

When the history books are written in the future, somebody will have to
say, "there lived a race of people, fleecy locks and black complexion," but
a people who had the marvelous courage to stand up for their rights, and
thereby they injected a new meaning into the veins of history and of
civilization. And we are going to do that.

Such a sense of messianic destiny, when tied to continuing acts of
courage and resistance, and spread broadside through the black community, was radical and shaking in the heart of the Deep South.

IV

Although the Montgomery Improvement Association's specific goals of bus desegregation were limited, the spirit of resistance that Montgomery symbolized had a dramatic, catalyzing, revolutionizing effect on the larger black community. Here, again, the role of television was critical, providing black people across the country with a sense of immediate participation in the struggles that that southern community represented. In the city, itself, men, women, and children discovered within themselves tremendous resources of courage and endurance. For nearly a year, in the face of beatings, bombings, legal and economic intimidation, and harassment, the black community of Montgomery stuck with their movement. At the same time, the black crime rate in the city plummeted down to a new low. Finally, near the end of 1956, the courts ruled in favor of the Montgomery Improvement Association.

By then, a certain fear was lost. On the night after the Supreme Court decision in favor of the black movement, the Ku Klux Klan scheduled one of its periodic marches through sections of the black community, meaning to let them know that nothing had changed in the balance of terror and power. But something had changed. One account says,

> Hooded and awesomely caparisoned, the Klan procession of forty vehicles entered the black neighborhoods, expecting the mere news of its coming to broadcast paralyzing fear. Instead, porch lights remained lit, and a few black spectators lined the sidewalks to jeer or gesture good-naturedly. Many people went about their business as though oblivious to this intrusion. After a few blocks, puzzled and embarrassed, the procession abruptly turned into a side street and was engulfed by the darkness from whence it came.

Unfortunately, as black people began to act with new courage, determination, and unity, such representatives of the old white order did not remain on side streets. Throughout the section, as they caught the intimation of where black people were going, their puzzlement and embarrassment were easily transmuted into fear and acts of terror.

In 1954, shortly after the *Brown* v. *Topeka* decision, a more respectable version of the Ku Klux Klan had been born when the White Citizens Councils organization was formed. Made up largely of businessmen and professionals, they took off the hoods of the Klan. They now came out from the side streets, and walked the main thoroughfares, entered the city halls, and the corridors of the United

States Congress. Before long, the White Citizens Councils had become a major organizing point for much white resistance in the South.

Between 1956 and 1958 especially, this white resistance focused itself against the schools. Token desegration was beginning in the border states, where heroic black children and their parents and friends were committed to break down the bars, to test the will of the courts, to assert their freedom of choice, to escape the trap of the "colored schools" which white power had set for black spirits. In once obscure places like Clinton, Tennessee, Sturgis, Kentucky, and Little Rock, Arkansas, these black young people became the key participants in the struggle for freedom.

Ranging in ages from six through seventeen, they somehow found the strength to face hatred and fear in the mouths and faces of adults and children. They listened to dynamite blasts shattering the darkness of their towns, shaking their homes. They felt hot soup and cold ink poured down their backs, rotten eggs spattering against their bodies. Some had to walk to school for many weeks in the company of armed national guardsmen. Others walked the lonely white gauntlets alone, feeling the searing hatred against their tender flesh.

They were not alone. Inevitably, an often-frightened, but still determined cadre of family, friends, church members, and others in the local community were with them. Thus, with names like Minnie Jean and Ernest, Elizabeth and Jonathan, Amanda Melinda and Jimmy, the children were walking into a history their people had created for them. Sharing that common experience with their people, thrust into hundreds of thousands of living rooms and bars through the medium of television, the black children of the South could not be alone. Indeed, millions of persons surely felt what Paul Robeson said when, in his autobiographical statement, he addressed the black children of Little Rock, who represented all the tender young warriors for black freedom. Robeson said,

> Dear children of Little Rock—you and your parents and the Negro people of your community have lifted our hearts and renewed our resolve that full freedom shall now be ours. You are the pride and the glory of our people, and my heart sings warm and tender with love for you.

Then Robeson added these significant words,

> You are our children, but the peoples of the whole world rightly claim you, too. They have seen your faces, and the faces of those who hate you, and they are on *your* side.

This sense of the international context of the black struggle for freedom in America was being heightened and expanded during these years. An intensified consciousness of the African and Asian struggles was clearly at work. Though there was as yet no common acceptance of the colonial analogy for the black situation in America, many persons sensed that the common concerns, conditions, and aspirations were unmistakable. And as the power of the southern struggle mounted, it helped to beat back the fears of the anti-Communist crusades.

Meanwhile, the black movement continued and expanded, constantly bringing more persons into its ambit of commitment and action. The Deep South had been broken open by Montgomery, and in spite of the White Citizens Councils it would not close up again to smother black struggle. Men like Fred Shuttlesworth in Birmingham, Amzie Moore in Mississippi, women like Septima Clarke in Charleston—these and hundreds more had determined that the fight would continue and build, even if it must be built on their bodies. Making tremendous sacrifices of jobs, family, and physical safety, they pressed court cases, voter registration campaigns, protests, refusing to allow the black momentum to be halted. In all of this, they found their ally, the federal government, characteristically lethargic, moving only when forced to—as in Little Rock in 1958.

VI

The new sense of movement that had been seeping through the South was also present in unexpected places, such as Kansas and Oklahoma. In 1958, in cities like Kansas City, Wichita, Tulsa and Enid, NAACP youth groups began pressing for enforcement of antidiscrimination laws in public facilities. They sat in restaurants until they were served. They visited all-white churches. In 1958 and 1959 national marches were staged in Washington on behalf of integrated schools, with the largest attracting at least twenty-five thousand persons.

Although the ferment in the black community in the half decade after the 1954 decision was unmistakable, it was not uniform in its thrust towards freedom and independence. Indeed, the rising black attack on the structures of segregation, and the often ferocious white resistance to black participation had opened the way for a new series of calls for black solidarity and independence. Often referred to as black separatism, this emphasis was as old as Garvey and Delaney and the black community itself. In the late 1950s, its archetypical expression was found in Elijah Muhammad's Nation of Islam.

The leader's imprisonment during World War II had immeasurably increased his status among the black community's Islamic cults. After he was released, Elijah Muhammad carried on a tireless campaign of organizing, publicizing, and teaching. Moving from city to city, he had established congregations of Muslims in nearly a dozen urban areas by the time of the court decision. Then, as explosive white resistance met black campaigns for desegregation, the Honorable Mr. Muhammad found increasingly fertile territory for his teachings.

He taught that blacks should not go where they were not wanted. He urged them to seek and support "your own." He embellished on the organization's dogma, that whites were "devils" incarnate who had been created by a rebellious black scientist. He challenged black people to meet white violence with "an eye for an eye and a tooth for a tooth." He called for a separate black nation, and he predicted that any attempts at integration would prove useless, for the destruction of white America at the hands of Allah was due in 1970.

In spite of his critical role as leader and teacher, it was not Elijah Muhammad who provided the dynamic for the rise of the Nation of Islam as a national force in the post-1954 period. That role was played by one of the most fascinating and charismatic leaders produced by the black community: Malcolm X, who had once been Malcolm Little, and whose father had marched with Garvey. The tall, vibrant, and attractive young man had been converted from the dissipated criminal life of "Detroit Red" while in Massachusetts prisons. Through an experience that was a combination of classic religious conversion and hard-won self-transformation, he had emerged from six years of prison a new man, devoted to Elijah Muhammad, and the truth of his teachings. Before long, he was the major messenger of the Messenger.

At the end of the 1950s, Malcolm was not yet a figure of general national renown, but he was already marked with a uniqueness among leaders of the struggle for black freedom in America. At least three important elements contributed to this unique position. Even until his death, Malcolm remained the only major black leader-spokesman who had gone through the dehumanizing criminal experiences of the northern ghettos and survived them to create something new and supremely human. Second, aside from Elijah Muhammad, he was the only one of these leaders who passed through the additionally harshening and honing experiences of a significant prison term, thus sharing a way of life familiar to hundreds of thousands of black men. Finally, he was the only one of the post-1954 leaders who had submitted himself to the requirements of membership in a disciplined, sometimes ascetic religious movement. All these qualifications would serve him well in the days ahead.

VII

The rise of the Muslims in the late 1950s was a reminder that while the post-World War II phase of the other American revolution was based in the South, its connections and vibrations were nationwide. They also served to draw attention to the lack of concensus concerning the way of nonviolent struggle that Martin King represented. Not only did dissent from that position arise in the North, it came also out of the South.

That period's most notable challenge to the way of nonviolence arose from Monroe, North Carolina, where Robert F. Williams, the former United States Marine had come home to claim the freedom and the citizenship that he had dreamed of in May, 1954. In the face of white resistance, Williams was forced to turn to the methods he had learned so well in America's service. He organized an NAACP chapter that was filled with veterans like himself and soon had most of them also enrolled in a "rifle club" that was committed to armed self-defense of black freedom. Before long, he was pressed into a series of armed confrontations with the white forces of his community and at one point he called publicly for black people "to meet lynching with lynching." Williams was attacked by the national office of the NAACP, hounded out of the state and out of the country, and soon was on his way to Cuba.

Of course, his call for armed self-defense and retaliation was no new voice in the traditions of the other American revolution. But again, television was critical. Never before had such a voice been able to reach black people across the nation and throughout the world. Exile did not silence Williams's voice, but his call was largely unheeded at the time. Instead, in the next year, a dramatic movement of black students across the South carried the struggle for black freedom beyond the levels that either King, Elijah Muhammad, or Robert Williams had foreseen. With this striking development, men and women were able to gain some real sense of the power and potential that was in the movement that Montgomery had inaugurated.

Chapter 26

"... Want My Freedom Now":
The Student Revolutionaries
(1960 — 1963)

I

During the first few days of February, 1960, the House Committee on Un-American Activities, still caught up in the spirit and mythologies of the cold war period, was carrying on an interesting investigation. Using a paid informer, they were seeking to ferret out information concerning the nature of the revolutionary activities that the Communist party of the United States was supposedly carrying on among the black young people of Harlem. In characteristic form, they did not know that the genuinely revolutionary activity taking place among black people in 1960 had little or nothing to do with the moribund Communist party. Nor did they dream that its major contemporary manifestation was just then erupting in so unlikely a place as Greensboro, North Carolina—a long way from Harlem.

Black folks knew Greensboro best for its North Carolina State Agricultural and Technical College, but no one expected radical departures to spring from the sleepy campus. Indeed, no one expected much in the way of social or political action from any college students in those days when a "silent" campus generation seemed still frightened into apathy by the repression and alarums of the cold war. Nevertheless, the other American revolution had persistently been marked by events and explosions that surprised the wielders of conventional wisdom, and this stage proved no exception.

The impact of the 1954 decision, the exhilarating example of Montgomery, the inspiring example of Dr. King, the rise of a renewed spirit of hope and assertion in the black community—all these signs and symbols had established themselves in Greensboro. At least such things had begun to touch the lives of four freshmen, Ezell Blair, Jr., David Richmond, Franklin McCain, and Joseph McNeill, and they decided that they must respond. None of the quartet was more than eighteen years old, but they were ready to seize the time. So they went downtown to sit at a segregated lunch counter in a five and dime store, determined to challenge the power of white supremacy over this highly symbolic and therefore deeply felt aspect of their lives.

That first action on the afternoon of February 1, 1960, soon became a catalyst that moved a generation. A steadily growing stream of students from their own campus joined the initial four; then students—some of them white—came from other campuses in the city. Soon, as the words and images flashed by television and by the grapevine, hundreds and thousands of other young people, in other towns and cities, on other campuses, were seized by the rising spirit of movement and freedom. (Part of it was just being in style, but it was a great style to be in; better than anything they'd ever found.)

Lunch counters, restaurants, motels, pools, beaches, churches, filling stations—no public places were safe from the rising river of black students pouring out of campuses across the South. In Richmond and Petersburg, in Rock Hill and Charleston, in Atlanta and Savannah, in Birmingham and Mobile, in Nashville and Memphis, in Little Rock and Pine Bluff, in New Orleans and Baton Rouge—across the sweep of the South, black students were moving to challenge the power of white supremacy, to test the real intentions of the federal government, to determine whether any life still remained in the traditions of the white American revolution.

II

Even more important was the life they carried within them. The black students were filled with vitality and passion, with belief and cascading hope. They overflowed with songs and sermons from all the deep wellsprings of their people's long struggle. And in the vortex of their own tremendous, energizing thrust, they grasped the lives of thousands of whites who were deeply moved and overwhelmed by this black flood of human struggle and commitment.

If there was any life in the old revolution, they would resurrect it. If not, it did not matter; for they had so much of their own. Properly guided, carefully channeled, it might lift the other American revolution to a position of dominance and redefinition in America. Within a year, more than fifty thousand persons had participated in some kind of demonstration, many of them acting in the North in solidarity with the southern movement.

That spring, while the movement was bursting towards its greatest excitement, some of the students, following the advice of adults long experienced in the struggle, decided to organize, to form a coordinating committee. Out of a meeting on the campus of Shaw University, the Student Nonviolent Coordinating Committee (SNCC) came into being. Nonviolence, love, reconciliation, and justice were the major themes in their search for ideology. Martin King, in spite of certain disappointments, was still their model. But they were destined to push beyond his point, to press him into radical directions, to become the shock troops of the other American revolution.

There was indescribable hope, idealism, courage, and determination in those early months of organizing, marching, singing, and going to jail. There were heroes and heroines of every kind at every turn in this new student movement. Names could fill a long roster—names like Jim Forman, Ruby Doris Smith, Julian Bond, Bob Moses, Ella Baker (who was their most crucial nonstudent advisor), Marion Berry, John Lewis, James Bevel, Diane Nash, Charles McDew, Charles Sherrod, Charlie Jones, Prathia Wynn, Curtis Hayes, Bob Zellner, Hollis Watkins, Cornell Reagan—to name a few.

They were believers. When they sang in jail, in mass meetings, in front of policemen and state troopers, "We Shall Overcome," they meant it. Few were certain about details, but they *would* overcome. Vaguely, overcoming meant "freedom" and "rights" and "dignity" and "justice," and black and white together, and many other things that people in a movement feel more than they define. But they knew they were part of a revolution, and they believed that if they only persisted in courage, determination, and willingness to suffer, they would make it over.

Their belief and courage were contagious. The students convinced many elements of a generation of adults that they were really right, and they drew them into the struggle in ways that had not been possible before. They served as a natural magnet for high school students who had been waiting for their role. They encouraged black people all over the North to believe anew that there was a common struggle.

III

In 1961, some of these northern blacks (many of whom were not long out of the South) worked with white allies to create the freedom rides. Black and white groups were to board interstate buses in northern or border cities and then head South, testing the federal ordinances against segregation in interstate carriers. By law and tradition, blacks had had to move to segregated seats after the invisible Mason Dixon line was crossed and the South was breached. The freedom riders would not be moved. The nonviolent action group called the Congress of Racial Equality (CORE) took the lead, but like so much else at this stage of the struggle, organizational labels meant very little. What counted most was sheer courage, courage to board buses headed into a hostile territory still dominated by white fears, hatreds, and ignorance, courage to face men and women who were determined to crush the black uprising.

Again, partly because of the unique power of television, and largely because of the unquestionable heroism of the freedom riders, the movement came to even wider national and international public attention. The price for the publicity was very high. Buses were firebombed and destroyed. Busloads of riders were attacked with wanton savagery in terminals. Blood poured out of cracked skulls. Hundreds of riders ended in jails. But the rides continued. (At one point, when the largely northern contingents seemed stymied in Alabama, a group of the Nashville sit-in students put aside their worst fears and forayed into Alabama to take up up the pilgrimage.) Entire towns and cities of black folks were mobilized around the freedom rides. Old men and women cried and renewed their determination to be free when they saw the naked courage of the riders in face of death. Through the freedom rides, the Deep South had been penetrated by the spirit of the modern movement as never before.

Then, beyond the spectacular action of the rides and the sit-ins, as beachheads were being slowly but clearly won in the realm of public accommodations, new decisions had to be made. SNCC, especially under the quiet, reluctant, charismatic leadership of the New Yorker, Robert Moses, began to press even more deeply into the black heartland. Many persons were convinced that black people had to be organized to move beyond the issues of public accommodations and to thrust themselves into the arena of political power, challenge, and control. It was ultimately the vision that Delany and young H. Ford Douglass had seen more than a century before; it had been part of

Reconstruction's best hopes: if they were to remain and be free in America, black people must become a part of the ruling element of their society.

Now in the 1960s, if that direction were to be developed again, the critical issue of the broken black right to vote had to be faced head on. So the freedom movement, with SNCC taking the lead, pressed its way into some of the hardest territory of the black belt. Small teams of young men and women went to places like Amite County, Mississippi; Lowndes County in Alabama; Sumpter and Baker Counties in Georgia. Every one of these places—like many others around them—had harsh and hard-earned reputations for destroying black resistance, for killing black leaders. Nevertheless, the young people went. If they could gain victories in these places, then the entire racist structure would be undermined.

The students knew that singing, enthusiasm, and hope were not enough. They would have to take their youth, their strength, and their hope into the bastions of white power, into the centers of black population strength. They would have to convince black people that a new day had indeed come. They would have to walk down terrifying country roads and face hostile white officials and stand by all those first black folk who would break the white control over the ballot box. They would have to organize with wisdom, courage, and patience. Some of them would probably have to die. Nevertheless, the young people went.

As they moved into these hard places, the black freedom workers were constantly struck by the knowledge that they were not alone, that they were not pioneers. In each place, there were men and women who had continued to hope and work—against great odds, often in the face of threats of death and economic destruction. They met Amzie Moore and Medgar Evers and Fannie Lou Hamer in Mississippi. They met Fred Shuttlesworth, Mrs. Amelia Boynton, and S. S. Seay in Alabama. They met Slater King and Moma Dollie in southwest Georgia. And these were only representatives of the hundreds of others who stood openly with them, and the thousands who came surreptitiously to their side.

Not only were individuals prepared to offer tremendous support to this newest thrust of the struggle, but in all these small towns and villages, on plantations in the heart of nowhere, the voter registration organizers found help from black institutions. Churches, schools, fraternal lodges, families, all provided persistent examples of courage, resistance, and material aid.

IV

Somehow, everyone seemed to sense the great importance of this campaign to register black people in the heart of the South. There were counties where blacks often outnumbered whites by ratios ranging from two to one, to eight to one, in towns where a registered minority black vote would become a power to deal with. In Fayette County, Tennessee, one white man put the issue as clearly as anyone else in those times when he said to a white reporter,

> I reckon its all right for a nigger to vote if he wants to and it don't harm nothing, but what if they all begun to vote here! We'd be swamped. You put *yourself* in our *place* and you'll see why we got to keep *them* in *their* place.

After decades of white control, every move by black people out of the place that whites had assigned to them, culturally, politically, or economically, was essentially a revolutionary move. For blacks to demand simple, elementary rights, like the right to vote, would obviously "harm" something—the unchallenged power of white supremacy. Thus white resistance continued to be harsh. But the movement had gathered too much momentum to be stopped. In places like McComb, Mississippi, Rock Hill, South Carolina, Americus and Albany, Georgia, the combined force of the sit-ins, freedom rides, and voter registration campaigns set entire communities into motion, sent scores of people willingly to jail.

In the course of these brutal local campaigns for registration, desegregation, and resurrected black hope, there were persistent examples of tremendous courage in the face of menacing white power. Out of thousands of possible examples, one may suffice. Sam Block was a native of Mississippi, and in 1962 the twenty-two-year-old young man was a field organizer in SNCC's voter registration campaign in his native state. Working in Greenwood, accompanying some local black folk to the voter registration office, Block was accosted by the locally feared sheriff. This exchange took place:

> SHERIFF: Nigger, where you from?
> BLOCK: I'm a native of Mississippi.
> SHERIFF: I know all the niggers here.
> BLOCK: Do you know any colored people?
> (The sheriff spat at him.)
> SHERIFF: I'll give you till tomorrow to get out of here.
> BLOCK: If you don't want to see me here, you better pack up and leave, because I'll be here.

The next day Sam Block was there, bringing more folk down to register. It was he and his co-worker Willie Peacock who created one of
Mississippi SNCC's most popular songs, a line of which ran, "I ain'
scared of your jail, cause I want my freedom . . . want my freedom
now."

The loss of the fear of jail, of the fear of sheriffs, of the fear of death
was central to the transformation of many lives in the course of the
struggle in the South. And for those who did not entirely lose the
fears, they learned to subject them to their will, to their determination
to be free. Most often, the results were the same, for the power of
white terror was broken. The making of slaves was ended.

V

In the North, men, women, and children were thrilled by the tremendous battle being waged in the southern states. Lines of association between the two sections which may have been broken or badly
frayed were recreated, just as the pre-Civil War fugitives had tied the
black community of the North to the southern experience. In response
to television, to lecture and freedom song concert tours, in response to
their own memories and longings, blacks in the North sought out ways
to become more fully involved in this magnificent battle for freedom.
They sent food, clothing, people, money. They expanded their support
demonstrations. Most important, they took a new look at their own
situation.

Since 1950, more than a million and a half black folk had moved out of
the South, and when the sit-in movement began only 59 percent of the
nation's black people still lived in the region. Wherever they went in the
North and West, blacks had become almost exclusively urban dwell-
ers, with five cities like New York, Chicago, Philadelphia, Detroit, and
Washington, D.C., accounting for some 15 percent of the nation's total
black population. When blacks looked around at this northern situation
what they saw was disquieting, to say the least.

For a long time, especially since the relative prosperity of World War
II broke the hold of the depression, many blacks in the North and West
had tended to play down the real extent of white racism and oppression
in their section. Now, the insistent freedom movement of the southern
forces shook them into a new attention, forced them to recognize that
many of the traditional problems of the urban North were still present
for blacks; in fact, some had been exacerbated with the continuing
movement of migration.

The school systems were controlled by whites, and almost invariably it was true that those schools where blacks were in a majority were in the poorest condition and received the smallest proportion of attention, skills, and finances. As ever, black people had far less living space available to them than their numbers and percentages required, and their housing was usually the oldest, the least cared for, the most dangerous—and the most expensive. In spite of continuing economic expansion of the nation, blacks still found that they were the "pockets of unemployment" that were always the exception to prosperity, and even on the jobs, advancement and power were denied to them. Indeed, the access to significant decision-making power was blocked in every area, and it was especially obvious in the political arena.

Taking their cues from the southern demonstrations and from the direct action heritage of their own prewar history, northern blacks developed forms of protest and struggle to deal with the joint issues of racism and powerlessness. The schools formed one critical focus, and in cities like Chicago, New York, and Detroit, demonstrations in mounting intensity began to develop, often taking tens of thousands of black people out into the streets. Rent strikes and housing demonstrations were a part of the action now taken up by the black community of the North. New challenges to urban redevelopment placed crowds of people in front of bulldozers. Acts of civil disobedience in cities like New York threatened to create disruptions that were previously unheard of. Meanwhile, pickets and sit-in demonstrators attacked the tough, unyielding white areas in the North where blacks were still refused service in restaurants, skating rinks, motels, and a variety of other public accommodations. Repeatedly, the fury of the white reactions in the North led men like Malcolm X to declare that there was really no difference in the racism of the North and the South.

VI

All the paradoxes of the white democracy were being pressed to the surface, and the hypocrisy of the North was among the most important rediscoveries. In such a situation, the Nation of Islam flourished. By the early 1960s, it was estimated that it had grown from the few thousand members of a decade or so before, to more than one hundred thousand members in some twenty-seven states. Their best propaganda was provided by white America and its refusal to follow the logic of its own revolutionary documents and its court pronouncements. Every new white bombing, every black church burned in the South, every beating in a county jail, every dynamiting of a black family's house in a white northern suburb provided grim testimony to their conviction that whites were essentially devils. So their call for separation intensified. Their demand for land to establish a separate black state seemed to carry a certain growing appeal. Their conviction that Allah would wreak vengeance upon white America seemed consistent with much black preaching, and necessary for any belief in a just God. In the light of contemporary American developments their rejection of Christianity seemed logical. And Malcolm made it most logical of all.

From a larger perspective, though, as one looked at the kaleidoscopic, explosive struggle for black freedom in the early years of the 1960s, it was not the logic that was most impressive. Rather it was the movement, the ferment, the new power that had arisen out of the black people of the South. In the breathtakingly brief period of seven years since the first meetings in Montgomery, a massive social movement had been released, with many manifestations and many parts. Starting from its unexpected southern base, it had shaken a nation out of a period of fear, conformity, and reaction. In its swelling powerful movement, it had revealed the potentials and great strength of an entire people. It had challenged a nation to respond and caught the attention of a world. Now it was being called a black revolution. But no one knew where it led.

VII

In a series of meetings near the end of 1962, a small group of people at the heart of the southern movement revived an earlier idea, the prospect of developing a well-trained, highly disciplined, nonviolent "army" of a thousand or more veterans of the southern struggles. This army, after other lesser missions, would finally march on Washington and become the cadre for a massive civil disobedience campaign that would paralyze the nation's capital until congressional legislation and presidential executive orders broke down all external racial barriers. It would remain in Washington until a clear dynamic had been set in motion for the dissolution of all other structural obstacles to true racial equality in America. No one avoided the question of the risks involved, but they saw no other direction for a nonviolent, revolutionary movement. Predictions were that the nonviolent seige would have to last at least a year.

Black people, with their white allies, were planning sustained, open confrontation with the American government. Was that where the revolution was leading?

Chapter 27

From Birmingham to Atlantic City:
The Testing of America (1963 — 1964)

I

Birmingham. Ever since the 1920s, whenever the word was sounded in the black communities of North and South it conjured up all the worst images of southern white urban racism. Unyielding white supremacy, blatant segregation, brutal police, easily organized white mobs, unresponsive elected officials—all these were part of the story. Every black person seemed to know someone who had been beaten, bombed, raped, or murdered in Birmingham. Yet, at the same time, because this was the heart of the coal mining and steel-making industry of the South, it had provided certain economic opportunities for black people which were not available in many other southern cities. It was paradoxical. It was the South.

So it was appropriate that the post-Montgomery civil rights struggle in the South should reach its apex in Birmingham. All the elements were present, beginning with the city's history. Then there was the safety commissioner, Eugene "Bull" Connor, representing the epitome of unenlightened white racist law and order. Behind him was a largely silent, acquiescing segregationist majority and a vicious, smaller band of white bombers and marauders. Far in the background, making uncomfortable noises, was a group of white "moderates." And furthest of all from the public eye, but wielding great power, were the northern white industrial concerns, like United States Steel, who owned so much of the life of Birmingham.

The tough, outspoken, and absolutely courageous Fred Shuttlesworth had repeatedly placed his wiry body on the line for black freedom in the city. He had been the key force in organizing the Alabama

167

Christian Movement for Human Rights when the state's courts out-lawed the NAACP. Together with a relatively small group of followers and associates, he kept a movement going against great odds, continu-ing to press the issue of desegregation in the schools, in the downtown stores, in the city hall, wherever they could raise a picket sign and present a petition. Repeatedly the white response was a mixture of brutal resistance, unseeing apathy, and minute concessions. Then Shuttlesworth, a key participant in Martin King's Southern Christian Leadership Conference (SCLC), convinced SCLC that Birmingham was the place for the organization's big move.

II

In the spring of 1963, the move began. Keying on many lessons that had been learned in the last major campaign in Albany, Georgia, King and his organization attempted to raise a broad set of issues and chal-lenges. Desegregation of public facilities was only one element. The movement had exploded beyond that level. Employment in the downtown stores and in city hall, the use of black policemen, the estab-lishment of a biracial negotiating committee to move the city from white supremacy to some kind of pluralism—all these and more were part of the barrage of demands that were raised. For the ordinary black people of Birmingham, the heart of the issue was freedom.

They spoke the word with a loving, possessive familiarity. They sang it in the crowded, rocking churches:

> Over my head, I see freedom in the air
> There must be a God somewhere.

They chanted it in ecstatic unison in response to the corps of speakers and exhorters who came before them: "Everybody wants freeDOM! Birmingham wants freeDOM!" (And their accent on the last syllable sounded very much like the way it was then being shouted in Ghana and other parts of Africa.) The aged deacons and deaconesses prayed for freedom, in their ritualistic cadences, and they didn't mind when the young people took the old song, "Woke up this morning with my mind stayed on Jesus," and made it "Woke up this morning with my mind stayed on Freedom." Jesus, Freedom . . . Didn't it all mean the same thing?

Then when Martin King or Fred Shuttlesworth or Ralph Aber-nathy—or anybody else—told them that it was time to put on their "marching shoes," they knew that they must now march for freedom . . . or Jesus. Didn't it all mean the same thing? They knew Bull Connor was outside. They knew hundreds of policemen were outside. They knew that these white men were armed with pistols and shotguns and centuries of hatred and fear. They knew that the crippling high power fire hoses and the vicious dogs were outside. They knew the jails were waiting outside. But they also knew that there would be no freedom for them or for their children unless they went outside too.

So, following their leaders into the face of white power, following the dictates of their faith in the liberating God, they marched for freedom. Children from elementary and high schools marched. Brothers and sisters from the streets and poolrooms marched (stashing their knives in boxes first—trying to keep straight with this man King and his strange teachings). Teachers marched. Maids marched. Garbage men marched. Preachers marched.

"Everybody wants freeDOM! Birmingham wants freeDOM!"

On the streets came the confrontation that the world witnessed on television. Unarmed, singing, often frightened, but uncowed black people (and a few white allies) were marching, demanding with their bodies the freedom their fathers had lived and died for. Right into the face of the police they marched. Up to the dogs they marched. Children walked into hundreds of pounds of water pressure, but held on to each other and to the hope of freedom through it all. Other, even more dauntless children and young people ran around it all and found their way downtown and sat on the floors of the fine, segregating stores and went on singing about freedom. When the dogs snapped, men and women did not forget freedom. When the billy clubs fell, freedom was still on their minds. When the vans and buses came to take them to jail, they went as free people, having broken the chains of fear. Watching it all, fighting against an irrepressible force, Bull Connor said more than he knew when he exclaimed, "If this is religion, I don't want no part of it."

III

As the jails filled, as the marches continued, as men, women, and children submitted their lives to this strange religion of freedom, the nation surged with responses. King's eloquent *Letter from Birmingham Jail* became a rallying point. Demonstrations took place across the nation. Fiery, black anger flared up in North and South. Responses came from all over the world. Millions of people asked what the American government was going to do. In Washington, in New York, in

Pittsburgh, in Chicago, men and women who supposedly wielded real power in America wondered about where this black revolution was leading. The pressure the black movement was building was of undeniable depth and power. Finally, in Birmingham, Washington, Pittsburgh, New York, concessions began to be made.

Martin King and his cohorts were also unsure about where the revolution was going. They had obviously unleashed a power that was beyond their imagination. Often, on the streets of Birmingham it seemed as if the people were leading the leaders in their rush to freedom. Then, at what was supposed to be the end of the campaign, after compromises had been outlined and speeches made, a midnight bombing smashed at the house of Martin King's brother, a pastor in Birmingham's black community. That night, a quick, lightninglike, but fierce confrontation took place out on the streets between the police and a group of black men and women who could hold their rage no longer. It was a fiery intimation of things to come in cities far away.

Where was this revolution going? Partly because they were not sure of the answer, partly because they were afraid to consider fully what it might be, King and his associates did not attempt to build any new, forward thrust on this erupting spirit. Because neither the leaders nor the majority of their followers were honed for the long, hard, disciplined movements of those next stages of the revolution that seemed to be suggested on Birmingham's streets, they accepted the white concessions and accepted too little. Everything was at the token stage. But a wedge had been driven, irrevocably. A people's spirits had been lifted and could not be crushed again.

IV

Of course, the southern struggle for black freedom was not confined to Birmingham. Indeed, that city became a source of great concern to the nation's leaders largely because it was simply the most prominent manifestation of an explosive series of harsh battles that were being waged across the South during that crucial spring of 1963. While SCLC concentrated its energies and attention on Birmingham, SNCC, CORE, and many local groups were digging in and meeting vicious white violence in cities and towns from Virginia to Arkansas. In Danville, Virginia, and Cambridge, Maryland, in Gadsden and Selma, Alabama, in a dozen counties in Mississippi, in Knoxville, Tennessee, in Pine Bluff, Arkansas, the struggle for votes, for jobs, for open accommodations, for space to live and be human went on. Invariably, in all of these places the freedom fighters met gassings, beatings, assassinations, and bombings from the forces of authorized and unauthorized white order. It was as if these white people knew that critical changes in the old order were coming, and they determined to make the price high.

Somehow, as has often been the case throughout the history of the other American revolution, the cost of the struggle for black freedom was focused on the death of one black man. Late that spring, Medgar Evers, veteran NAACP official in Mississippi, was cut down by an assassin's bullet in the driveway of his home. On June 15, 1963, after thousands of black mourners had followed his body to the funeral home, nearly a thousand mostly younger marchers broke from the line and surged towards the main section of town. They were filled with rage and shouted to the advancing policemen, "We want the killer!" But they were also filled with hope, and shouted, in the Africanlike cadences, "FreeDOM! FreeDOM! FreeDOM!" In this atmosphere, bloody confrontation with the frightened, trigger-ready Jackson police force was only narrowly averted. But when the incident was over, and only the heated feelings remained in the air, a young black man stood in a doorway and said, "The only way to stop evil here is to have a revolution. . . . Somebody have to die."

Where was this revolution leading? Many persons were asking that question. They saw and felt the rising level of anger and militance in the faces and actions of the black young people who manned the front lines of the movement. They could not miss the rising sense of frustration with liberal solutions, the sense of betrayal of the federal government, the futility of any appeal to the conscience of the white nation. As had happened many times before, the movement for black freedom was releasing forces that were terrifying to men who valued law and order more than justice and humanity.

V

In the light of this dangerous situation, three connected developments emerged from the keepers of the liberal conscience in America. Together and separately they dissipated much of the black power that was building in the South. The first was the introduction of a civil rights bill into Congress by the Democratic administration. Instead of first using the many executive powers which were available to him, John F. Kennedy responded to the insistent pressures of the black freedom movement by calling for congressional passage of new civil

rights legislation that would deal primarily with public accommodations, an arena of struggle that many blacks had already passed by.
From that point on, a tremendous amount of black movement energy
was spent on pushing the bill through the reluctant Congress. Of even
more importance were the moves that black leaders were urged to
make to weaken the raw power and reduce the rage of the movement,
to avoid giving ammunition to critics of the bill.

The second event was attached to this concern about critics. The
earlier movement discussions concerning a nonviolent army and a
campaign of civil disobedience in Washington, D.C. had been picked up
again during the Birmingham movement. All over the South the mood
seemed right and necessary for such a militant, disciplined action
against a federal government that was recalcitrant at best and in
staunch opposition at worst. But such a campaign of civil disobedience
would obviously lose a host of congressional "friends" and stir up the
nation against the movement even more. Since highest priority was
now placed on the passage of the bill and the building of as large a
reservoir of white liberal support as possible, the original proposal for
an extended nonviolent confrontation with the federal government was
scrapped. In its place, primarily through the work of A. Philip Randolph and Bayard Rustin, a massive, friendly one-day demonstration
in Washington was arranged. The abandonment of the nonviolent army
project was a critical loss to the power of the other American revolution.

Finally, to orchestrate and guarantee the civility of the new march
on Washington, the movement spent tremendous amounts of man-
power, energy, and money—all of which were diverted from the
thrusts of direct action and voter registration in the South and elsewhere. At the end of August, when a well-integrated throng of some
three hundred thousand persons marched and sang and listened to
speeches (some of which, like that of John Lewis of SNCC, were
sanitized in the cause of unity with new white allies), the southern civil
rights movement had passed its peak of power.

A few weeks later, it had no strength to respond in any serious way
when a bomb blasted the side out of Birmingham's Sixteenth Avenue
Baptist Church, and took the lives of four of its Sunday school girls.
Somehow, it seemed as if the movement—at least temporarily—was
like the large stained glass picture of Christ on the blasted side of the
church—a huge imposing figure, with its heart blown out.

VI

The struggles went on all over the South, but a certain weariness, a bone-tiredness was setting in, especially among those who had been the shock troops. The dreams they had dreamt three years ago at Raleigh, in Nashville, in Atlanta did not seem to be working out on schedule. The struggles for votes, for jobs, for a way to be human were far longer and more complex and far less romantic than they had thought. Many persons seemed unprepared to face a struggle that might demand all the rest of their lives.

Meanwhile, the power that had been building in the spring, though not ultimately lost, seemed dissipated. It was a time for new thoughts, for the entertainment of ideas and dreams that had not been permissible before. It was in this period that many participants in the southern movement were introduced to Frantz Fanon's *The Wretched of the Earth*, and at times, they examined it more for his reflections on violence than for his call to create new men and women and a new world.

This was the time that they began to take Malcolm X more seriously than ever before, not the mythology about black scientists, but the calls to black solidarity and black nationhood. After the Washington march and the Birmingham bombings, more than ever before, the hard, touchy question of the role of whites in the movement for black freedom was raised. At the same time, in a related reaction, the SNCC forces and others repeatedly identified the federal government as more enemy than friend. (Ironically the assassination of John Kennedy seemed only to confirm such beliefs.) Beneath the level of all these connected, disconcerting thoughts they toyed with the idea that James Baldwin had popularized in his widely read essay, *The Fire Next Time:*

> The Negroes of this country may never be able to rise to power, but they are very well placed indeed to precipitate chaos and ring down the curtain on the American dream.

But in the fall of 1963 the young veteran freedom workers were only pondering such thoughts (while the names and the dying cries of Cynthia Wesley, Denise McNair, Carol Robertson, and Addie Mae Collins screamed in their ears).

In Mississippi, SNCC was still trying to understand what it might mean for some black people to "rise to power" where they were. Following Bob Moses's leadership, they were now convinced that voter registration was only a means to an end, and that the end was certainly not the delivery of black people into the hands of either of the major

political parties. Thus they began to experiment with the development
of an independent, predominantly black political thrust in the state. To
help develop that thrust, SNCC decided, after much debate, to work
with CORE and the NAACP to bring a corps of largely white volunteers to Mississippi in the following summer.

VII

While the way was being prepared for this explosive development,
the new civil rights bill cut a tortuous path through Congress. On July
2, 1964, with representatives of the civil rights movement surrounding
him, and with visions of the November presidential elections dancing
in his head, Lyndon Johnson signed the bill for which so many persons
had worked and died. But if he thought that that was the way the black
revolution was going, he was wrong.

Beginning almost simultaneously with the movement of the presidential pens, a series of black eruptions broke out in the North. From
Harlem, New York, to Dixmoor in Illinois, usually goaded by charges
of white police brutality, thousands of black people attacked police,
looted stores, threw Molotov cocktails, and generally announced a new
phase of the other American revolution. A civil rights bill would not cut
it. Birmingham was not forgotten.

Meanwhile, in Mississippi, nearly a thousand predominantly white
volunteers came to work. They were admittedly serving as hostages
for the life and safety of the black people who sought to build their
political power in the state. The assumption was that since white lives
were more valuable to America than black ones, these white students,
housewives, artists, and teachers would be a protective covering for
black movement. In an even more chilling calculation, it was thought
that the death of any one of these whites in action in Mississippi would
probably bring more national attention and federal response than the
murder of several black workers.

In the course of Mississippi summer the white worker-hostages
taught freedom schools, registered voters, operated recreational centers, gathered research materials, learned something about life in Mississippi, became politically radicalized—and some of them died. Then,
in a cruel coincidence, on the day that the badly bludgeoned, lifeless
bodies of the three of the freedom workers were identified, Lyndon
Johnson announced the American bombing of North Vietnam.

VIII

In the summer of 1964, the connections between the struggle for black freedom and the bombing of North Vietnam were not very clear to most persons in the movement. They could only feel instinctively that wherever white America claimed to be protecting the freedom of nonwhite peoples with troops and planes, something was wrong. For instance, that August, the young black warriors from SNCC and CORE had sent a "loyal" delegation of blacks and whites from the Mississippi Freedom Democratic party to claim their seats in Lyndon Johnson's Democratic convention at Atlantic City, New Jersey. In the light of the refusal of the all-white "regular" Mississippi delegation to abide by the party's rules for racial justice, here was Johnson's chance to protect democracy in his own country, in his tightly controlled convention. But the party that could support the bombing of North Vietnam in the name of democracy could not support a new democratic force in America. They were not ready to pay the price. And leaders like Martin King and Bayard Rustin allowed themselves to be used on the wrong side of that struggle.

After the brutal Mississippi summer, the betrayal at Atlantic City proved to be the decisive turning point in the minds of many young movement veterans. The system itself was structured against black freedom, against serious exercise of democracy for black folk. Under the scrutiny and pressure of black struggle, the entire system, including its "liberal" Democratic party, and its far-flung wars for democracy, appeared bawdy and corrupt. In the light of such terrible knowledge, where could the other American revolution go?

Chapter 28

Black Power and Urban Rebellion: The Struggle Transformed (1964 – 1967)

I

Some persons had begun to refer to the post-Montgomery freedom movement as the Second Reconstruction, and in spite of many important differences in the two eras of struggle, they were more accurate than they knew. During both periods of radical transformation, the urgent black demand for full participation in the life of the society— starting with the South—formed the bedrock of the struggle. In the 1950s and 1960s, no less than a century before, such a black thrust into the heart of a racist society was profoundly revolutionary, requiring the reshaping of minds, institutions, and systems. In both periods, many black people recognized that they were pressing America to fulfill its own uncompleted and distorted revolution.

By 1965, it was evident that some of the essential faults that had appeared in the structure of the first Reconstruction were breaking to the surface again. Now, as before, the South could not be transformed unless the nation were transformed. For Mississippi was connected to Atlantic City, by way of Washington, D.C. The South could not be reconstructed and the nation could not be broken out of its racism unless the men at the head of the federal government were prepared to press an uncertain, often fearful, resistant white society to take risks with the future. The radical change could not be accomplished unless America's leadership was ready to transform itself, its

177

priorities, its foreign policies, its expenditure of funds, its essential national image and goals.

Although the words were not used as often as in the nineteenth century, the majority of American society still conceived of this as a white man's country. And if they did not use Abraham Lincoln's mystical language, nevertheless there could be no doubt that the national leaders who sent hundreds of thousands of men into Vietnam still believed that this white-dominated nation was, indeed, "the last, best hope of earth." For the masses of black people to jam their way into the life of this society, to become—in the words of Delany and H. Ford Douglas again—an integral part of "the ruling element," required fundamental changes from bottom to top.

By and large, in that time of decision the white nation lacked the leadership, the courage, and the will to wrench itself open. Some men and women in the churches, a few in the universities, others scattered through the institutions of the society seemed momentarily to be prepared for the long struggle for radical change, but the vast majority of leaders and people were not. Once more, the white North was refusing the demands that were made upon it. The federal leadership was forcing itself more deeply into the quagmire of an imperialist war; and even as he signed civil rights bills and almost sang "We Shall Overcome," Lyndon Johnson was seeking a way to co-opt (or undermine) the other American revolution, to turn it from the radical logic of its demands.

II

Of course, there were several critical differences in the development of the two reconstructions, the most important of which was the position of the black population itself. By 1965, almost three hundred and fifty years after Jamestown, the children of Africa in America were well over twenty million strong. More important, the demands of two world wars and the rapid, explosive internal changes in America had spread this black community across the face of the nation, with at least 40 percent of them now out of the South.

In many northern cities, black voting power was crucial to the turning of elections, and black buying power was a critical factor in the profits of business concerns. Black labor was deeply embedded at the point of production in many basic industries. Of greatest significance, though, were the power and momentum that the post-Montgomery movement had built, and the transformation that had taken place in the mind and self-image of the Afro-American community. It was a community in movement, in motion, with powers not yet realized or channeled. Almost all of its post-World War II children had grown up in a setting of challenge, where exclusive white prerogatives were under attack, all over the world.

Paradoxically this explosive momentum presented one of the central problems faced by the black struggle for freedom. Though black people formed a nation in one real sense of the word, though there was a national sense of identity, ferment, and movement among them, there was no overall sense of direction, no clarity on where the revolution was going and how the various segments of the black community might go forward with maximum power to force change in the society. There was no leadership that had grasped sufficiently the black and white realities of the entire nation to mobilize and organize this great momentum on a national scale to define and secure justice.

The civil rights movement was groping, puzzled, searching for ways to move beyond the issues of public accommodations, voter registration, and token integration, to the deep, structural racism of the society. Constantly there was talk of the triple conundrum faced by blacks in jobs, schools, and housing, and some persons—like Bob Moses—were becoming more active in the antiwar movement, but no one seemed certain how to use the tremendous energies built by the southern movement to strike at the heart of America's life.

Back in 1963, shortly after the March on Washington, one of Martin King's key assistants, Wyatt T. Walker, had voiced the frustration and the searching of the nonviolent movement. At an SCLC convention that year, he said the question was "whether we want to continue local (nonviolent) guerrilla battles against discrimination and segregation or go to all-out war." Then he dramatically asked the convention,

> has the moment come in the development of the nonviolent revolution that we are forced . . . on some appointed day . . . literally (to) immobilize the nation until she acts on our pleas for justice and morality? . . . Is the day far off that major transportation centers would be deluged with mass acts of civil disobedience; airports, train stations, bus terminals, the traffic of large cities, interstate commerce, would be halted by the bodies of witnesses nonviolently insisting on "Freedom Now." I suppose a nationwide work stoppage might attract enough attention to persuade someone to do something to get this monkey of segregation and discrimination off our backs, once, now and forever. Will it take one or all of these?

Those were the questions and the dilemmas men still faced in 1965. How could the freedom movement be transformed into a national revolutionary force capable of "all-out war" on behalf of a new society?

Walker's flailing about for appropriate actions indicated how great a reservoir of imagination and courage was required among movement leadership to deal with the very changes it had helped to create, and to carry them to the deepest levels of American politics, economics, and culture. At the same time, his vague references to persuading "someone to do something" was another testimony to the lack of clarity, ideology, and program that plagued the religiously oriented organizations of the southern struggle.

Because there was no overall sense of direction, no larger strategy, because they were often afraid or unable to follow the logic of their own movement towards mass revolutionary action (whether armed or unarmed), the leaders of the civil rights movement were poorly prepared for the next stages. They had helped to release forces that were now surging out beyond them, just as the students had done in 1960. There was a growing sense that the future of the next period was developing in the northern cities, but there was no real understanding of how those cities might be tied to their roots and the roots of the struggle in the South. So, episodic attempts at "relevant" action were made, but the true revolutionary potential of the next period was often wasted and misdirected.

III

Because of his central role in the struggle, Martin King's activities provided a vivid testimony to the confusion and ferment of the explosive year of 1965. In the fall of 1964, King had gone to Oslo, to receive the Nobel Peace Prize. When he returned to America, it often appeared that the search for humane, just peace in his native land would overwhelm him. As the power of the southern movement poured out into the North and West, as it gathered its own distinctive, new momentum in the cities of the North, King began to appear increasingly driven from place to place, like a small ship, uncertain of its direction, continually in danger of destruction.

He had announced a new voter registration campaign in Selma, Alabama, and early in 1965 he was flying and driving in and out of that black belt community, helping to build for a traditional series of marches and demonstrations. In a now established pattern, various national leaders and celebrities came to Selma briefly, to offer their word of support and encouragement, to renew their credentials. Among the visitors was Malcolm X. In 1964 he had broken loose (if not free) from the constraints of Elijah Muhammad and the Nation of

Islam, and had made journeys to Africa and to Mecca. Now, his life endangered from many sources, he had decided to seek for ways to stand in solidarity with King and SNCC and the troubled southern movement.

Momentarily, this fascinating overture by Malcolm suggested the ties that might be established between the northern and southern struggles, between the slashing, politically conscious searching of the North, and the great concentrations of potential black political power in the South. Two weeks later, in New York City, that moment of opportunity was shattered by the blasts from the guns of a squad of assassins and Malcolm became a myth, eventually providing sustenance and hope for a generation of black young people. But myths could be no substitute for the linkages so badly needed in the movement. (In contrast, the immediate forces released by his death were a powerful cresting of antiwhite and black nationalist feeling, and eventually these did offer certain new, temporary grounds for unity between the black North and South.)

Meanwhile, King went on with Selma, but a certain critical quality of life, hope, and direction was missing. Especially among the veteran participants, there was a powerful, sad sense of déjà vu. So much of the activity seemed locked into the past. Partly as a result of this lack of fresh power, some serious mistakes were made, and the harsh, festering disagreements between SCLC and SNCC were pressed up to the surface.

King made the mistake of being absent from a demonstration in which scores of black people fell beneath the galloping horses, the flailing billies, and the tear gas of state troopers. Heads—including that of John Lewis—were cracked, and King, the leader, was in Atlanta. Then when he came, hundreds of northern whites and blacks, mostly church people, were mobilized to join the local black forces to face the next onslaught of Alabama troopers. But when the time came to assert their right to march for freedom, there is every evidence that King backed off. Listening to mediators from President Johnson, he refused to press the movement into so harsh and predictably bloody a confrontation.

Many sagging spirits were finally broken with that act of retreat, and the distrust that had been building against King, SCLC, and the Johnson administration since Atlantic City poured out in deep anger and disgust. Though there was eventually a well-orchestrated march from Selma to Montgomery, the powerful, forward thrust of the southern civil rights struggle had now been finally broken, and that turned out to be the last traditional, major march of the southern movement.

Everything after that was transition, a shifting back and forth, a searching towards the new time.

IV

By then, the Deacons for Defense and Justice had spread from Louisiana through Alabama, Mississippi, Arkansas, and Texas, providing a late manifestation of the armed self-defense doctrines of Robert F. Williams. Other, similar groups were organized in the South to protect the unarmed freedom workers, at times creating an element of confusion in style as well as in goals. Now self defense began to be spoken of as if it were an end, a laudable goal in itself, a put-down of nonviolence, an object of revolutionary struggle. Young men and women who knew no history believed that this was the first time that black people had decided to defend themselves. Meanwhile, in Lowndes County, Alabama, Courtland Cox and Stokely Carmichael, two of SNCC's most aggressive and articulate field secretaries, were pushing forward the concept of independent black political power, organizing the Lowndes County Freedom party, whose emblem was a black panther. Up in the northeast a handful of politically conscious black radicals met in the spring of 1965 to form a coalition called "The Organization for Black Power."

One of the major external contributing factors to the searching, confusion, shifting, and loss of focus in the movement was the expanding Vietnam War. The constantly escalating American intervention in this long Vietnamese revolutionary struggle demanded attention at every level of the society. Funds, energies, and moral force were drained.

Early in the history of American involvement, some of the most sensitive and politically conscious members of the black freedom movement had participated in antiwar meetings and demonstrations. In his local Atlanta church, King had long been an opponent of the American role, and after his Nobel Peace Prize, he began to make occasional public references to it. Then in July, 1965, a leaflet appeared among the voter registration forces in McComb, Mississippi, providing one of the first, studied statements on the relationship between the black freedom struggle and the war.

The leaflet, bearing a fresh, unprofessional quality about it, appeared after the black people of McComb received word that one of their boys, a former participant in the movement there, had been killed in Vietnam. Readers were presented with "five reasons why Negroes should not be in any war fighting for America." These were:

1. No Mississippi Negroes should be fighting in Vietnam for the white man's freedom, until all the Negro people are free in Mississippi.
2. Negro boys should not honor the draft here in Mississippi. Mothers should encourage their sons not to go.
3. We will gain respect and dignity as a race only by forcing the United States government and the Mississippi government to come with guns, dogs, and trucks to take our sons away to fight.
4. No one has a right to ask us to risk our lives and kill other colored people in Santo Domingo and Vietnam, so that the White American can get richer. We will be looked upon as traitors by all the colored people of the world if the Negro people continue to fight and die without a cause.

Fifth, urging black young men who were already in the army to follow the example of a white soldier who had gone on a hunger strike for a discharge, the leaflet said to parents,

> write and ask our sons if they know what they are fighting for. If he *(sic)* answers Freedom, tell him that's what we are fighting for here in Mississippi.

V

While these echoes from Paul Robeson and W. E. B. Du Bois were sounding in southwest Mississippi, another war broke out—or was it simply the latest battle in one of the world's longest wars? In the middle of August, fire and death tore loose like a raging flood in a dreary-looking, lower middle class black community in Los Angeles called Watts. Once again, the occasion was the action by the occupying army of police, but the forces had been seething, surging for a long time.

For five days, fighting went on. Black people attacked police, firemen, white stores—but no white civilians. Flames from dozens of fires lighted the nighttime skies. Bullets, tear gas shells, screaming sirens, and shouting men and women poured out a cascade of sounds closely approximating those of battlefield. And it was. When police and thirteen thousand national guardsmen finally quelled the uprising, thirty-four persons were dead, more than one thousand were wounded and nearly forty million dollars in property had been destroyed.

As Watts was burning, smaller scale uprisings against white law and order took place in Chicago and Philadelphia. King and other veterans of the civil rights movement flew from place to place, seeking a way to communicate, to mediate, to understand. But they could do none of these things. In a deep sense, these young urban rebels were Martin's children, products of the long struggle that began in Montgomery a decade before, but in the frenetic style of northern life many of them were short-circuiting his approaches, seeming to believe that freedom was on the streets for the taking, that "the man" would cave in at the sight of a Molotov cocktail and a .38 revolver. Others were searching for nothing more than an opportunity to be seen and heard, to assert their visibility, their existence. Some were after the loot.

White America responded to the early urban explosions with a volatile mixture of fear, anger, and confessions of guilt. Tensions were high. Predictions of racial warfare spread about. Professionals in the human services were beseiged for their opinions. Millions of persons who had previously ignored the cry of the black cities now opened their eyes and ears. Traditional black leaders were torn between a facile condemnation of the violence and a desire to use it to argue for the funds, the laws, and the programs they had been advocating. Not one to be left behind, President Johnson announced a great war on poverty. Meanwhile, back in Los Angeles, a former director of the Central Intelligence Agency was assigned to investigate what had happened in Watts.

By the end of the year, still searching for the connections between Montgomery and Watts, Martin King announced he would move to Chicago at the beginning of 1966 to confront the network of problems faced by blacks in that city. Though he actually rented, and periodically occupied, an apartment on the West Side, and his family came once or twice from Atlanta to visit, the move turned out to be largely symbolic. It represented his deep and anguished search for the answers to Wyatt Walker's (and his own) earlier questions about the need for "all-out" war against black oppression. It was symbolic of his sense that something had to be done about the tremendous racism and alientation faced in the northern black communities. It was symbolic of his unpreparedness for the harsh realities of Chicago, its subterranean politics, its widespread, variegated black community, the highly organized, deadly power of the Daley machine, and the need for years of hard, meticulous movement organizing towards goals that were understood by all. In 1966, King had neither the sense of coherent direction, the cadre of long-range organizers—nor the time. Thus he had to fail, and the movement he represented had to continue to flounder and search.

VI

While the pressures built up in the North, essential transformations were taking place in the southern movement as well, especially in the ranks of SNCC. As the once-exciting months stretched into hard and brutal years, many persons backed off, sought more "normal" lives, turned away from the lifetime of revolutionary commitment that was demanded from those who would transform a nation.

The frustrations were racking on body and soul. Every movement forward had been purchased at great cost. Bleeding ulcers, nervous breakdowns, mysterious, incurable ailments took their toll on young lives. All the high-speed escapes in the night, all the exposure to rain and hunger, all the confrontations with death could not be forgotten. Then, to make it even more murderously difficult, every time they smashed away some obstacle to black freedom and equality, another larger, newly perceived hindrance loomed before them, challenging the last ounce of their strength and their spirit. Now, those full-time workers who were left, those mostly young persons who had been forced to press decades of life into a few short, explosive years, were angrily, desperately groping, trying to find where their revolution led.

For many reasons, some less substantial than others, they searched for links to the rebellious young people of the urban ghettos. They began to identify the streets of the black communities of the North as the new frontiers of the black struggle. Beyond these shores, they sought identification with the liberation movements of other colonized peoples, especially those of Africa; and the freedom songs began to take on an international flavor, a harsher, more abrasive ring.

At the same time, SNCC and CORE were exploring levels of nationalism and black solidarity that would not have been imagined three years earlier. A SNCC black paper produced in Atlanta proposed that "our organization should be black-staffed, black-controlled and black financed." Only in this way could blacks work out their necessary destiny in America, the document said. Then in the spring of the year, Stokely Carmichael, who reflected much of the thinking represented in the paper, was elected chairman of SNCC.

VII

Not long after Carmichael's election, the roads of Mississippi provided the arena for a remarkable, unsettling confrontation among past, present, and future in the post-Montgomery black struggle. In June, 1966, James Meredith, who had braved a mob four years earlier to become the first known black student at the University of Mississippi, returned to his native state to begin a "march against fear." He planned to walk along the public highways from the northern to the southern border of Mississippi. Shortly after he set out, Meredith was cut down by a shotgun blast from a would-be assassin. While his wounds were being treated in a Memphis Hospital, television cameras recorded for the world what was already a general suspicion: the dissolution of the traditional civil rights movement in the face of the newer, slashing currents of the struggle.

The leaders of CORE, SCLC, the NAACP, SNCC, and the Urban League had dutifully hurried to Memphis, partly in response to news that Meredith was more seriously wounded than he turned out to be. Immediately, dissension arose over the most appropriate form of protest and solidarity. SNCC and CORE wanted a march with whites excluded, one that would not be pledged to nonviolence in the face of the expected provocations. Finally, after long hours of argument and negotiation, it was decided that the new Meredith march (without Meredith) would be interracial and nonviolent. But the manifesto that defined the march frightened off Roy Wilkins of the NAACP and Whitney Young of the Urban League with its unsparing criticism of the Johnson administration. In part, the manifesto declared,

> This march will be a massive public indictment and protest of the failure of American society, the government of the United States, and the state of Mississippi to "fulfill these rights" [referring to a slogan of the Johnson administration].

The harsh debates that had begun in Memphis were carried on all the way down the Mississippi highways, in the face of tear gas, death threats, and provocative, club-wielding sheriffs and state troopers. Carmichael and King were the protagonists, with King being forced into an overzealous defense of the past. Because the motion of the march was towards the future, Carmichael emerged as the dominating figure, and the cry of "Black Power!" that he thrust into the consciousness of the world became the major public legacy of the march.

"Black Power!" replaced "FreeDOM" as the dominant chant. The words, "Ho-ho, whata you know, white folks gotta go," repeatedly rang out in the night, usually sung by the young people who dominated the march. Perhaps a greater honesty was also achieved when new stanzas were added to one of the older movement songs. After

> I love everybody,
> I love everybody,
> I love every body in my heart,

the marchers quickly added:

> I just told a lie,
> I just told a lie,
> I just told a lie in my heart.

On a more frightening level, but one that testified to the mood of the march and the times, young people were also heard singing:

> Jingle bells,
> Shotgun shells,
> Freedom all the way,
> Oh what fun it is to blast
> A trooper man away.

VIII

It was hard for King to counter this mood, partly because he had to shuttle back and forth between Mississippi and his new northern base in Chicago. There, even while the march was going on, the lightning of the northern movement struck again in uprisings in several black and Puerto Rican sections of the city. Throughout the summer, rebellions spread across the North again, hitting such places as Cleveland, Ohio; Lansing, Michigan; Omaha, Nebraska; Dayton, Ohio; and then sparking into new and more widely spread disorder in Chicago, itself, later in the summer. By the time King led a series of demonstrations for open housing in some of the tough white suburbs of the city, many persons were asking whether the movement had passed him by.

The times seemed much more propitious for the tall, supremely self-confident Stokely, not only because he appeared to be more closely in touch with the street forces of the North, but because he seemed to sense more fully the needs of the new time of the struggle. For instance, below the provocative rhetoric of his language, there was a deep insight into the nature of the black predicament in America when he said,

> I've had so much law and order, I swear before God I want some chaos! I want some chaos so bad I can taste it on my lips, because all I see is law and order everywhere I go. Law and order, from Canton, Mississippi to Watts, Los Angeles, to Harlem, to Chicago—nothing but law and order.

Somehow the statement tied him to the brothers in Watts, to the black soldiers in Houston, to the outlyers in the Dismal Swamp of Virginia, to the insurrectionary Africans on board the many ships of the middle passage. With them, he was saying that where law and order support oppression, then chaos is a necessary step toward justice.

There seemed to be no want of chaos in America in the summer of 1966, but the black cities were only a part of the nation's profound disorder. By the fall of the year, some three hundred and fifty thousand American military personnel were in Vietnam, creating a chaos of their own, and throughout the black movement the cry for antiwar dissent and draft refusal was reaching new levels, joining the rising nation-wide ferment. Stokely was condemning America's role as imperialist and racist and shouting the slogan to black and white young men: "Hell no! We won't go!" Floyd McKissick of CORE was voicing the same sentiments in his even more abrasive style. And both men were pressing Martin King, the chief spokesman for peace and nonviolence, towards the edges of dissent, helping to hasten a sharp break with the Johnson administration. Only those who loved security more than truth and justice could deny what black men and women had long seen and known: The struggle for freedom was indivisible. Watts, Chicago, Mississippi, and Vietnam were part of one bloody ground.

Chapter 29

Vietnam, Detroit, and Memphis: The Indivisible Movement, The Indivisible Man (1967 – 1968)

I

At every point in the history of black struggle in America, the nation's wars had had a profound effect on the life of the movement, transforming, diverting, intensifying, opening new avenues and understandings, shutting other channels of growth. The war in Vietnam was no different. At times it seemed like some huge, sprawling rock, growing in size and intensity every day, smashing, crushing, destroying all hopes for justice and renewal in America. Sometimes its visage was that of a gigantic sponge, sucking in money, energies, lives, and moral concern. Whatever its form, it was of course a natural outgrowth of the decisions the nation had made and refused to make about liberation movements, communism, nonwhite peoples, manifest destiny, and about the power of American presidents to destroy both truth and life.

By the beginning of 1967, there were more than four hundred thousand persons in the American military forces in Vietnam, including all the tragic ironies of major black participation. Still, in spite of a mounting and ever more aggressive national antiwar movement, there was an overwhelming majority of persons who refused to see the injustice of the war and its horrendous effects on the moral, economic, and political life of America. Even more vital here, important segments of leadership in the black protest–civil rights mainstream refused to raise any independent criticism to the war, and claimed that

there was no intrinsic connection between the struggle for racial justice and the movement against America's racist, imperialist war. For
the most part, their real concern was to be free to continue seeking and
finding the favor of the federal government, especially its larger-than-
life head, Lyndon Johnson.

As in every other war, the pressures on black leaders for conformity
and silence were enormous, and some of those leaders were deeply
troubled by anyone who broke out of their circle. SNCC and CORE
had clearly done so—but they had broken out in many other ways, and
they were paying a tremendous cost in the loss of financial supporters.
In contrast, Martin King was still the symbolic leader, the major single
spokesman of the deeply troubled freedom movement. So men like
Whitney Young of the Urban League, Roy Wilkins of the NAACP, and
A. Phillip Randolph and Bayard Rustin tried to rein him, in warning
him, among other things, of the loss of funding for the movement, the
loss of public sympathy, and the danger of incurring the great and ugly
anger of Lyndon Johnson.

King was deeply concerned about all these things, more than many
of his younger, more radical colleagues might have liked. But King had
too much conscience to allow these threats to control him. In the spring
of 1967, he launched his major public attacks on the war and the administration. He had been raising the issue, stating careful public criti-
cisms for some two years, but never before had he lashed out with such
righteous anger, indignation, and radical power.

II

In a series of speeches and press conferences in April, King un-
equivocally condemned his own nation as the aggressor in Vietnam. He
called America "the greatest purveyor of violence in the world," and
indicated a deep sympathy for the sufferings of the entire Vietnamese
people and a notable understanding of the justice behind the anti-
Saigon forces. Moreover, King made it clear that he saw an intimate
connection between the war in Vietnam and the struggle for black
freedom in America, excoriating a society that sent young black men
"8,000 miles away to guarantee liberties that they had not found in
southwest Georgia and East Harlem." Beyond speeches, King participated in peace demonstrations, and finally made it clear that he would
urge draft resistance and other forms of antiwar civil disobedience,
especially to black people.

King's dramatic and outspoken stand was not the first in the movement, but it was clearly the most influential, and he was met with a storm of criticism and many bitter, vituperative attacks. They came from inside his own organization as well as from the more "moderate" elements of the traditional civil rights establishment. It was reliably reported that Lyndon Johnson, incensed and deeply cut by King's words and actions (because they were so true?), broke off all relations with the black leader from that point. But King stood fast, never retreating an inch from his principled position.

Still, in the new movements of the freedom struggle, there were positions far to the left of King's, far more radical in their critique of America and in their break with the nation's foreign policy. In 1967, Stokely Carmichael toured many parts of the socialist and anticolonial world, including Cuba, Algeria, and North Vietnam. In Vietnam he made it clear that he hoped not simply for peace, but for the defeat of America in the war. Using the editorial "we," he said, "We are not seeking the end of the bombing or the end of the United States policy of aggression in Vietnam. We want to see the Vietnamese win the war, defeat the United States, and drive it out of the country."

In Cuba that summer, Stokely spoke to a meeting of Third World revolutionaries and said,

> we have a common enemy. Our enemy is white Western imperialist society. Our struggle is to overthrow this system.

Then, speaking more specifically about his own sector of the struggle, and using more than the editorial "we," Carmichael said,

> We are moving into open guerrilla warfare in the United States. We have no alternative but to use aggressive violence in order to own the land, houses, and stores inside our communities and control the politics of those communities.

(Meanwhile, H. Rap Brown, Stokely's successor in the leadership of a rapidly declining SNCC, was writing letters to offer the services of black American young men to the active liberation armies of Africa.)

III

Was this where the other American revolution was going? Would it erupt into a "classic" nationwide explosion of coordinated, black urban guerrilla warfare? Would it become a war for national liberation within

America? From his base in China, Robert F. Williams was sending back instructions and encouragement for blacks to take this direction, to form a serious movement for national, armed revolutionary struggle. Many persons, black and white, believed this was the only logical denouement of the drama that had been building in the struggle for black freedom. Some viewed such an eventuality with fear and trembling, others with a strange, desperate hope, believing anything was better than the continued pressure of white oppression.

In the course of the year, it was revealed that a clandestine operation known as the Revolutionary Action Movement (RAM) had been at work in the black community, and in spite of the ambiguous nature of its activities, RAM's activities were interpreted in the heated context of the time. There was, however, nothing clandestine about what took place in Sacramento, California that spring. On May 2, 1967, a group of twenty-nine young black men and women marched into the state legislature building. They wore black leather jackets and black tams. They looked very serious; and twenty of them were armed with pistols, shotguns, and rifles.

With that audacious—and foolhardy—move, the Black Panthers barged into the attention of the nation and the world. The immediate black and white reactions were a mixture of shock, excitement, fear, pride, and a good deal of romantic hope. In a period when men and women seemed to be in a state of constant expectation, waiting for some kind of messianic, revolutionary deliverance, the question was raised again: Were these impressive young men and women the shock troops of the new stage of the revolution?

Then, in the summer of 1967, the flames of new black urban uprisings swept the nation with an unparalleled force and power, appearing at times as if they would engulf the society in chaos. Beginning in Boston, where a demonstration of black welfare mothers was transformed into three nights of open rebellion, the conflagrations tore through every part of black America. From Tampa, Florida, to Milwaukee, Wisconsin, from Buffalo, New York, to Waterloo, Iowa—in every conceivable kind of community where Afro-Americans lived and experienced the nation's racism—the fires of that summer shot up into the sky.

Almost always, the initial provocation for the black community was some encounter with the local law enforcement officials, usually white officials. An arrest, a beating, a shooting—then all the rage of decades would break loose. Blacks, especially young people, ran shouting, exalting through the streets, feeling a freedom they had not felt before, giving way to urges and fulfilling long-felt needs to be seen, to be heard, to be known, "to get whitey off our backs." They set fires and broke into stores. They taunted police, National Guardsmen, and firemen; but often they had no other weapons than sticks, cans, rocks, and homemade Molotov cocktails. At times there was sniping, but not nearly as much as white America wanted (and yet did not want) to believe. Mostly there was burning, and looting, and believing that the revolution was at hand, that sustained, but unfocused black violence could "bring America to her knees."

IV

Nearly one hundred and fifty cities were hit by the rebellions that summer, but none matched the intense ferocity and widespread destruction that took place in Newark, New Jersey, and Detroit, Michigan within two weeks in July. These cities, with their large black populations, had long histories of movement and struggle, from the days of Noble Drew Ali and the early Temple People, to the violent racial warfare of 1943 and the bitter conflicts of the 1960s. In Newark, fighting raged for six days, involving a determined and incensed black community against the police and some three thousand National Guardsmen. When it was over, twenty-six persons were dead (24 of them black) and more than fifteen million dollars of property damage was estimated.

But neither Newark that summer nor Watts in 1965 could prepare the nation for the warfare that took place in Detroit less than a week after the fighting in New Jersey had ended. For five days, it seemed as if the whole city was aflame. There was no section where black attacks on property were not made, where fire did not burn—sometimes over blocks at a time—where uneven battles between blacks and the forces of America's law and order did not rage. And for the first time since 1943, federal troops were brought in: almost five thousand paratroopers. With helicopters probing the sky, with tanks and other armored vehicles on the streets, and American soldiers engaged in battles and patrols, it looked as if the other American revolution had entered its final stage. America was at war with itself.

Near the end (does it ever end?) of the Detroit rebellion, as the dead were being counted (there were at least 43), and the two hundred million dollars of damage was being assessed, Lyndon Johnson made a special address to the nation. Referring to Detroit and all the other uprisings, he said,

> The only genuine, long-range solution for what has happened lies in an attack—mounted at every level—upon the conditions that breed despair and violence. All of us know what those conditions are: ignorance, discrimination, slums, poverty, disease, not enough jobs. We should attack these conditions—not because we are frightened by conflict but because we are fired by conscience. We should attack them because there is simply no other way to achieve a decent and orderly society in America.

But he was frightened, and so was all of America. Johnson suspected that a black revolutionary conspiracy was at work. His intelligence apparatus was busily probing, tracking, listening. Meanwhile, the president tried to buy time by appointing a national advisory commission on civil disorders.

Besides, he could not have meant what he said about attacking the conditions. For within the next few days, Johnson announced that the American troop level in Vietnam would be raised to 525,000, and there was no way that a nation engaged in that level of overseas imperialist warfare could possibly attack the real problems of its own internal black colony at home.

V

The nation was frightened, confused, and disorganized. For better or worse, much of the same condition existed in the black community. In spite of what Lyndon Johnson suspected, there was no organized, national black revolutionary movement. If the struggle for black freedom was moving in that direction, then it was moving without guidance, without discipline, without control. There was tremendous power at work, and there were many persons who took seriously the episodic incitements of Stokely Carmichael, his successor at SNCC, H. Rap Brown, and scores of other militant exhorters. But there was no national revolutionary organization, no centralized development of strategy, no cadre of organizers, no clear and common sense in the black community about where this revolution ought to be going.

Many of the strengths and weaknesses of the new, uncertain period of the struggle were vividly displayed at a national Black Power conference that was held in July in Newark, convened almost precisely between the cooling of that city and the eruption of Detroit. On display at the conference was the tremendous anger and rage that moiled the black community at the time—but too much of it was turned inward, and too much more was wasted in rhetoric. Still, the mercurially rising influence of black nationalist thought and culture since the death of

Malcolm was demonstrated by the fascinating variety of African costumes, the dominance of the Afro hairdoes and the powerful presence of politically conscious black artists in the meeting.

If the Newark conference could be accepted as a testimony of the times, then several things were clear. The traditional civil rights movement of the 1950s and early 1960s had been transcended by another stage of the black struggle for freedom. In this new period (which still held many manifestations of the old), the search for identity and solidarity was central. The rejection of any role for whites in the struggle, the refusal to assimilate into American culture, the rediscovery and affirmation of the Africanness of their heritage were also critical elements. Over all the discussions, the smoke and fire from the urban rebellions cast an aura and a pall of dramatic urgency, militant seige, and great danger. The images of conflagration, the romance of the gun, the threat of apocalypse, were all part of this strange, new mix. None of the traditional civil rights leaders were present at Newark, but some of the younger, more radical members of the organizations were there. They could not afford to miss it.

The Black Power conference, however, produced no clarity of direction for the next stages, for these new times (of course, conferences of a thousand persons rarely offer any clarity, if it is not first in the minds of the leadership). The official conference document testified more to a heightened consciousness than to a strategy of movement. It said, for instance,

> Black people who live under imperialist governments in America, Asia, Africa, and Latin America stand at the crossroads of either an expanding revolution or ruthless extermination. *It is incumbent for us to get our own house in order to fully utilize the potentialities of the revolution or to resist our own execution.*

(In a calmer moment, the writers of the document might well have recognized the false dichotomy they had established, and would have affirmed that in a racist society, for black people to resist their execution was an act of revolution.)

VI

Meanwhile, back on the streets of the black communities, the unbearable tensions of the summer of 1967 had not been resolved, the search for revolution continued. A study of the rebellions described "the typical rioter" as a teenager or young adult, a lifelong resident of the city in which he rioted, a high school dropout; he was nevertheless, somewhat better educated than his nonrioting Negro neighbor. . . . He was proud of his race, extremely hostile to both whites and middle-class Negroes and, although informed about politics, highly distrustful of the political system.

By and large, that was an accurate description of the brothers (and sisters) the Black Panthers were recruiting.

Therefore, it should not have been surprising to find that in their earliest manifestation they embodied many of the contradictory tendencies that were then shaking the black community. For instance, the Panthers carried on a profound, and ultimately destructive romance with the gun, in true American style. They mistakenly saw the rebellions (and all of the world's revolutions) as a testimony to the power of the gun. At the same time, they tapped into the tremendous, justified antipolice hostility that existed in the black community. Their promise to defend the people against the police made them immensely popular figures, especially after their famous stand-offs and armed confrontations. Mixed with all this, was the strong hand of Fanon and the anticolonialism of the Third World.

For a time there was something attractive about their eclecticism. For instance, their ten point program was obviously modeled in style on the Nation of Islam's "What the Muslims Want" and "What the Muslims Believe." But the Panthers put forward a fascinating and far more politically sophisticated program than did the Nation. It included the call for self-determination, a guaranteed income, reparations, "decent housing," black-conscious education, exemption of black men from military service, "an immediate end to police brutality" and the freedom of all black men serving in the nation's jails, penitentiaries, and prisons.

When, in the fall of 1967, the jailing of Huey Newton brought him and the party to new heights of national notoriety and fame, there was renewed speculation about whether or not the Panthers represented the "vanguard" in the struggle for black freedom. Nervously, frightenedly, persistently, the rulers of white America watched the young, self-proclaimed revolutionaries, and plotted their destruction. Unfortunately, the Panthers were destined to offer great cooperation in that task.

VII

Twelve years had passed since those magnificantly orderly meetings in the churches of Montgomery, Alabama. There had never been a comparable period of extended, tumultuous struggle, transformation, and change in the history of the other American revolution. Everywhere white America turned, angry, determined black people were moving. The new poets were shouting words like bullets from the stages, calling on crowded audiences for acts of revolutionary courage and violence. The playwrights were killing more white people in public view than any time in man's memory. Students, elected public officials, teachers, preachers—everyone seemed fiercer, more troubled, more black conscious, more prepared to speak of revolution on the one hand and genocide on the other, than whites could bear to hear. On the white side, there was talk of concessions, investigations, jobs, scholarships, poverty programs, money—but also talk of "backlash" and irritation, impatience, and tremendous fear—and concentration camps. Under it all, growled the ferocious monster of the Vietnam war, standing like a sentry between the two American revolutions.

This was the America, this was the black struggle that Martin King had helped to create. These were the forces that his courageous bands of black singers and marchers had pressed into existence out of the bomb-pocked nights of Montgomery, Alabama. Almost all of the early targets of the public accommodations battle had been reached. In the course of a dozen years many other public and private bastions had been challenged, broached, and severely weakened in their power to discriminate against and exploit black people. But the soul of America had not been redeemed. As a matter of fact, its deepest character had only been fully revealed, and all the long-held suspicions of black people concerning the nature of white racism North and South were being confirmed.

Besides, in spite of concessions and half-hearted wars on poverty, there seemed no great force of will in white America radically to change its ways, either at home or abroad. At the same time, black people appeared determined to break through to new levels of freedom, power, self-determination, and human dignity. The future held promises of much trouble, blood, and death, and Martin King regularly admitted that his dream of 1963 had turned into a nightmare.

What had actually happened, of course, was that the sweeping, driving revolutionary energies of the black community had pressed Wyatt Walker's 1963 vision to a strange fulfillment. For he had talked about a nation being immobilized, about "major transportation centers [being] deluged with mass acts of civil disobedience." He had envisioned "the traffic of large cities, interstate commerce [being] halted by the bodies of witnesses nonviolently insisting on " 'Freedom Now.' "

The top-level leadership of the nonviolent civil rights movement had neither the courage, the imagination, nor the disciplined organization to bring that off, but it had happened in its own way. Because there was no leadership, no discipline, no training for unarmed struggle, the widespread chaos came in ways that were deeply disturbing to Martin King. But he could not ignore the forces of history that were leaping beyond the capacities of the old movement.

VIII

It was in that setting of tremendous crisis and magnificent possibilities that King began to put forward a slightly updated version of the nonviolent army idea. At the same time he placed great emphasis on the need for the forces of black struggle to forge new alliances. In his staff meetings during the 1967 summer uprisings and in the SCLC convention near the end of August, King had begun to follow more closely the logic of his own condemnations of American imperialism and militarism. For instance, he claimed that America was "preoccupied with war and . . . determined to husband every resource for military adventures rather than for social reconstruction." As a result, he came to the chilling conclusion that

> Negroes must therefore not only formulate a program; they must fashion new tactics which do not count on government goodwill but serve, instead, *to compel unwilling authorities to yield to the mandates of justice.* (my italics)

In King's opinion, black people could develop the necessary, compelling force only in alliance with others; but now the alliance he proposed was no longer focused on the middle-class white liberal forces of "goodwill." Instead, he declared,

> The dispossessed of this nation—the poor, both white and Negro—live in a cruelly unjust society. They must organize a revolution against that injustice, not against the lives of the persons who are their fellow citizens, but against the structures through which the society is refusing to . . . lift the load of poverty.

Indeed, he placed the black struggle in America not only in the context of the fight of the nation's dispossessed, but he drove it into the international arena as well. For King declared he was convinced that

> The storm is rising against the privileged minority of the earth, from which there is no shelter in isolation or armament. The storm will not abate until a just distribution of the fruits of the earth enables men

everywhere to live in dignity and human decency. The American Negro
. . . may be the vanguard of a prolonged struggle that may change the
shape of the world, as billions of deprived shake and transform the earth
in their quest for life, liberty, and justice.

For King, the first step of this new stage of struggle would be a
campaign of nonviolent direct action in Washington in 1968. He admitted that this truncated revival of the nonviolent army was a desperate
move, a "last chance for nonviolence." More important than the details
of the program, however, was that King had evidently begun to steel
himself for the necessary chaos of revolutionary struggle; he had chosen to seek out new allies in the struggle for black freedom, and he had
declared himself an implacable foe of the policies of the American government.

Once again, he came under blistering attack from every side. Those
who talked of "armed struggle" for freedom saw this idea of nonviolent
revolution as a return to a land that was now forever gone for them
(repressing any memory that most of them had never visited it). On the
other side, his liberal "allies," both black and white, recognized the
new move by King as another step out of the arena of the "political
process," the "system." They said it would create chaos and destruction in the pressurized situation of America. Naturally, the federal
government brought harsh pressure to bear against any projected action that had such potentials for revolutionary confrontation in the
nation's 70 percent black capital.

Added to all this was the massacre of black students at South
Carolina State College in Orangeburg in February, 1968. Ironically
enough, thirteen years after Montgomery, they were shot in the wake
of a demonstration to integrate a local bowling alley. Amid such confusing signs and signals, buffeted by one of the most chaotic periods in the
struggle, King's staff gave only dispirited attention to the preparation
for the Washington demonstration. Many of them were uncertain that
they were prepared for such clearly revolutionary action at that stage
of history; besides, King, himself, seemed unclear about how far he
really wanted to go.

IX

Then the call came from Memphis, to assist an overwhelming black
union of garbagemen in their strike for just wages and humane working conditions. When police provoked some of the city's black young

people, they turned a march led by King into a frightening, portentous experience for him. Stubbornly, courageously, against the advice of many persons, a few days later he returned to Memphis to try again. Stubbornly, courageously, he died.

Even a confused, beleaguered, searching Martin Luther King, Jr. was too great a threat to the forces of racism, injustice, and exploitation in America. They could only suspect what energies he might release in Washington, D.C.; and their suspicions were enough to cost him his life.

For a time, after word of his death stabbed its fiery way through the black community, it appeared as if the greatest irony of an ironic struggle might be developing. As fires raged and guns sounded and screams filled the night in scores of black neighborhoods, King's death seemed to be sparking the confrontation that would open the next levels of urban insurrection and revolution.

Once again, because there was no leadership prepared for the tremendous forces that the black populace thrust forward, and because the American nation placed more armed men around the black ghettos than ever before, the irony did not work its way out. But King's death remained in the heart of the black community, like a great unhealed wound, like an explosive that had been only partially spent. Neither the half-hearted Poor People's Campaign, which his organization finally led, nor the unexpected quietness of the following summer expended that charge or healed that wound.

Chapter 30

The Wedge and the Winter: Reflections on the Search for Meaning

(The original text of The Other American Revolution *ends with the assassination of Martin Luther King, Jr. and the painful failure of Resurrection City. Even at the beginning of the 1970s it was obvious that these events did not, could not mark the end of the black struggle for freedom in America; but from such an intensely close distance it was hard to sense the meaning of such tragedies and what they might augur for the next stages of our continuing quest for liberation.*

The two documents that follow are in some sense attempts to gain a clearer perspective on the explosive period that began in the mid-1950s, to try to assess its meaning for black people, for the United States, and for a larger community as well. The first document is the concluding portion of an essay written in 1975, "The Black Wedge in America," and published in The Black Scholar, *December, 1975. The second document, "A Long, Hard Winter to Endure: Reflections on the Meaning of the 1970s," represents the complete text of an article that appeared in* The Black Collegian, *December/January, 1979/1980. Taken together, they represent a tentative assessment of this stage of our struggle, its relationship to the not-so-distant past, and its possible uses for the creation of a new future. V.H.)*

THE BLACK WEDGE IN AMERICA (excerpts)

Brown v. Topeka: Opening the Way

If we examine the 1954 decision carefully, then, it is evident that what the court originally intended was the creation of a narrow, legalistic slit in the democratic façade of America, hoping thereby to meet both domestic and international demands. The court did not—and still does not—intend to be a handmaiden to basic social transformation.

But what we also realize now is that the black struggle for freedom has never been limited by what white leaders intended, wanted, or allowed. So, black people, beginning in the South, took a legal decision that was meant to open a slit, and we transformed it and ourselves into a black wedge, driving deep into the center of American society, helping to split open the sham American dream, the American myth. Then, as our struggle joined with other movements of this generation—movements that we have helped to create and enliven—we made it increasingly impossible for the old America ever to come back together again.

Deaths and Transformations

When Malcolm X attempted to tie together the meaning of our public movements in America with the worldwide struggle for self determination, and with the internal black struggle for integrity and self-discipline, he was assassinated. Three years later, as Martin King sought to bring the power of the black movement to bear against America's racist imperialism in Vietnam, and threatened to call for black draft resistance, he was gunned down. Then on the night of King's death, in 1968, the federal and state military forces put more troops and equipment out on the streets (and in the skies) of America than we had ever known since the Civil War, effectively blunting and cordoning off the terrified and painful anger of black America.

These deaths, and the display of raw military power that we saw before and after them, hit hard against us. Along with the brutal harassment and killing of the Panthers and other forces, they presented the black community with a stunning, sometimes numbing reality—and we were unprepared for it.

In spite of all the rhetoric about revolution, we were too American to believe that revolution in this country might take at least a generation of disciplined, organized, sacrificial struggle. At times it seemed as if we were more prepared to die on the streets than to struggle against long, hard odds, for long years—far from the appealing eye of the television cameras.

Not only did we fail to count on the force, the extent, and the subtlety of the opposition, but when our movement was at its height, we had not really organized ourselves or our thoughts for the next stages. For instance, we had not raised sufficiently with ourselves the question: what kind of America are we seeking for? What are the next goals of this struggle that began in Montgomery? How shall we organize ourselves for the transformation from a period of mass movement to a time of grueling protracted struggle? And even among that very small minority which raised such questions, too many were seeking answers from revolutionary situations which could not be applied to the unique, concrete realities of America.

As a result, deep waves of discouragement, fear, apathy, and copping-out soon began to overwhelm us. Many of those who had been active in the movement often sought to return to more "normal" lives. Others were physically and psychically wounded. Moreover, there was no long-range organization or sense of direction remaining. Instead, cynicism became the style. Talk of "genocide" and "survival" on the one hand, and do-your-own-thingism on the other reflected a great weariness and disarray. For some the answer was now to be found in various forms of religion, from astrology to the Nation of Islam. The talk of "our real struggle" being in Africa too often became another sign of despair.

Besides, in those places where they had been forced to make concessions to the sheer power of the black movement the ruling forces met with some real success in their attempt to co-opt. In a broad set of institutions, especially in the public sector, they relented before the pressure and created new openings for the black middle class to move up and into certain positions within the cracking American system. They made available opportunities for blacks to affirm their loyalty to the system or to take their paychecks with a cynical grin and try to build their own private bastions of "security." Thus another element of the movement-created unity seemed broken, as the black middle class expanded away from the life of the majority of the people, as the movement lost its force.

Of course, many of our deepest troubles came from within, for we were confused and unclear. Too often, as we moved beyond the range of older principles and goals, we failed to create new sources of strength and direction. Thus, "Up against the wall, MF," was too easily transformed into "Up against the wall, brother/sister." And the gun we picked up was usually used in defense or offense against one another rather than for any of the revolutionary fantasies we had once created. And, more often than not, Black Power became the power to exploit black people.

Meanwhile, the mass media which seemed like such an important tool in the development of our struggle was turned vigorously against us. Its owners and managers, often using black music as a come-on, and black faces as sops, began to bombard the minds of the black masses through television, movies, and other elements with all the most deadly values of American capitalism: greed, individualism, fear, disunity—and a positive love of violence.

Farewell to the Invisible People

Where are we now? Surely we are at a point where all of this current evidence of disunity, disarray, regression, and self-destruction might easily overwhelm us, push us more deeply into the hole of despair. But it can only do that if we misapprehend the history, the power, and the profound significance of the black wedge. What we need to see clearly is what we have done, how our own action has transformed us, and what is happening all around us in America and in the world.

We have transformed ourselves in the course of this past twenty years. Make no mistake about that. The transformation carries both positives and negatives, but it is there, and the negatives are not the full story. There is, for instance, a consciousness of roots and origins that is more widespread than ever before, which cannot be denied or passed over in shame. There is a new sense of open defiance, hostility, anger, that was not present before this period in anything like the current extent. There is a veiled but clearly present sense of our power, usually seen in only destructive terms, but now to be reckoned with. On another level, it is important to realize that the institutions we have built during this period of struggle (even those that have failed), the words we have written, the ideas we have put forward, the revolutionary connections we have made in the rest of the world—all of these are part of the transformation, and bear within themselves great potential value, provide many lessons for those who seek the next stage.

At the same time, we are now scattered over the length and breadth of the society more fully than ever before. We are wedged into its inner cities, sprawling into their outskirts. We are entrenched in many parts of the public sector of the political, economic, and cultural life. Nowhere can we ever be invisible again.

The resultant swelling of the black middle class, with all of its problems, also presents a crucial reservoir of possible strengths for the next stage. The army of unemployed is frightening and tragic on one hand, but there too is a source of certain potential power. Both groups have seen much about America, from Vietnam to Dubuque, from Westchester to Five Points. If we are honest with ourselves, we bear insights and powers that our parents cannot have experienced. (Just as they bore scars that we do not know.)

Equally important, we have remolded the nature of America. Nowhere can anyone ever think of this country as they did before Montgomery—despite all the yearnings of white nostalgics. And perhaps the greatest significance of that still ambiguous transformative process is the fact of our part in the struggle itself, and the new authenticity and authority it provides to black leadership in the continuing struggle to remake America.

We have been central to the re-creation of post-World War II America. We have provided the nation's single major impetus for change towards basic human justice over this period. Therefore, if we are conscious of what we have done, we have won the right and the responsibility to claim leadership in the struggle for that future radical transformation that is necessary to fulfill and move forward the history we have already made.

This process of struggle to transform America, and our role in it, has necessarily had implications for the world, especially the nonwhite world. But the greatest implications are for us, and they need very careful consideration. For when a people become a crucial force in history they are no longer responsible solely to and for themselves. Thus, through our movement, we have helped develop and release creative/disruptive elements in this society that we must now face and deal with. These elements go beyond what we have done within the black community; indeed, they press us into arenas of struggle and responsibility which threaten the security of the identity that we found and shaped for ourselves in these last two decades.

What are some of the forces that we have helped to create and embolden in the heart of America, these powers for breaking and building with which we must now conjure? Any listing would be incomplete, but it would certainly include such movements as:

The white students who were politicized and radicalized in the southern black movement and who then went on into Students for a Democratic Society, the Weathermen, and other forms of white radical activity are part of the list.

The antiwar movement took much of its leadership from that same group of radicalized young people, and a great deal of its inspiration from the black freedom movement.

The various, stumbling attempts of poor whites to organize against oppression in places like Appalachia and in the northern cities were clearly patterned after and inspired by our movement.

The newly found force of the Chicanos, the Native Americans, Puerto Ricans, Asian-Americans grew out of their often ambiguous relationships to our struggle and their desire to develop strong movements of their own. But all of them acknowledge the importance of the black movement in leading the way.

The Welfare Rights Movement, almost entirely black in makeup, was a direct spin-off from the freedom movement. Much of its leadership had known experience in southern and northern struggles.

The newest, more radical stages of the women's liberation movement clearly owe elements of their style, and—more importantly— their content to the Black Power and Black Liberation stages of our struggle.

The Gay Liberation movement grew out of the same black-tilled soil, emboldened by our successes and our demands for rights.

The prisoner rebellions which will not allow the penal system of this country to rest in its medieval and racist forms, pay continual homage to the black movement's inspiration. The rebellions in America's military forces are also directly a part of the black wedge, and have forced fundamental changes in the nature of the military establishment.

Even the largely white movements that some of us have too glibly identified as cop-outs, like the consumer rights groups, ecology forces, communes, and new, nonwestern religious searchings, owe much of their origins and force to the churning of America which the black movement carried forward.

Indeed, even the resurrection of the Communist party of the United States of America—and the Socialist movement generally—can be attributed in large part to the reviving power of the black wedge—and not vice versa, as some would seem to think.

Now, we may not like all these forces, or others which have emerged; and we probably should not like them all. But the fact is that these elements are now loose, and it was the power of our shattering thrust into America which played a crucial role in their development. Singly, jointly, they have all participated in some aspect of an essentially unorganized, but very real movement towards the cracking of the old America—the mythological, democratic, free-enterprise, melting-pot, just-and-good, white-male dominated America.

All of these developments, together with the basic contradictions endemic in America's economic and political system, are part of the forces which now jam their way into the core and cause the traditional center of America to fall apart. And all around we see the results: on the one hand, a society of people who have nothing in which they really believe, not even themselves, not even while they mouth slogans of bicentennial and revolution. On the other hand, all these forces of disruption also carry elements of hope, new possibilities, suggestions of other ways ahead for a new America—if new people with a new consciousness and a new politics (principles) take responsibility for a struggle to redirect it.

Once in motion, history cannot be turned back—neither by presidential order nor by our own wish to escape the judgment of history. Many of us long to go back to the good old days when we seemed able to make revolution by shouting; when we could lump all white folks together and blame everything on them; when we could bogard our way into the chambers of power and financial resources; when "unity" based on common suffering and persecution seemed sufficient; when we had responsibility for nothing in America other than ourselves.

Only through debilitating fantasy can we now recapture or reuse that past. But such longings remind us that we are not only the wedge, we are also part and parcel of the old society. Its ideas, ideals, and temptations fill us. We are often trapped in our own best black past. Thus we, too, must be cracked open; many of our old questions, answers, and solutions must be blasted away. The identity for which we fought so hard must not become an antiquated haven but a base of operations, a beachhead on the future.

The Awesome Responsibilities of Blackness

The vast responsibilities we opened up by the very power of our own wedge are now upon us. We played the leading internal, human role in bringing on the crisis of purpose, identity, and direction that America now faces. We must also face the awesome new burdens such developments now thrust upon us.

At this point, there seem to be a limited number of choices available to those of us who have any sense of the history we have made:

1. We may continue to sink into apathy and the dehumanization it brings into our lives. From that position, we may assume the traditional victim's perspective and mentality, a black worm's eye view of the world, blaming everything on The Man, seeking everything from him, refusing to believe anything else is possible—or desirable.

2. We may continue to reach for a "piece of the action," seeking to fit ourselves into America's structures as we know them, making ourselves "marketable commodities," raising no fundamental questions about the structures which have absorbed us. Of course, for many of us, this path can be nothing more than a cynical acceptance of an eternal tokenism, for by now it should be clear that the vast majority of our people can never participate in "the action" of a society that is willing to accept up to 50 percent unemployment among our youth, that is willing to allow vast sectors of black America nothing more than a future of welfare, warfare, or prisons. This choice also means acceptance of the fact that the American economic and political action is intrinsically tied to the exploitation of critical sectors of the nonwhite world, and to the support of repressive antirevolutionary governments. It is, as well, bound to a brutal exploitation of the earth's environment itself. Ultimately, then, this position is self-destructive, for such political and economic structures—such "action"—have no healthy future.

3. Some of us may instead go off into the so-called counterculture, moving to a future that tends largely towards drift without mastery. Thus we shall be drawn into searches for essentially private and semireligious solutions through drugs or new forms of transcendental consciousness, or to a kind of privatistic communalism. Essentially, this will likely mean that we have refused to enter (or remain in) the struggle to create a new history, a new future.

4. For many persons, the greatest temptation may be to cling to an unexamined, defensive black nationalism whose historical movement forward has stopped, a nationalism which refused to struggle for hegemony over the entire American future. Thus we may encourage fantasies which ultimately envision some kind of separate black detente with America as it is, a truce that cannot transform the situation of the vast majority of our people in this country, and does not speak to America's worldwide exploitative role.

5. Others may tend to one of the varieties of authoritarian solutions, which require little personal struggle with the issues facing American society. Thus the Nation of Islam leadership can present as a *fait accompli* a transformation in its fundamental doctrines and its members are expected to accept it. For they have joined a faith in which it is their responsibility to submit to higher authority, not to struggle jointly for the new truths of this time. Or we can find solace in the possibility that there are "scientific" certainties in the realm of human relationships, and seek for a way through a black

Marxist-Leninism which may be no more examined than the nationalism it harshly, cruelly castigates. Here, again, the temptation to find ready-made solutions, prefabricated analyses, and models from other times and places may be overwhelming. But often they are another form of the escape to authoritarianism—or to fantasy. (At the same time, let it be clear that I believe the basic, nonpersonality questions that are being raised in the best parts of the nationalist-Marxist debate are crucial, and necessary, if we are to move to the next stage of our struggle. For, among other things, they can force us to deal with the questions of what is the nature of the society we seek to create, and what are the quaifications of our own internal forces and of the allies we want to draw into the struggle.)

6. There is another, less clearly outlined choice that is available to us, and I think it is the most consistent with our best history. That is to recognize where the tired, courageous marchers of Montgomery have led us. It is to face the fact that a history that we helped to create has now pressed us forward into a position in which there are no certainties (scientific or otherwise), no comforting answers, no familiar solutions—at least not for those who insist on maintaining the tension between their own personal integrity and their sense of social responsibility.

This choice is essentially to begin to face the lineaments of the new time, the new ground to which we are moving. For we are now being pressed toward an uncharted future where the only real maps are the ones we will create out of the struggle to find our way. Thus it is necessary now to take and use this time of seeming limbo to begin to try to make sense out of the recent past, to ask new questions about ourselves, our future, the future of all the black, white, and other people of the society that we have helped to unhinge.

Following this path, *our only real choice is to create new theory, to create new practice, to create new ideology, to create new hope, to recreate ourselves, building them all on the solid reality and particularities of our terrifying and glorious black experience in this land.* In this way, the roots we have in Africa shall continue to be important, necessary, life-affirming sources. But roots are ultimately for trees; and we must become new trees, striking out, reaching out, seeking new levels, new possibilities, here on these still new shores. (For a two-hundred-year-old country is still very young, still in the process of creation, needing creators more than victims.) All the things we must learn from Africa, Europe, Asia, and Latin America will thus become resources, transformed by us to our needs, not manuals to be copied.

For we must finally ask ourselves what kind of human society we want here, in America. We must enter into the hard process of determining how we shall move from the history we have already made to the future we have yet to make. And we must ask ourselves—not once, but continuously—how much we are prepared to pay for the creation of a new society in America.

If we are ready to engage in that struggle, to ask those questions, to study carefully what others have said and done in revolutionary struggles, if we are prepared to experiment with new paths, to pay whatever cost is necessary in sacrifice and self-transformation, then we may be ready to create a new revolutionary force in America. Such a force will likely not be drawn from a particular class, shaped by a special relationship to production. Instead, it will probably emerge, and create itself in the course of a struggle for a unique and unwavering commitment to radical transformation.

If we are prepared to move from wherever we are in that direction, then we shall find there are comrades who are prepared to join us in the way ahead. By now, it should be clear that the way leads directly from Montgomery, 1955, and builds on much that has happened since then. But where it is going is far less clear. That is what we shall have to decide and create.

Only those persons who are ready for such a new departure, a new beginning, based on our past, leaping beyond our past, should choose it. But to choose it may be the only way left for us to become the humans we were meant to be, the only way to vindicate those who helped to create this new edge of history on which we perilously, hopefully stand, the only way to reclaim/create this land.

A LONG, HARD WINTER TO ENDURE: REFLECTIONS ON THE MEANING OF THE 1970s

For those of us who lived and struggled through the momentous years of the 1960s, with all of their inspiriting sense of collective action, transformative power, great victories, and tragic wounds, these past ten years have been a perplexing and difficult time to weather, a long, hard winter to endure. Now, as the 1970s draw to a close, as we reflect on some of the significant events of that period, it is no less difficult to assess their essential meaning, to understand what we have been and done, what has been done to us.

Of course, this is partly a matter of our vantage point. Still standing as we do within the chronological confines of the seventies, we are much too close to have the advantage of any sure perspective. Moreover, the decade is too deeply embedded in our lives and consciousness for us to make any claims at objectivity or precision as we examine its essential contours. Nevertheless, none of this should keep us back from the responsibility of trying to begin to forge some understanding out of the materials of the 1970s. For such an assessment of where we have been is a responsibility—to ourselves, to our forebears, to our children, especially if we dare to hope that we can again lay our hands upon the forces that will shape the future. Understanding our limitations, but recognizing our responsibility, it may be possible to make a few suggestions, to put forward a tentative, sometimes impressionistic set of proposals that may help us all to identify and understand some of the crucial events of this decade and their possible meaning for black people in the United States.

First, it is important to be more specific about what we mean by the decade of the 1970s. Chronology has never controlled history, and in our own time there is every reason to suggest that what we call the decade of the 1970s actually began somewhere between the death of Martin Luther King, Jr. in April, 1968 and the convening of the National Black Political Convention in March, 1972. Sometime in the midst of those explosive years, unhindered by the numbers on calendars, we moved precipitately from one period into another, entered the new decade.

View from the Mountain Top:
The Assassination of Our King

It is understandable then that we cannot really comprehend our current decade except as we place it against the panorama of the 1960s, cannot grasp its meaning unless we see its integral links to that earlier time. So it is no surprise that almost every thoughtful attempt to define the 1970s has involved a comparison with the high tide of the black mass movement of the previous decade. Indeed, by the time King was assassinated, by the time his death was joined with the police assassination of Black Panther leaders Fred Hampton and Mark Clark in Chicago (by the time other men and women tried to understand where the killing of Bobby Kennedy fit into all of this), one of the most important elements of the 1960s had become fully manifest. Beginning in the chronological 1950s as a hopeful mass movement for an equal place within the mainstream of an expanding, potentially democratic

American society, by the end of the sixties the modern black struggle for freedom had broken all the traditional American traces. By the time of those killings our movement was raising fundamental questions about the political, social, economic, and moral structures of American society, was pulling the covers off the confused ineffectuality of its elite educational institutions, was daring to attack its foreign policy and to open serious dialogues with the government's avowed overseas "enemies."

In other words, we can actually say that the sixties ended when black folk, joined temporarily by hundreds of thousands of white people—especially young ones who had created their own version of "The Movement"—jammed themselves against the limits of this country's liberal vision of itself. We can say that the sixties ended because we had begun to sense the costs of creating a just and "beloved community" out of an unjust, racist, and deeply fearful society. (We saw and tasted and felt some of the cost as we recognized part of ourselves stretched out on a Memphis motel balcony, or penned up in a Chicago tenement room sprayed with police bullets; we could not miss the cost if we looked at the spotlights of the helicopters over our communities and in the regiments of troops who were sent out to contain our funeral pyres the night when they killed brother Martin.)

Early in the 1970s, one of King's closest and best known co-workers reflected on the direction his friend and leader had been taking in those last, perilous years of his life. He said, "In a way, it was probably best for many of us who worked with Martin that he was killed when he was, because he was moving into some radical directions that few of us had been prepared for." The man paused. Then he added, "And I don't think that many of us would have been ready to take the risks of life, possessions, security, and status that such a move would have involved." Then another pause, and the final reflection: "I'm pretty sure I wouldn't have been willing."

That was how the sixties ended and the seventies began. For Martin Luther King was not the only one, certainly not the first one who had begun to look with different eyes at this nation, its values, its structures, and its effects on the world. So, when he began consistently to preach about the need for a new economic ordering of society to provide jobs for all, when he began to call for housing and health care for all the people of the nation who needed it, and demanded drastic steps towards disarmament to make funds available, when he condemned the government's imperialist destruction of Vietnam and increasingly urged black and white young men to refuse to participate, when he determined to stand with the poor of the society until their just needs were met, then he had to be killed. When he began to preach vaguely but full of feeling about organizing a predominantly black "nonviolent army" ready to engage in revolutionary civil disobedience in the cause of a just and compassionate society in the United States, when the struggle for his great dream of the "beloved community" seemed to be moving to harder, harsher, more fundamental levels than in the early 1960s, King was representing many, many more than himself. He was a touchstone of the potential direction of the movement in the 1970s.

His associate understood that, understood that he was talking about much more than Martin and the somewhat reluctant revolutionaries of the SCLC cadre, but about a direction, an opening that we black people had created by the logic of our demands and challenges to the United States of America. Thus, the story of the 1970s can be seen in large degree as the story of what happened when black folk of many kinds and convictions began to recognize the frightening, challenging depths and the momentous implications of our own most fundamental challenges to the nation. This decade has been the time when we, like King's reminiscing associate, had to count the cost of continuing our forward movement, had to ask what was really involved in following the logic of our own deepest insights concerning the racism, militarism, injustice, and fear that are built into the structures of the United States. This was the decade when we had to face the radical changes that would be required within us and in this country in order for black people and others like us to become fully participating citizens of a truly just, humane, and creative national community.

On the Edge of History: The Challenge of Gary

That quieter, but deeply troubling and almost contemplative, searching mode of the 1970s was not clear at first. In those earlier eruptive, transitional years between the Memphis assassination and the 1972 convention in Gary, there were many tendencies, many actions, many ideas and modes at work. The period of changeover was filled with much of the residual energy of the confrontations and challenges that indelibly marked the 1960s. There were echoes of the urban rebellions, as black people and police continued in sporadic armed conflicts, both in the North and South. On hundreds of college campuses black students organized and fought for changes in curriculum, administration, admissions policies, and basic ethos. In the South, at places like

Jackson State and Southern University in Baton Rouge, local police forces responded to the students by invading their campuses, shooting to kill.

Nowhere were the physical confrontations of those years more dramatic and costly than the ones that took place on the great gathering and killing grounds of the nation's prisons. In 1970, the Soledad brothers of California streaked blood across the sky in their bold and recklessly doomed attempt to seize justice at any cost. One year later the cry of "Remember Attica!" rang out like a great death knell from the East as more than forty men were cut down like so many trees at the order of Nelson Rockefeller, surrogate executioner for the fearful majority of the white nation. Though the connections were sometimes hard to grasp and though it was too easy to romanticize their actions, it is nonetheless true that these black men, fighting for justice, dignity, and hope in the heart of the American darkness were tied to Martin King, to Bob Moses and Fannie Lou Hamer, to Ella Baker and Charles Sherrod, to all the creators of the southern struggles of the sixties. They had simply chosen and been chosen by another battleground.

The complexities of all the connections among the events of that transitional period are still sometimes dense, but always fascinating. For instance, the California Soledad action eventually brought Angela Davis to national and international attention, providing impetus to the black reexploration of Marxist alternatives. While at Attica, men who were deeply affected by the surge of Pan-Africanism took on new names in the prison, fashioned their own neo-African garb, and called for relocation in a "nonimperialist" nation. So, all the currents at work in the larger black community had their manifestations in the prisons.

By then, the Black Power conferences, which tended to emphasize struggle in the United States, had been transmuted into the Congress of African People; but the direction of our convention movements was not clear, for after the Congress's beginning in Atlanta in 1970, the next year's feature was Jesse Jackson's Black Expo in Chicago, carrying an obvious appeal to those structures of American private enterprise capitalism which we had recently and bitterly condemned. Meanwhile, as the black power/black solidarity thrust burned its way into the life of the black professional classes, black caucuses were being formed everywhere that these professionals found themselves in white institutions; but their purposes beyond an immediate, passionate, reactive movement were not always clear.

Then, in the late winter of 1972, almost all of the tendencies from the past and some from the future came together at Gary, Indiana, in the watershed experience that was the National Black Political Convention. Among many other meanings that it had, the convention in Gary—where Richard Hatcher had become the city's first black mayor—was a reminder of one of the crucial but ambiguous tendencies of the seventies. For while black men and women were being shot down in the streets and in the jails, while black unemployment figures continued to mount and real black income began to drop, while black students were taking over administration buildings and having their campuses invaded, while James Forman and the Black Economic Development Corporation were demanding half a million dollars in reparations, while some black intellectuals were looking again at Marxist ideology as a way of dealing with the American reality—while all of these things were happening, on another level black men and women were being elected to a variety of public offices on the strength of the new black voting power that emerged out of the southern voter registration struggles and out of the continuing black migration to the cities of the North and South. Here, then, was another potential challenge to white American hegemony, another tendency within the time of transition. (Even in those days there were many questions about how important such electoral challenges actually were in the light of the continued financial domination exercised by white private businesses or by white-controlled state and federal funding agencies over the decaying urban areas.)

Much could be said about the fact that the call to Gary went out over the names of Imamu Baraka, Charles Diggs, and Richard Hatcher, poet-organizer, member of Congress and mayor, but for the moment we can only afford to look at one element of the meaning of Baraka's leadership. His tough-minded and powerful presence, based in a highly disciplined, Newark-based black nationalist organization, was the central force in the convention's leadership. As such, he symbolized one of the most significant developments of the 1960s—the evolution of several black artists into the role of organizers of their people. Men and women like Haki Madhubuti (Don L. Lee), Sonia Sanchez, Askia Toure, Mari Evans, and Kalamu ya Salaam—to name only a few of the best known artist-activists—brought an important tradition into the seventies. Only rarely had this combination of functions taken significant life before. (Our minds quickly move back to the nineteenth-century writer, Frances Ellen Watkins Harper, and her sacrificial anti-slavery and post-Civil War activity; also to Claude McKay's and Langston Hughes's association with the Communist party in the late 1920s and early 1930s, or Paul Robeson's powerful role as spokesperson for—not organizer of—the oppressed.) Never had it taken on such widespread power. The presence of such politically active artists was of tremendous importance in the world of black youth.

Their engagement at Gary, symbolized most fully by Baraka, was also a testimony to the black challenge to white America that went down deeper than politics, economics, or race. Rather, the artists reminded us that black people were laying seige to the fundamental arsenals of spirit, morals, and hope, discovering large, empty, lifeless arenas as they moved. In earlier times such deep levels of encounter had been approached only by religiopolitical forces like the Nation of Islam and its inventive, idiosyncratic cosmology. By the time of Gary, however, the word had been given—at least temporarily—in many other places, in seminaries and taverns, on campuses and in prisons: the white god was indeed dead; his reign of unlife was essentially over; new forces, with profound potentials, were on the rise. Black people by way of the artists and seers, by way of their prisoners and preachers, brought the announcement, joining with other prophetic voices in the nation. So, when we all gathered at Gary, many persons instinctively seemed to sense something of the powerful meaning of the last words of the preamble to the convention's declaration: "We stand on the edge of history. We cannot turn back." Is this what Malcolm and Martin had seen and felt before us? Was this the vision that so troubled each of them in the last churning months of their lives? Were they struggling with the inward urge to turn back? Was this the vision that finally drew them forward?

The edge of history. No turning back. Much of the meaning of the events of the 1970s is to be found in our struggle to come to terms with the new realities we helped to create, the old bridges we helped to burn, the stark vision of the United States we did so much to reveal, the forces we worked to unleash, forces that have undone the old America. For it is not only we but the nation at large which stands on the edge of a new, uncharted history. (And what of the world, of the cosmos? Are we all on the edge of history, invited to be co-creators of a relentlessly pressing new time?) In the light of that reality we can see the 1970s as an intimation of the new directions. We can see the 1970s as a time, a space that opened for us to decide whether we will take the risks of entering/reentering the struggle to re-create this nation as a humane society, one in harmony with the coming age. We can see the 1970s as a sampling of the various ways in which we have already either tried to move forward, or to turn back to the safety and security of our old and limiting ideas, aspirations, friendships, and hopes.

Gary, itself, revealed much of the black response to the challenge of the new age. For instance, the conference declaration called for disciplined national black organizing and teaching around the set of revolutionary goals for human development which were put forth. By and large, beginning with the conference organizers (who, of course, bore many of the contradictory tendencies of the entire gathering among themselves) that summons was ignored. Instead, in response to the most fundamentally challenging calls of the convention's black agenda, many persons turned back to politics-as-usual, turned aside to the demands of private self-interest, or wandered off into unclear, necessarily solitary ways, searching for their own best responses to the new time.

To look at some of those responses is to look at some of the major developments of the 1970s for black America. Even before the convention had ended, the majority of delegates had rejected the call for independent black political organizing, for a national black political party (more in the revolutionary than the electoral mode); rather, they returned to the all-too-familiar presidential politics of 1972. Shirley Chisholm's campaign was a part of that returning, perhaps its most refreshing part, but it was still a return to the past. (Later the black community at large showed what it thought of American presidential politics in that year when less than half of our registered voters bothered to go to the polls.)

At the same time, in the dialectic common to our life, black folk were exploring other paths, attempting to hold the past and the future in creative tension. So, even as the delegates were meeting at Gary, even as American presidential politics held the national spotlight, thousands of black persons from one coast to another were being mobilized by a national African Liberation Support Committee to stand and move in solidarity with the struggles of our people on the African continent. Then in May, 1972 nearly ten thousand black men, women, and children marched in the streets of Washington, D.C.—accompanied by thousands of others across the country—in the first and most ideologically united of several annual African Liberation Days. This was, among other things, an expression of the latest surge of Pan-Africanism, a concern that never dies among the children of Africa in the United States, one that erupts in unpredictable ways and times, and which continually opens new doors of thought and action from deep within the heart of the black community.

Nevertheless, the path of electoral politics, of attempting—often with a sincere sense of devotion—to gain leverage for black people

from within the American political party system, continued to be a
major element for the 1970s. This was encouraged and symbolized by a
string of mayoral victories in such diverse cities as Newark, Detroit,
Atlanta, and Los Angeles. Two of the symbols worth pondering were
the emergence in 1973 of Bobby Seale, former leader of the Black
Panthers, as an unsuccessful Democratic candidate for mayor of Oakland, and the success of Marion Berry, former SNCC chairperson, in
his race for mayor of the District of Columbia. At the head of the list of
former movement leaders who turned to electoral politics was Andy
Young, who was elected the first black congressman from the South
since Reconstruction.

Destined to play a major role in the events of the 1970s, Andy was
central in rallying black voters to give their decisive support to the
election of Jimmy Carter in 1976. Now, looking back on a beleaguered,
ineffective Carter, his string of broken promises to black people, his
readiness to accept the forced resignation of Andy Young, there is
something inherently sad in the sound of the voices already rising at
the end of the 1970s, debating again about which white Democratic
presidential aspirant black people should follow. In the presence of
such voices it may be important to remember *again* one of the challenges of Gary to the black folk in the seventies:

> If we have never faced it before, let us face it at Gary: The profound
> crisis of black people and the disaster of America are not simply caused
> by [individual] men, nor will they be solved by [individual] men alone.
> These crises are the crises of basically flawed economics and politics, and
> of cultural degradation. None of the Democratic candidates and none of
> the Republican candidates—regardless of their vague promises to us or
> to their white constituencies—can solve our problems or the problems of
> this country without radically changing the systems by which it oper-
> ates.

It was the movement of our own struggle which forced us, in our
most honest moments, to reach that conclusion, which smashed our
vague dreams up against the hard limitations of American structures.
On one level, then, the seventies have been essentially our attempt to
test whether we really believe what we discovered, what we declared
in the Gary declaration, to test what implications our agreement or
disagreement have for our lives as individuals and as a people. In
1975, the congressional Black Caucus gave its own public response in
the wording of the theme for its annual fund-raising event: "From
Changing Structures to Using Structures." How seriously the caucus
took that sentiment is not clear. (How it related to the socialist pronouncements of members like Ron Dellums and John Conyers is no

more clear.) But those words obviously expressed the feelings of many black persons as the decade wore on. It may not be wishful thinking, however, to suspect that such slogans were less statements of belief in the American political, economic, and social structures, but more the expression of weariness, the admission of unclarity and occasional despair about how change of this apparent colossus might be brought about.

The Marxian Maze:
To Be Black and Red

A different but no less significant development in the 1970s was the resurgence of Marxist thought among black people, at least one stratum of black people. This direction was represented and symbolized by such powerful figures as Angela Davis and the transformed Baraka, as well as by the brilliant scholar-activist, Abdul Alkalimat (Gerry McWhorter) and the revived, older doctrinaire party men like Harry Haywood and Hosea Hudson. It was pressed forward by a score of competing small organizations as well as by the temporarily energized Communist party of the United States. For a variety of reasons, this way of defining and organizing reality attracted the minds and lives of many persons, including those who demanded clarity in an unclear time.

Here was a world view that was at least theoretically prepared to deal unflinchingly with the necessity of revolutionary structural change in the United States. Its resurgence sparked both helpful and unnecessarily acrimonious debates across the nation, and raised many high hopes. But somehow, those who tried to organize black people at the grass roots around this framework seemed unable to make any significant advances. Partly that was because many of the organizers had not yet freed themselves from the conceptual models, social vision, and political jargon that grew out of encounters with early European capitalism. Partly it was because they still did not know how to come to terms with that continuing anomaly, "the white working class" of the United States. And in some part, the problem went deeper, to their refusal to recognize any realities that could not be approached from a materialist base.

The difficulties were, of course, quite understandable. For the combination of affluent, wasteful consumerism, the paper orientation and service orientation of so much of the nation's work and its "workers," the abiding racism of the society, and the complex development of the transnational corporations that are based in the United States, all these helped to create a model of a capitalist society that was unlike anything Marxism had had to deal with before, and required leaps of the imagination that were not easy for the doctrinaire. Moreover, in a society in which many persons were engaged in profound spiritual searching and were asking new questions about the unity of all existence, an ideology that was uneasy or off-handed with such issues was at a disadvantage. Meanwhile, in the 1970s, powerful segments of the white working class continued to resist any identification with black aspirations, and, on the contrary, attacked black children and their itinerant school buses in cities across the country, and fearfully denied black men and women access to working and living spaces. Obviously much organizing and teaching needed to be done among those workers before any connections could be made that would lead to a significant black and white challenge to the keepers of American society.

The serious inadequacies of the traditional approaches to white workers and the profound dangers of a dependence on old-line, "militant," provocateur-type actions were harshly brought home to us in Greensboro, North Carolina, as the decade ended. There, one black and three white members of a Marxist group were killed in an unnecessary, uneven, and unplanned confrontation with a group of heavily armed Klan type white men. (How some of the anti-Klan group had moved from leadership in the all-black Malcolm X Liberation University at the end of the 1960s to such current Marxist organizing is, in itself, a major expression of our political movements in the 1970s.)

The Death of the Devil:
A Nation Dies

Interestingly enough, there appeared to be a revived openness toward those interracial alliances in the black community, coming in at least one case from a most unexpected source. In the 1960s, there had been a renascence of black nationalism, deeply related to the flowering of Black Identity, Black Consciousness, and Black Power. Often, these developments were connected to expressions of hostility against whites or against premature alliances with whites, and it is impossible to understand such directions without a recognition of the crucial role played by the continuing presence, message, and power of what was then the Nation of Islam, popularly known as the Black Muslims. Under the sometimes eccentric but powerful leadership of the Honorable Elijah Muhammad—focused for a critical period in the brilliant prime ministerial role of Malcolm X—the Nation formed the continuing, traditional core of much of the new explosions of blackness.

Then in the 1970s everything seemed to change, the organic center fell apart, perhaps in preparation for the development of a new center of consciousness. Whatever the meaning, the critical single event was the death of Mr. Muhammad in February, 1975 (ironically almost ten years to the day from the still unexplained assassination of Malcolm X). From that moment, the only predictable element in the bulwark of the nationalism and black consciousness was precipitate change. The first and most disruptive transformation was announced before the year was over by Wallace Muhammad, son and successor to Elijah. Wallace told the Nation and the world that white people were now eligible for admission to their organization.

Though the evidence is not fully available, it is likely that that move marked the beginning—or at least the point of critical acceleration—of the end of one of the most powerful movements in the black world. The reorganization, decentralization, denationalizing, and orthodoxing of the World Community of Islam in the West left the group in painful, often bitter disarray. It also removed one of the single most important structural underpinnings from the already shaky house of nationalism in black America. In spite of a valiant attempt at a competing revivalist movement led by Minister Louis Farrakan, this transformation of the old Black Muslims (who called whites "devils," traced their evil origins back to the activities of a rebellious black creator-scientist, and depicted them in cartoons with tails) into a respectable, "integrated" orthodox Moslem grouping (which now celebrates the American flag and boasts of its business dealings with the Department of Defense) is at once part of the cause and part of the result of the new movement of history which black people have helped to create and which we were painfully called upon to face in the 1970s. A movement like ours which often struck out forcefully against white racism, which called for the breaking down of all racial barriers, which insisted on the presence of black people in all the structures of American life, finally had to deal with some of the by-products of its own action. We had to ask how it would be possible to create the open, pluralistic society we championed and at the same time maintain certain bastions of black solidarity of our own. While the answers were not impossible to find, the process of asking the questions and opening ourselves to new directions was filled with understandable distress.

But it was more than the belief in black nationalism and our need for black solidarity which were threatened by the transformation of the Muslims into the World Community of Islam in the West. Something deeper may have been involved. For at the height of the 1960s, the Nation and Malcolm had represented what seemed to be a total black, religiously based challenge to the structures of white American life and thought. (Properly understood, Martin and the southern-based movement carried that potential as well.) Then, late in the 1960s, somewhere between the death of Malcolm and of King, the voice was changing. For instance, criminal and anarchic elements were reported in frighteningly high places in the Nation. Mr. Muhammad seemed increasingly to be courting favor and approval in the world of the white "devils." Then the word itself disappeared from the paper. The tails disappeared from the cartoons. Early in the 1970s, the picture of Chicago's notorious mayor, Richard Daley, appeared on the front page of *Muhammad Speaks*, seeming almost to be in exchange for Daley's pro forma proclamation of an Elijah Muhammad Day in Chicago. So the breaking of the center had been anticipated (hadn't Malcolm seen it?) and what it seemed to mean to many black persons was a retreat from speaking the truth in the face of white American power. In their minds, it meant that a fundamental black politicoreligious challenge had been withdrawn in the face of the harsh realities of white force and white blandishments. (Did it also mean that there was something in us which stubbornly refused to be ready for the changes we had forced on the society—that we really hoped that official Chicago would never "recognize" the honorableness of Mr. Muhammad? Or did we refuse to admit the possibility of corruption in a dictatorial organization that had essentially separated itself from the day-to-day political struggles of our people?) It means the loss of a community that most blacks never formally joined, but which seemed to exist—sometimes romantically—on behalf of certain unspoken feelings and desires in millions of hearts and minds.

My Lord, What a Mourning: Jonestown Is America

So it was not surprising that one of the major developments of the 1970s was the proliferation of essentially apolitical groupings of black people who were in search of some significant expression of black spirituality. Some went the way of Islamic-type splinter movements. Some searched for other African-rooted alternatives. Many persons looked again towards the modernized versions of the essentially conservative Christian churches that emphasized charismatic experiences of heartwarming but privatistic salvation and renewal. Still other black people were scattered among the millions of seekers after the revived truths of the various eastern religions that were rapidly spreading across the United States in the 1970s. Few, if any, of the black participants in these numerous experiences seemed to see their faith as a basis for continued confrontation with and challenge to "the basically flawed economics and politics" of America, the "cultural degradation" of America, or "the profound crisis of black people" in America. So the historic connection between black religion and black struggle for change which had been magnificently represented in their different ways by Malcolm and Martin and their companions was in jeopardy in the seventies.

Perhaps the new time will require a new kind of connection, a new kind of community, a new basis for challenge and hope. For at least three crucial developments of this decade have worked against reliance on the old connections, communities, and hopes. First is the absence of mass movement, which serves inherently as a creator of at least a temporary set of connections, community, and hope. Second is the corollary tendency to individualism and privatism that marked so much of the decade. Third is the black victory in breaking the power of segregation at crucial levels in the public and private sectors of the society. That victory carried with it a certain draining off of the solidarity that the black community had once been forced to experience. In a time when all traditions are under attack and serious reexamination, could we black people have expected to escape with our own intact, even the precious tradition of community, even the traditional religious grounds of our hope? In the seventies, we were forced to ask for the first time serious questions about the possible need for alternatives. That was a major event, largely interior, but no less crucial.

Unfortunately, it took a major disaster to emblazon on our minds the importance of that search for new grounds for hope, new bases for community, and new connections between spirituality and struggle. But for anyone who was listening and watching carefully, Jonestown brought it all home. Whatever else may be said about the men and women who were part of the People's Temple movement, it was obvious that many of them were still in search of that connection between religion and radical social concern which large numbers of us had abandoned. Thus, there is a sense in which Jim Jones was a judgment on us, especially on the structures of black religion, as well as on those of us who claim to believe in the necessity for fundamental structural transformation in the United States.

For in his terribly flawed and destructive way, Jones was nevertheless speaking to the issues that Malcolm, Martin, and Elijah at their best had raised—and, like them, he was acting as well. He was challenging men, women, and children to reject the spiritual, economic, and political structures and ethos of the American way of life and give their lives to the creation of real alternatives. In its actual manifestation, much of Jones's alternative vision was deeply warped, but apparently hundreds of spiritually starved people saw in it the promise of a life that would combine membership in a nurturing, creative religious community with persistent struggle for fundamental, humane political change in the world around us. The horrible tragedy of Jonestown and the degradation and destruction of so many of our people should not allow us to forget the essential message that still remains: Nothing in the arid materialism and individualism of the 1970s has eliminated the fundamental hungers in the human spirit for a deep sense of a caring, responsible, disciplined community and a great human cause to which a person may give himself or herself at the risk of "life, possessions, security, and status." Indeed, perhaps we have learned again that people become truly human only as such hungers are fed, a lesson that black folks once lived out as part of the natural necessity of our being. (Perhaps it would be well to point to one other critical lesson from Jonestown, a lesson black folks have not learned so well: Beware of charismatic leaders of any color, creed, or claim who demand unquestioning loyalty. At best, they hinder our own highest development as magnificently gifted human beings; at worst, they lead us down the path of self-destruction.)

In the 1970s, the pressures of cynicism, materialism, hedonism, and despair all tended to force us away from that enduring human reality. Thus one of the most crucial "events" of the 1970s came in the form of another essentially internal development—a dangerous loss of hope among black people, hope in ourselves, hope in the possibility of any real change, hope in any moral, creative force beyond the flatness of our lives. Our loss was, of course, intimately related to a similar depletion of moral energy (by far the most important energy crisis) throughout the mainstream of the nation. Nor is this mysterious. For the instruments of mass education, information, and entertainment have tied us more deeply to the American mind than ever before. And in a period where there is no mass countermovement and where men and women with both vision and leadership capacities are rare, then the sources of hope are not easy to find and maintain. Thus the search for a supportive community of people who are still committed to walk a different path, who seek the creation of a radically humanized version of the United States becomes even more important. For without such support we are unprepared to face the realities that Malcolm and Martin and all the participants in our driving, pressing movement finally opened up before us.

Needed—A New Vision

Fortunately, there are small but important signs that such a network of supportive counterforces is beginning to emerge from the cost-counting, contemplative period of the 1970s. On local levels, we have seen serious extended families and politically responsible communes and communities developing among black and white people in various places in the country, clearly committed to the ongoing struggle to create a new society. We have seen radical movement-born institutions—like the Third World Press and the Institute of the Black World—valiantly fighting to endure and to open themselves to the new questions of the new time. On the national level we have seen a group like the Organization for a New American Revolution which James and Grace Boggs have done so much to shape, and which seeks to develop the men and women who will grapple with the critical issues and fundamental struggles of the next decades. These are men and women who will neither back away from Martin and Malcolm, from DuBois or Robeson, from Fannie Lou or Ella Baker, nor make them idols. Rather they will confront the harsh and compelling American realities with these forerunners, and then move toward the twenty-first century.

Meanwhile, scattered all around the landscape of the 1970s, we have also seen the needy, broken, often wasted lives of our own people, facing a future in which new issues, new questions, new threats and new problems are constantly emerging, matters that go beyond the best conservative, liberal, or radical thinking we have known. Perhaps the greatest challenge of the coming decades will be to find some vital ways to join those unchallenged, temporarily passive, millions of men and women in a search for new and humane directions of our time. Coming out of the groundings of the 1970s we will be seeking with them for new ways to work, to travel, to nurture children. We will be searching to know how we can care for the earth and all its living parts. We will be searching to know how we can care for ourselves and our communities in a humane and nonexploitative manner, how we can jointly share responsibility for the raw materials of the world and not assume they belong to the highest bidders.

Perhaps if we have used well the sometimes-unwanted gift of relative quietness that has marked this decade we shall know how to look for new ways to live without the threat of war or starvation, new ways to heal ourselves and others, to banish fears and remove from power all who nurture fear to maintain their power and their weapons of coer-

cion, control, and destruction. If the intimations of the 1970s offer any
real hints, then those who are committed to the healing transformation
of this land must search out new ways to work for justice and compas-
sion, new ways to distribute our population, new and just ways to
define and distribute our national wealth, new ways and just ways to
relate to the natural wealth of other lands. Moving against the grain of
much that we have learned in this decade—drawing close to other
lessons that are no less available—we must find new ways to develop,
nurture, and strengthen the courage we need to press forward. We
must build the communities of struggle we need to advance past the
dead ends, to begin to see ourselves, this nation, this world, and even
the cosmos in ways we have not seen them before. If we learn our
lessons well, we will find ways to be prepared to participate in, to take
responsibility for, the next stages of struggle for those humanizing
transformations of a nation that we shall one day be proud to claim as
our own.

Without such a new vision of ourselves and the world beyond the
borders of our persons, many of the events of the 1970s become nothing more than frustrating repetitions of history, new signs of white
racism or mystifying novelties and epiphenomena. So, for instance, a
series of accidents, investigative reporting, and court cases throughout
the decade has revealed that there was a massive array of spying,
disruption, and destructive force set in place against our movement at
its height. Military intelligence, the FBI, the CIA, and local "law
enforcement" agencies were all involved in the action. Now, approach-
ing such information from a less reactive perspective, we may take this
evidence as an impressive testimony to the threatening power that our
movement represented in the eyes of the keepers of the status quo in
the United States, a power sometimes unrecognized by us. Indeed, if
we ponder these developments carefully, their most important significance is not as still another evidence of white perfidy, but in the fact
that this network of spying and deceit against us and others eventually
became one of the major handles by which the series of events known
as "Watergate" exploded on the nation and the world. In other words,
it was the residual power of our movement which helped to throttle the
rise of the imperial presidency and which helped open the minds of
many disparate persons to an emphasis on decentralized government
in the United States, an emphasis that will likely be part of the development among us of any truly new and democratic national state in the
future.

So, too, unless we press ourselves beyond the best cliches of the past
to envision the creation of an education that will help us all to contrib-

ute to a nurturing, pluralistic and nonexploitative society, then the question of busing or no busing, the furor over court decisions and metropolitan boundaries becomes literally academic. For they divert us from the main question that we must face here, the question of what kind of education do we really want and need for the kind of society we envision. Of course, that question is obviously secondary to the more fundamental one that we have begun to raise: what kind of a society do we want, and are we willing to struggle for? Without a nationwide pressing of that question among blacks and whites, then we do not know what kind of education we need, and we surely would not recognize "integration" if we saw it.

Learning to See in New Ways:
Black and Other Studies

In the same way, a new depth of vision that the seventies may have made available will allow us to look at an experience like the rise and fall of Black Studies and see its relationship to the larger struggle out of which it came. Just as the nation has been deeply affected by the mass black struggle of the last twenty-five years, so, too, the universities will never be the same again—though they may try very hard— after the movement of black people and ideas into their formerly essentially white precincts. It is also true, however, that just as many of the energies of the middle-class black freedom movement leadership have now been absorbed into the middle level structures of the American nation, so, too, the phenomenon that we called Black Studies—and many of its similarly middle-class proponents—has been absorbed into the structures, ethos, and aspirations of the American university system.

A clarity of vision is necessary to grasp the connections between these two crucial events of the 1970s. With it, we may begin to understand, for instance, that Black Studies was absorbed (with a few important partial exceptions) for many of the same reasons that we experienced in the larger area of national struggle. Essentially, it happened because the Black Studies movement failed to carry to their logical, radical ends many of the challenges to the assumptions, ideology, and structures of American higher education, failed to continue to press the critical issue of the relationship between black people inside the universities and those who will never make it. It was absorbed because it failed to deal unflinchingly with the connections of the American university to the American political, economic, and social system, failed to organize nationally to deal with such questions, failed because many black persons wanted nothing more than to be absorbed into tenure tracks, systems of status, and communities of academic unreality.

But the seventies may also have taught us to recognize the relentless nature of certain issues. And like its macrocounterpart, this one cannot ultimately be avoided. The role and function of the mainstream universities, their capacity to become truly pluralistic in their governance, curriculum, and ethos, the responsibilities of the universities to the changing national and international community, the meaning of the universities in a time of moral crisis, spiritual upheavals, and economic chaos—all these are issues that Black Studies came close to addressing, and they are issues that will not go away. Indeed, those black people who are now wedged into the universities and their systems have begun to sense the relentless nature of the questions and the inadequacy of so many of our answers—just as those persons who have moved into the arena of electoral politics are becoming aware that they are now jammed very close to the limits of the structures, and yet the crucial needs of the majority of black people are still essentially unaddressed. Where do we go from here?

Unless the more interior events of the 1970s release us to address such questions and grasp such connections, then we are tempted to see Supreme Court decisions like those related to Bakke and Weber as far more significant than they really are. For if we view them only as manifestations of white backlash and resistance, then they divert us from the crucial debate over the meaning of justice, over the obligation of a nation to its most exploited people, a debate that the courts have been asked to carry on only in the absence of a national forum of the people. (Indeed, most of the people are so lulled to sleep by television and other narcotics of the spirit that they cannot even conceive of such debates as being possible, much less that they might be essential to the establishment of a truly democratic citizenry in this country.) If such court cases were of any importance to us in the 1970s, their main value was as testimonies to the inadequacy of the judicial process to deal with issues that must be addressed by a conscious and informed citizenry. How we do that, how we get beyond mock television debates to real encounters is one of the questions we must address when we evaluate the usefulness of our present structures for the development of a democratic society.

In the same way, black folks who seek to learn from the developments of this decade must look in new ways at the rise of other social forces in the nation. In almost every case, these forces were either revitalized by or remodeled on the movement of our people toward freedom. Native Americans, Asian Americans, Chicanos, women, Latinos, members of the Communist party of the United States of America, gays, the ecology movement, the antinuclear movement do more than sing our songs and borrow our sometimes antiquated style. They also testify to the openings that we helped to create for others as the power of our struggle lay seige to so many of the traditional ways of American life. They remind us that the questions we raised about the essential values of America and its leaders were soon picked up and made the property of many others.

Now, they in turn offer new possibilities to us, if we will learn. Seeing ourselves and them in a new way, we will realize how deeply the Native American movements and the ecology forces are tied to the best insights of our own African forebears regarding the mutually nurturing relationships of human beings to the spirit-filled earth, waters, and skies. We will recognize how much unfinished business there is between black men and black women and how grateful we must all be for a women's movement whose most recent state and shape owe so much to our own struggle.

Similarly, when we look closely at all the current strivings for a new connectedness with the universe by way of the revised Eastern religions among us, and by way of the revived native American spirituality, we can see fascinating patterns of interpenetration. For it was our movement that raised some of the most insistent and radically effective questions about the adequacy of mainline white American religious faith and action for the coming new day. We pointed to its failure to respond adequately to the national and international struggles for justice. We were the local bearers of the challenge to Western cultural, political, and economic hegemony. It was we who had long demanded a closer look at the white American Christ, suggesting his inadequacy to the needs of the majority of God's dark-skinned world. The unsettling of the foundations, the opening to new fountains of spirituality cannot be understood apart from the religiously based struggle that we carried on. Thus we cannot afford to ignore the new developments of the 1970s. Instead, we need to ask what they can now teach us about the adequacy of our own traditions of spirituality, what they may demand of us concerning our need to expand and deepen the capacities of our own vision of the cosmos.

Without a transformed sense of the meaning of this age and our own role in it, we are of course, unable to understand the great African chorus that has lifted its voice and its arms continually throughout this decade. The sounds of struggle and victory and renewed struggle which have arisen out of Mozambique, Angola, and Zimbabwe, the cries of anguish and pain which have come to us like a wailing wind from across the Sahel, like the cries of the dead from the ancient land of Ethiopia, the voice of Steve Biko and the clenched fists of the children of Soweto as they faced the guns of their murderers—all these and more could be nothing but confused, episodic events or grist for some predigested ideology unless the 1970s have helped us to begin to see with new eyes and hear with new ears. For few of the responses of traditional Christianity, Marxism, Pan-Africanism, or a vague anti-imperialism will do as we stand on this newly native ground and try to know what has happened in this decade in the land of our forebears.

In the same way, it is crucial that we see clearly the epochal significance of the victory of the Vietnamese in their struggle against this nation and its chosen role as the last bastion of white Western domination in the world. Somehow, neither the rapidity of subsequent events nor the great human suffering that continues to rake that entire war-ravaged Indochinese peninsula (especially Kampuchea/Cambodia) should prevent us from understanding how crucial was that victory, that exemplary resistance. And certainly nothing should hinder us from a recognition of the role that our black struggle played in inspiring the Vietnamese to continue with their own struggle, until the United States was defeated and forced to withdraw. Properly understood, such connections may remind us of the profound ways in which our movement has contributed to a continuing fundamental change in the very course of American history; indeed, they suggest to us how our struggle has flowed into the creation of a new world situation.

So, too, while our current black adventures in the Middle East may stimulate some long-avoided discussion concerning the independence of our judgment and our organizations, it will ultimately be filled with no more than sound and fury if it is not informed by a new way of seeing this nation at work in the world. Our need for new questions, for fearless challenges to our own traditional thinking is no less when we turn to Vietnam or Cambodia, to China or Korea, to Jamaica, Cuba, or the nations of Latin America. All across the globe, new realities are being created, new relationships are being developed, new connections are being forged, new questions are being asked, new demands are being made which go deeper than the politics and economics we have been taught. Arising out of our foundation-shaking movement and others like ours in the anticolonial struggles of the last forty years, the activities of the 1970s and the reverberations of the 1960s cannot be confined to this continent. No, it is more likely that the 1970s may have signaled a fundamental turning point in the political, economic, ecological, and spiritual relationships of the world, bearing the intimations of a transformation that is destined to take us beyond the civilization of the industrial revolution, preparing us for the demands of the twenty-first century.

A Time of Turnings:
Which Way Shall We Go?

If we are actually in the midst of so elemental a time of turning, if indeed we stand at the edge of history, then the central question for us all, but especially for those of us who are young, is, how shall we live responsibly in this momentous period of humankind's evolution? In the light of what we have seen and been and done over the last twenty years, what is our best response to this hour, to our forebears, to our children—to our own deepest hopes and human longings? Considering the lessons of the 1970s, how do we move forward?

Do we turn aside into diversionary and essentially private pursuits, refusing to face our need for solidarity and community, resisting the struggle-honed development of our own most humane and creative selves? Or do we move forward, emerging renewed and enlarged out of the spiritual pilgrimages of this decade, ready to advance in the company of our brothers and sisters into the uncharted arena of the new time?

At the edge of history, how shall we move? Do we continue to trail behind the most revolutionary insights that our struggle has already achieved; do we turn away from the radical directions that Malcolm, Martin, and Fannie Lou had already approached in the 1960s? Or do we stand with them, move with them, move beyond them, move on for them and for ourselves and our children to remake this nation?

Absorbing the meaning of the 1970s, do we ignore the call of Gary? Or do we take its best insights and press on to create our own courageous summons to the newest stages of our struggle? How do we take all that we have learned and move it into the deeper internal spaces of our beings which this decade of winter has allowed us to explore? How, from so spacious and solid a center do we then move forward, beyond our best leaders of the past, beyond our best declarations, beyond our best actions, beyond our best dreams, to participate fully in the creation of a fundamentally new reality, in ourselves, in our people, in this nation, and in this world?

These are no longer wild and visionary questions. The winter of our constrictions is finally passing. Are we ready for all the necessary birth pangs, all the searching floodlights, all the unexpected new pathways of spring?

Come, then, comrades; it would be as well for us to decide at once to change our ways. We must shake off the heavy darkness in which we were plunged, and leave it behind. The new day which is already at hand must find us firm, prudent and resolute.

Frantz Fanon

Into your palm I place the ashes
Into your palm are the ashes of your brothers
burnt in the Alabama night
Into your palm that holds your babies
into your palm that feeds your children
into your palm that holds the work tools
I place the ashes of your father
here are the ashes of your husbands
Take the ashes of your nation
and create the cement to build again
Create the spirits to move again
Take this soul dust and begin again.

Ed Bullins

Bibliography

Adams, Henry. *The United States in 1800*. Ithaca, New York, 1955.

Allen, James S. *Reconstruction, The Battle for Democracy*. New York, 1937.

Allen, Richard. *The Life Experience and Gospel Labors of the Rt. Rev. Richard Allen*. New York, 1960 (originally published in 1793).

Allen, Robert L. *Black Awakening in Capitalist America*. New York, 1970.

———. *Reluctant Reformers*. Washington, D.C., 1974.

Allen, William F. *Slave Songs of the United States*. New York, 1965.

Ames, Mary. *From a New England Women's Diary in Dixie in 1865* Springfield, Mass., 1906

Anderson, Osborne P. *A Voice from Harper's Ferry*. New York, 1974 (originally published in 1861).

Andrews, Sidney. *The South Since the War*. Boston, 1866.

Anstey, Roger. *The Atlantic Slave Trade and British Abolition, 1760–1810*. Atlantic Highlands, New Jersey, 1975.

Anthony, Earl. *Picking Up the Gun*. New York, 1970.

———. *The Time of the Furnaces: A Case Study of Black Student Revolt*. New York, 1971.

Aptheker, Herbert. *American Negro Slave Revolts*. New York, 1963 (originally published in 1943).

——— (ed.) *Documentary History of the Negro People in the United States*. 2 vols., New York, 1951.

———. *Nat Turner's Slave Rebellion*. New York, 1966.

——— (ed.). *One Continual Cry*. New York, 1965.

Attica. New York State Special Commission, *Attica*, 1972.

Baird, Robert. *Religion in America*. New York, 1969.

Baldwin, James. *The Fire Next Time*. New York, 1963.

———. *Nobody Knows My Name*. New York, 1961.

Bancroft, Frederic. *Slave Trading in the Old South*. New York, 1959 (originally published in 1931).

Barbour, Floyd B. (ed.). *The Black Power Revolt*. Boston, 1968.

Bartley, Numan V. *The Rise of Massive Resistance*. Baton Rouge, Louisiana, 1969.

Basler, Roy P., *et al.* (eds.). *The Collected Works of Abraham Lincoln*. 9 vols. and index. New Brunswick, New Jersey, 1953.

Bates, Daisy. *The Long Shadow of Little Rock*. New York, 1962.

Bearse, Austin. *Reminiscences of Fugitive Slave Law Days in Boston*. New York, 1969 (originally published in 1880).

Belfrage, Sally. *Freedom Summer*. New York, 1965.

Bell, Howard H. (ed.). *Minutes of the Proceedings of the National Negro Conventions, 1838–1864*. New York, 1969.

———. *A Survey of the Negro Convention Movement, 1830–1861*. New York, 1969.

Bennett, Lerone Jr. *Black Power USA. The Human Side of Reconstruction, 1867–1877*. Chicago, 1967.

———. *Confrontation: Black and White*. Chicago, 1965.

———. *The Negro Mood*. Chicago, 1964.

———. *The Shaping of Black America*. Chicago, 1975.

———. *What Manner of Man*. Chicago, 1965.

Bergman, Peter M. *Chronological History of the Negro in America*. New York, 1969.

Berlin, Ira. *Slaves Without Masters*. New York, 1974.

Bernstein, Barton J. (ed). *Politics and Policies of the Truman Administration*. Chicago, 1970.

Berry, Mary Francis. *Black Resistance, White Law*. New York, 1971.

Berwanger, Eugene. *The Frontier Against Slavery*. Urbana, Illinois, 1967.

Bibb, Henry. *Narrative of the Life and Adventures of Henry Bibb*. New York, 1850.

Bittle, William E., and Gilbert Geis. *The Longest Way Home*. Detroit, 1964.

Blassingame, John. *The Slave Community: Plantation Life in the Antebellum South*. New York, 1973.

Bond, Horace Mann. *Negro Education in Alabama*. New York, 1969.

Bontemps, Arna. *Black Thunder*. Boston, 1968 (originally published in 1936).

Bontemps, Arna, and Jack Conroy. *Anyplace But Here*. New York, 1966.

Botume, Elizabeth H. *First Days Amongst the Contrabands*. Boston, 1892.

Boyer, Richard O. *The Legend of John Brown*. New York, 1973.

Bracey, John H., Jr., *et al.* (eds.). *American Slavery: The Question of Resistance*. Belmont, California, 1970.

———. *Black Nationalism in America*. Indianapolis and New York, 1970.

———. *Black Workers and Organized Labor*. Belmont, California, 1971.

———. *Blacks in the Abolitionist Movement*. Belmont, California, 1971.

Brawley, Benjamin. *A Social History of the American Negro*. New York, 1970.

Brazeal, Brailsford R. *The Brotherhood of Sleeping Car Porters*. New York, 1946.

Breitman, George (ed.). *Malcolm X Speaks*. New York, 1965.

———. *By Any Means Necessary*. New York, 1970.

Brewer, Mason J. *American Negro Folklore*. Chicago, 1968.

Brink, William, and Louis Harris. *Black and White*. New York, 1967.

Brisbane, Robert H. *Black Activism*. Valley Forge, Pennsylvania, 1974.

———. *The Black Vanguard*. Valley Forge, Pennsylvania, 1970.

Broderick, Francis L. *W. E. B. Du Bois, Negro Leader in a Time of Crisis*. Stanford, California, 1959.

Broderick, Francis L., and August Meier (eds.). *Negro Protest Thought in the Twentieth Century*. Indianapolis, 1965.

Brotz, Howard (ed.). *Negro Social and Political Thought, 1850–1920*. New York, 1966.

Brown, H. Rap. *Die Nigger Die!* New York, 1969.

Brown, Sterling A., *et al.* (eds.). *The Negro Caravan*. New York, 1941.

Brown, William W. *Narrative of the Life of William W. Brown*. London, 1850.

Bunche, Ralph J. *The Political Status of the Negro in the Age of FDR*. Chicago, 1973.

Burchard, Peter. *One Gallant Rush*. New York, 1965.

Camejo, Peter. *Racism, Revolution, Reaction, 1861–1877*. New York, 1976.

Campbell, Penelope. *Maryland in Africa*. Urbana, Illinois, 1971.

Campbell, Stanley W. *The Slave Catchers*. New York, 1972 (originally published in 1968).

Canot, Theodore Captain. *Adventures of An African Slaver*. New York, 1969.

Cantor, Louis. *A Prologue to the Protest Movement*. Durham, 1969.

Carawan, Guy and Candy (eds.). *We Shall Overcome*. New York, 1963.

———. *Freedom Is a Constant Struggle, Songs of the Freedom Movement*. New York, 1968.

Carmichael, Stokely. *Stokely Speaks*. New York, 1971.

Carroll, Joseph C. *Slave Insurrection in the United States, 1800–1865*. New York, 1968 (originally published in 1938).

Carroll, Peter N., and David W. Noble. *The Free and the Unfree*. New York, 1977.

Carter, Dan T. *Scottsboro: A Tragedy of the American South*. Baton Rouge, 1969.

Catterall, Helen T. (ed.). *Judicial Cases Concerning American Slavery and the Negro* (5 vols.). New York, 1968 (originally published in 1926).

Cayton, Horace R., and George S. Mitchell (eds.). *Black Workers and the New Unions*. Chapel Hill, North Carolina, 1939.

Cheek, William F. *Black Resistance Before the Civil War*. Beverly Hills, California, 1970.

Cipolla, Carlo M. *Guns, Sails and Empires*. New York, 1965.

Clarke, John Henrik (ed.). *Marcus Garvey and the Vision of Africa*. New York, 1974.

———. *William Styron's Nat Turner: Ten Black Writers Respond*. Boston, 1968.

Clarke, John H., and Vincent Harding. *Slave Trade and Slavery*. New York, 1970.

Cleague, Albert B. *The Black Messiah*. New York, 1968.

Cleaver, Eldridge. *Soul on Ice*. New York, 1968

Cobb, Charles, *Furrows*. Tougaloo, Mississippi, 1967.

Cohen, Mitchell, and Dennis Hale. *The New Student Left*. Boston, 1966.

Cohen, Robert Carl. *Black Crusader*. Seacaucus, New Jersey, 1972.

Conant, Ralph W. *The Prospects for Revolution*. New York, 1971.

Cone, James. *A Black Theology of Liberation*. New York, 1970.

Conlin, Joseph R. *Bread and Roses Too*. Westport, Connecticut, 1969.

Conot, Robert. *Rivers of Blood*. New York, 1967.

Conway, Alan. *The Reconstruction of Georgia*. Minneapolis, 1966.

Conrad, Earl. *Harriet Tubman*. Washington, D.C., 1943.

Cooper, Wayne (ed.). *The Passion of Claude McKay: Selected Prose and Poetry, 1912–1948*. New York, 1965.

Cornish, Dudley. *The Sable Arm*. New York, 1965.

Corporation of Charleston. *An Account of the Late Intended Insurrection*. Charleston, 1822.

Courlander, Harold. *Negro Folk Music USA*. New York, 1963.

Cox, Oliver Cromwell. *Caste, Class, and Race*. New York, 1959.

Cronon, Edmund D. *Black Moses*. Madison, 1964.

Crossman, Richard (ed.). *The God That Failed*. New York, 1952.

Cruden, Robert. *The Negro in Reconstruction*. Englewood Heights, New Jersey, 1969.

Crummell, Alex. *Africa and America*. New York, 1969 (originally published in 1891).

Cruse, Harold. *The Crisis of the Negro Intellectual*. New York, 1967.

Curry, Richard O. (ed.). *Radicalism, Racism and Party Alignment*. Baltimore, 1969.

Curtin, Philip D. (ed.). *Africa Remembered*. Madison, 1967.

———. *The Atlantic Slave Trade*. Madison, 1969.

Curtis, Richard. *The Life of Malcolm X*. Philadelphia, 1971.

Dalfiume, Richard M. *Desegregation of the U.S. Armed Forces*. Columbia, Missouri, 1969.

Dangerfield, George. *The Era of Good Feelings*. New York, 1963.

Daniel, Pete. *The Shadow of Slavery: Peonage in the South*. Urbana, Illinois, 1972.

Dann, Martin E. (ed.). *The Black Press, 1827–1890*. New York, 1972.

Davidson, Basil. *A History of West Africa*. New York, 1966.

———. *Africa: History of a Continent*. New York, 1972.

Davies, K. G. *The Royal African Company*. London, 1957.

Davies, Peter, and the Board of Church and Society of the United Methodist Church. *The Truth About Kent State*. New York, 1973.

Davis, Angela Y. *If They Come in the Morning*. New York, 1971.

Davis, Benjamin. *Communist Councilman from Harlem*. New York, 1956.

———. *The Negro People on the March*. New York, 1956.

———. *Ante-Bellum Reform*. New York, 1967.

Davis, David B. *The Problem of Slavery in the Age of Revolution, 1770–1823* Ithaca, New York, 1975.

————. *The Problem of Slavery in Western Culture*. Ithaca, New York, 1966.

Davis, William W. *The Civil War and Reconstruction in Florida*. New York, 1913.

Dawley, David. *A Nation of Lords*. Garden City, New York, 1973.

DeCaux, Len. *Labor Radical*. Boston, 1970.

Delany, Martin R. *Blake or the Huts of America*. Boston, 1970 (originally published in 1859).

————. *The Condition, Elevation, Emigration, and Destiny of the Colored People of the United States*. Philadelphia, 1852.

Delany, Martin, and Robert Campbell. *Search for a Place*. Ann Arbor, Michigan, 1969.

Deming, Barbara. *Revolution and Equilibrium*. New York, 1971.

Dick, Robert C. *Black Protest: Issues and Tactics*. Westport, Connecticut, 1974.

Dickson, Moses. *Manual of the International Order of Twelve*. St. Louis, 1891.

Donald, David. *Charles Sumner and the Coming of the Civil War*. New York, 1960.

Donnan, Elizabeth. *Documents Illustrative of the History of the Slave Trade to America* (4 vols.). New York, 1965 (originally published in 1930).

Douglas, H. Ford. "Lincoln, Slavery and Equal Rights," in Norton Garfinkle (ed.), *Lincoln and the Coming of the Civil War*. Boston, 1959.

Douglass, Frederick. *My Bondage and My Freedom*. New York, 1968 (originally published in 1855).

————. *Narrative of the Life of Frederick Douglass*. Boston, 1845.

Dow, George F. *Slave Ships and Slaving*. Salem, Massachusetts, 1927.

Drake, St. Clair. *The Redemption of Africa and Black Religion*. Chicago and Atlanta, 1970.

Drake, St. Clair, and Horace R. Clayton. *Black Metropolis*. New York, 1945.

Draper, Theodore. *American Communism and Soviet Russia*. New York, 1960.

————. *The Rediscovery of Black Nationalism*. New York, 1969.

————. *The Roots of American Communism*. New York, 1957.

Drew, Benjamin (ed.). *The Refugee: Or the Narratives of Fugitive Slaves in Canada*. Boston, 1856.

Drimmer, Melvin (ed.). *Black History: A Reappraisal*. New York, 1968.

Duberman, Martin (ed.). *The Antislavery Vanguard*. Princeton, 1965.

Dubofsky, Melvyn. *We Shall Be All*. Chicago, 1969.

Du Bois, Shirley Graham. *His Day Is Marching On*. Philadelphia, 1971.

Du Bois, W. E. B. *The Autobiography of W. E. B. Du Bois*. New York, 1968.

————. *Black Reconstruction in America*. 1964 (originally published in 1935).

————. *Darkwater: Voices from Within the Veil*. New York, 1969 (originally published in 1920).

————. *Dusk of Dawn*. New York, 1968 (originally published in 1940).

————. *The Education of Black People: Ten Critiques, 1906–1960*. Amherst, 1973.

————. *In Battle for Peace*. New York, 1952.

————. *John Brown.* New York, 1962 (originally published in 1909).

————. (ed.). *The Negro Church.* Atlanta, 1903.

————. *The Souls of Black Folk.* Greenwich, Connecticut, 1961 (originally published in 1903).

————. (ed.). *The Suppression of the African Slave-Trade.* 1965 (originally published in 1898).

Dumond, Dwight. *Anti-Slavery.* Ann Arbor, 1961.

Durden, Robert. *The Gray and the Black.* Baton Rouge, 1972.

Duster, Alfreda M. (ed.). *The Autobiography of Ida B. Wells.* Chicago, 1970.

Ebony Editors. *The Black Revolution.* Chicago, 1970.

————. *A Pictorial History of Black America* (3 vols.). Chicago, 1971.

Edwards, Harry. *Black Students.* New York, 1970.

Elkins, Stanley M. *Slavery.* New York, 1963.

Ellison, Ralph. *Invisible Man.* New York, 1952.

Essien-Udom, E. U. *Black Nationalism.* New York, 1964.

Factor, Robert L. *The Black Response to America.* Reading, Massachusetts, 1970.

Fanon, Frantz. *The Wretched of the Earth.* New York, 1963 (originally published in 1961).

Fauset, Arthur Huff. *Black Gods of the Metropolis.* New York, 1970 (originally published in 1944).

Feagin, Joe R., and Harlan Hahn. *Ghetto Revolts.* New York, 1973.

Ferber, Michael, and Staughton Lynd. *The Resistance.* Boston, 1971.

Filler, Louis. *The Crusade Against Slavery 1830–1860.* New York, 1963.

Fisher, Miles Mark. *Negro Slave Songs in the United States.* New York, 1963.

Fladeland, Betty. *Men and Brothers, Anglo-American Antislavery Cooperation.* Urbana, Illinois, 1972.

Fleming, Walter L. (ed.). *Documentary History of Reconstruction.* Cleveland, Ohio, 1906–1907.

Fogel, Robert, and Stanley L. Engerman. *Time on the Cross* (2 vols.). Boston, 1974.

Fogelson, Robert M. *Violence as Protest.* New York, 1971.

Foner, Eric. *Free Soil, Free Labor, Free Men.* New York, 1971.

———— (ed.). *Nat Turner.* Englewood Cliffs, New Jersey, 1971.

Foner, Philip S. *History of the Labor Movement in the United States* (2 vols.). New York, 1962.

————. *History of Black Americans.* Westport, Connecticut, 1975.

———— (ed.). *The Life and Writings of Frederick Douglass* (4 vols.). New York, 1950.

————. *W. E. B. Du Bois Speaks: Speeches and Addresses, 1890–1919, 1920–1963.* New York, 1970.

————. *Organized Labor and the Black Worker, 1619–1973.* New York, 1974.

Foreman, Grant. *Indian Removal.* Norman, Oklahoma, 1953.

Forman, James. *The Making of Black Revolutionaries.* New York, 1972.

————. *Sammy Younge Jr.* New York, 1968.

Fortune, Timothy Thomas. *Black and White, Land, Color and Politics in the South*. New York, 1884.

Foster, Charles I. *An Errand of Mercy: The Evangelical United Front, 1790–1837*. Chapel Hill, North Carolina, 1960.

Fowler, Arlen. *The Black Infantry in the West, 1869–1891*. Westport, Connecticut, 1971.

Fox, Stephen R. *The Guardian of Boston: William Monroe Trotter*. New York, 1970.

Franklin, John Hope. *Reconstruction: After the Civil War*. Chicago, 1961.

———. *The Emancipation Proclamation*. New York, 1965.

———. *From Slavery to Freedom*. New York, 1967.

Frazier, E. Franklin. *Black Bourgeoisie*. New York, 1957.

———. *The Negro Family in the United States*. New York, 1948.

———. *The Negro Church in America*. New York, 1964.

Frazier, Thomas R. (ed.). *Afro-American History: Primary Sources*. New York, 1970.

Freedman, Jill. *Old News: Resurrection City*. New York, 1970.

Freedomways Editors. *Black Titan: W. E. B. Du Bois*. Boston, 1970.

Friedman, Leon (ed.). *The Civil Rights Reader: Basic Documents of the Civil Rights Movement*. New York, 1967.

Fullinwinder, S. P. *The Mind and Mood of Black America*. Homewood, Illinois, 1969.

Gara, Larry. *The Liberty Line*. Lexington, 1961.

Garfinkle, Herbert. *When Negroes March*. New York, 1969.

Garland, Phyl. *The Sound of Soul: The Story of Black Music*. New York, 1971.

Garvey, Amy Jacques. *Garvey and Garveyism*. Jamaica, 1963.

———. (ed.). *Philosophy and Opinions of Marcus Garvey*. London, 1967 (originally published in 1925).

Gatewood, Willard B., Jr., *"Smoked Yankees" and the Struggle for Empire*. Urbana, Illinois, 1971.

Genovese, Eugene D. *Roll, Jordan, Roll*. New York, 1974.

George, Carol V. R. *Segregated Sabbaths: Richard Allen and the Emergence of Independent Black Churches*. New York, 1973.

Gerteis, Louis S. *From Contraband to Freedman*. Westport, Connecticut, 1973.

Geschwender, James A. *The Black Revolt*. Englewood Cliffs, New Jersey, 1971.

Gilbert, Olive (ed.). *Narrative of Sojourner Truth*. Battle Creek, Michigan, 1878.

Gilbert, Peter (ed.). *The Selected Writings of John Edward Bruce: Militant Black Journalist*. New York, 1971.

Ginzberg, Ralph (ed.). *One Hundred Years of Lynchings*. New York, 1962.

Gipson, Lawrence H. *The Coming of the Revolution, 1763–1775*. New York, 1954.

Goddell, William. *The American Slave Code*. New York, 1853.

Goldman, Peter. *Report from Black America*. New York, 1970.

Goodman, Benjamin (ed.). *Malcolm X: The End of White World Supremacy.* New York, 1971.

Gossett, Thomas F. *Race: The History of an Idea in America.* New York, 1965.

Graham, Hugh D., and Ted R. Gurr (eds.). *The History of Violence in America.* New York, 1969.

Graham, Shirley. *Paul Robeson: Citizen of the World.* New York, 1946.

———. *There Was Once a Slave.* New York, 1947.

Grant, Joanne (ed.). *Black Protest.* Greenwich, Connecticut, 1968.

Gratus, Jack. *The Great White Lie. Slavery, Emancipation, and Changing Racial Attitudes.* New York, 1973.

Greene, Evarts, and Virginia Hamilton. *American Population Before the Federal Census of 1790.* New York, 1932.

Griffin, Clifford S. *Their Brothers' Keeper.* New Brunswick, New Jersey, 1960.

Griggs, Sutton. *Imperium In Imperio.* New York, 1969 (originally published in 1899).

Grubbs, Donald H. *Cry From the Cotton.* Chapel Hill, North Carolina, 1971.

Holt, Thomas. *Black Over White.* Urbana, Illinois, 1977.

Hansberry, Lorraine. *The Movement: Documentary of a Struggle for Equality.* New York, 1964.

Haraven, Tamara K. (ed.). *Anonymous Americans.* Englewood Cliffs, New Jersey, 1971.

Harding, Vincent. *Beyond Chaos: Black History and the Search for the New Land.* Atlanta, 1970.

Harlan, Louis R. *Booker T. Washington, The Making of a Black Leader, 1856–1901.* New York, 1972.

Harris, Sara. *Father Divine.* New York, 1971.

Harris, Sheldon. *Paul Cuffee: Black American and the African Return.* New York, 1972.

Harris, William C. *Presidential Reconstruction in Mississippi.* Baton Rouge, 1967.

Harrison, Hubert H. *The Negro and the Nation.* New York, 1917.

———. *When Africa Awakes.* New York, 1920.

Hayden, Robert. *Selected Poems.* New York, 1966.

Hayden, Tom. *The Love of Possession Is a Disease with Them.* Chicago, 1972.

———. *Rebellion in Newark.* New York, 1967.

Headley, Joel T. *The Great Riots of New York, 1712 to 1873.* New York: Dover, 1971 (originally published in 1873).

Heilbut, Tony. *The Gospel Sound, Good News and Bad Times.* New York, 1971.

Henry, H. M. *The Police Control of the Slave in South Carolina.* Emery, Virginia, 1914.

Hensel, H. V. *The Christiana Riot.* Lancaster, Pennsylvania, 1911.

Hepworth, George H. *The Whip, Hoe and Sword.* Boston, 1864.

Herndon, Angelo. *Let Me Live.* New York, 1937.

Herskovits, Melvin J. *The Myth of the Negro Past*. Boston, 1958 (originally published in 1941).

Hickey, Neil, and Ed Edwin. *Adam Clayton Powell and the Politics of Race*. New York, 1965.

Hicks, John D. *The Populist Revolt*. Minneapolis, 1931.

Higginson, Thomas Wentworth. *Travellers and Outlaws*. Boston, 1889.

Hill, Adelaide C., and Martin Kilson (eds.). *Apropos of Africa*. London, 1969.

Hilton, Bruce. *The Delta Ministry*. London, 1969.

Hinton, Richard J. *John Brown and His Men*. New York, 1968 (originally published in 1894).

Hobsbawm, E. J. *Primitive Rebels*. New York, 1959.

Hodges, Norman E. W. *Breaking the Chains of Bondage*. New York, 1972.

Hofstadter, Richard, and Michael Wallace (eds.). *American Violence*. New York, 1970.

Holly, James Theodore, and J. Dennis Harris. *Black Separatism and the Caribbean, 1860*. Ann Arbor, 1970.

Holt, Len. *The Summer That Didn't End*. New York, 1965.

Hopkins, Vincent C. *Dred Scott's Case*. New York, 1951.

Hornsby, Alton, Jr. (ed.). *In the Cage, Eyewitness Accounts of the Freed Negro in Southern Society, 1877–1929*. Chicago, 1971.

Horsmanden, Daniel. *The New York Conspiracy*. Boston, 1971.

Howard, Thomas (ed.). *Black Voyage: Eyewitness Accounts of the Atlantic Slave Trade*. Boston, 1971.

Howard, Warren S. *American Slavers and the Federal Law, 1837–1862*. Berkeley, California, 1963.

Howe, Irving, and Lewis Coser. *The American Communist Party*. Boston, 1951.

Howe, Julia Warde. *Reminiscences, 1819–1899*. Boston and New York, 1900.

Hudson, Hosea. *Black Worker in the Deep South*. New York, 1972.

Huggins, Nathan Irvin. *Harlem Renaissance*. New York, 1971.

Huggins, Nathan J., Martin Kilson, and Daniel M. Fox. *Key Issues in the Afro-American Experience*. New York, 1971.

Hughes, Langston. *Fight for Freedom: The Story of the NAACP*. New York, 1962.

———. *The Big Sea*. New York, 1963 (originally published in 1940).

———. *Good Morning Revolution—Uncollected Writings of Social Protest*. New York, 1973.

———. *I Wonder as I Wander*. New York, 1956.

Hughes, Langston, and Milton Meltzer. *A Pictorial History of the Negro in America*. New York, 1966.

Hurd, John C. *The Law of Freedom and Bondage in the United States*. Boston, 1858.

Hyman, Harold M. (ed.). *The Radical Republicans and Reconstruction, 1861–1870*. Indianapolis, 1967.

[Industrial Workers of the World], *Proceedings of the Founding Convention*. New York, 1969.

Jackson, George. *Blood in My Eye.* New York, 1972.

———. *Soledad Brother, The Prison Letters of George Jackson.* New York, 1970.

Jackson, Helen Hunt. *A Century of Dishonor.* Minneapolis, 1944 (originally published in 1885).

Jackson, James. *U. S. Negroes in Battle from Little Rock to Watts.* Moscow, 1967.

Jacobs, Andy. *The Powell Affair, Freedom Minus One.* New York, 1973.

Jacobs, Paul, and Saul Landau. *The New Radicals.* New York, 1966.

——— (eds.). *To Serve the Devil.* New York, 1971.

Jacobson, Julius (ed.). *The Negro and the American Labor Movement.* New York, 1968.

Jamal, Hakim A. *From the Dead Level: Malcolm X and Me.* New York, 1972.

James, C. L. R. *The Black Jacobins* (2d ed.). New York, 1963.

———. *A History of Negro Revolt.* London, 1938.

Jennings, Francis. *The Invasion of America.* New York, 1976.

Johnson, James Weldon. *Along This Way.* New York, 1965 (originally published in 1933).

———. *Black Manhattan.* New York, 1930.

Jones, LeRoi. *Blues People.* New York, 1963.

Jones, LeRoi, and Larry Neal (eds.). *Black Fire.* New York, 1968.

Jordan, Winthrop D. *White Over Black.* Chapel Hill, North Carolina, 1968.

[Josephy, Alvin M. Jr.]. *The Horizon History of Africa.* New York, 1971.

———. *Red Power, the American Indians' Fight for Freedom.* New York, 1971.

Katz, Jonathan (ed.). *Resistance at Christiana.* New York, 1974.

Katz, William Loren. *The Black West.* New York, 1973 (originally published in 1971).

Keating, Edward M. *Free Huey!* Berkeley, California, 1971.

Kellogg, Charles Flint. *NAACP: A History of the National Association for the Advancement of Colored People* (Vol. I). Baltimore, 1967.

Kerlin, Robert T. *The Voice of the Negro, 1919.* New York, 1920.

Kester, Howard. *Revolt Among the Sharecroppers.* New York, 1969 (originally published in 1936).

Killens, John O. *The Trial Record of Denmark Vesey.* Boston, 1970.

Killian, Lewis M. *The Impossible Revolution?* New York, 1968.

King, Martin L., Jr. *Stride Toward Freedom.* New York, 1958.

———. *Strength to Love.* New York, 1963.

———. *The Trumpet of Conscience.* New York, 1968.

———. *Where Do We Go from Here, Chaos or Community?* New York, 1967.

———. *Why We Can't Wait.* New York, 1964.

Koch, Adrienne, and William Peden (eds.). *The Life and Selected Writings of Thomas Jefferson.* New York, 1944.

Kolchin, Peter. *First Freedom.* Westport, Connecticut, 1972.

Kornbluh, Joyce L. (ed.). *Rebel Voices: An I. W. W. Anthology.* Ann Arbor, Michigan, 1964.

Kovel, Joe. *White Racism: A Psychohistory*. New York, 1971.

Kraditor, Aileen S. *Means and Ends in American Abolitionism*. New York, 1969.

Lacy, Dan. *The White Use of Blacks in America*. New York, 1972.

Lacy, Leslie Alexander. *Cheer the Lonesome Traveler: The Life of W. E. B. Du Bois*. New York, 1970.

Lafore, Laurence. *The Long Fuse*. New York, 1965.

Lamson, Peggy. *The Glorious Failure*. New York, 1973.

Lane, Ann J. (ed.). *The Debate over Slavery, Stanley Elkins and His Critics* Urbana, Illinois, 1971.

Langston, John Mercer. *From the Virginia Plantation to the National Capitol*. Hartford, Connecticut, 1894.

Lester, Julius. *Look Out, Whitey! Black Power's Gon' Get Your Mama!* New York, 1968.

———. *To Be a Slave*. New York, 1968.

———. (ed.). *The Seventh Son: The Thought and Writings of W. E. B. Du Bois* (2 vols.). New York, 1971.

Levine, Lawrence. *Black Culture and Black Consciousness*. New York, 1977.

Levy, Eugene. *James Weldon Johnson: Black Leader, Black Voice*. Chicago, 1973.

Lewis, Anthony (ed.). *Portrait of a Decade*. New York, 1964.

Lewis, David L. *King, A Critical Biography*. New York, 1970.

Lewy, Gunther. *Religion and Revolution*. New York, 1974.

Lincoln, C. Eric. *The Black Muslims in America*. Boston, 1962.

Litwack, Leon. *Been in the Storm so Long*. New York, 1979.

———. *North of Slavery*. Chicago, 1961.

Locke, Alain (ed.). *The New Negro: An Interpretation*. New York, 1925.

Lofton, John. *Insurrection in South Carolina*. Yellow Springs, Ohio, 1964.

Logan, Rayford W. *The Betrayal of the Negro*. New York, 1965.

Lomax, Louis E. *To Kill a Black Man*. New York, 1968.

———. *When the Word Is Given . . .* New York, 1964.

Louis, Debbie. *And We Are Not Saved: A History of the Movement as People*. New York, 1970.

Lovell, John Jr. *Black Song: The Forge and the Flame—The Story of How the Afro-American Spiritual Was Hammered Out*. New York, 1972.

Lubell, Samuel. *White and Black*. New York, 1966.

Lynch, Hollis. *The Black Urban Condition*. New York, 1973.

———. *Edward Wilmot Blyden, Pan-Negro Patriot, 1832–1912*. New York, 1967.

Lynd, Staughton. *Class Conflict, Slavery and the United States Constitution*. Indianapolis, 1967.

——— (ed.). *Non-violence in America: A Documentary History*. Indianapolis, 1966.

McCague, James. *The Second Rebellion: The Story of the New York City Draft Riots of 1863*. New York, 1968.

McClellan, George B. *Reports on the Organization and Campaigns of the Army of the Potomac*. New York, 1864.

MacDougall, Curtis D. *Gideon's Army* (3 vols.). New York, 1965.

McDougall, Marion G. *Fugitive Slaves*. New York, 1967 (originally published in 1891).

McFeeley, William S. *Yankee Stepfather: General O. Howard and the Freedmen*. New Haven, 1968.

McKay, Claude. *Harlem: Negro Metropolis*. New York, 1940.

———. *A Long Way from Home*. New York, 1937.

McKissick, Floyd. *Three-Fifths of a Man*. London, 1969.

McKitrick, Eric L. *Andrew Johnson and Reconstruction*. Chicago, 1960.

McLord, William. *Mississippi: The Long Hot Summer*. New York, 1965.

McManus, Earl J. *Black Bondage in the North*. Syracuse, New York, 1973.

McNeill, William H. *The Rise of the West*. Chicago, 1963.

McPherson, James M. *The Abolitionist Legacy*. Princeton, New Jersey, 1975.

———. (ed.) *Anti-Negro Riots in the North*. New York, 1969 (originally published in 1863).

———. *The Negro's Civil War*. New York, 1965.

———. *The Struggle for Equality*. Princeton, New Jersey, 1964.

———, et al. *Blacks in America: Biographical Essays*. New York, 1971.

McWhiney, Grady (ed.). *Reconstruction and the Freedmen*. Chicago, 1963.

Magdol, Edward. *A Right to the Land*. Westport, Connecticut, 1977.

Maglangbayan, Shawna. *Garvey, Lumumba, Malcolm: Black Nationalist Separatists*. Chicago, 1972.

Major, Reginald. *A Panther Is a Black Cat*. New York, 1971.

Malcolm X. *The Autobiography of Malcolm X*. New York, 1964.

———. *By Any Means Necessary*. New York, 1970.

Mandle, Jay R. *The Roots of Black Poverty*. Durham, North Carolina, 1978.

Marine, Gene. *The Black Panthers*. New York, 1969.

Marks, George P. III (ed.). *The Black Press Views American Imperialism (1898–1900)*. New York, 1971.

Marx, Karl, and Frederick Engels. *Letters to Americans, 1848–1895*. New York, 1953.

Mathews, Donald G. *Slavery and Methodism*. Princeton, New Jersey, 1965.

May, Samuel. *The Fugitive Slave Law and Its Victims*. Freeport, New York, 1970 (originally published in 1861).

May, Samuel J. *Some Recollections of Our Anti-Slavery Conflict*. New York, 1968 (originally published in 1869).

Mayer, J. P., and Max Lerner (eds.). *Democracy in America*. New York, 1966.

Mays, Benjamin E. *The Negro's God as Reflected in His Literature*. Boston, 1938.

Meier, August. *Negro Thoughts in America, 1880–1915*, Ann Arbor, 1963.

——— (ed.). *The Transformation of Activism*. Chicago, 1970.

Meier, August, and Elliot Rudwick (eds.). *Black Protest in the Sixties*. Chicago, 1970.

———. *CORE: A Study of the Civil Rights Movement, 1942–1968.* New York, 1973.

———. *The Making of Black America* (2 vols.). New York, 1969.

Miller, John C. *Origins of the American Revolution.* Stanford, California, 1959.

Miller, Floyd T. *The Search for a Black Nationality.* Urbana, Illinois, 1975.

Miller, William Robert. *Martin Luther King, Jr.: His Life, Martyrdom, and Meaning for the World.* New York, 1968.

Moody, Anne. *Coming of Age in Mississippi.* New York, 1968.

Moore, Gilbert. *A Special Rage.* New York, 1971.

Moore, Glover. *The Missouri Controversy, 1819–1821.* Lexington, Kentucky, 1953.

Morgan, A. T. *Yazoo.* Washington, D. C., 1884.

Morgan, Edward S. *American Slavery, American Freedom.* New York, 1975.

Muhammad, Elijah. *Message to the Black Man in America.* Chicago, 1965.

———. *The Fall of America.* Chicago, 1973.

Mullen, Robert W. *Blacks in America's Wars.* New York, 1974.

Mullin, Michael [Gerald W.] (ed.). *American Negro Slavery.* New York, 1976.

Mullin, Gerald W. *Flight and Rebellion, Slave Resistance in Eighteenth Century Virginia.* New York, 1972.

Muse, Benjamin. *The American Negro Revolution from Non-Violence to Black Power.* New York, 1970.

Nash, Gary B. *Red, White and Black: The Peoples of Early America.* Englewood Cliffs, New Jersey, 1974.

National Advisory Commission on Civil Disorders. *Report.* New York, 1968.

Navasky, Victor S. *Kennedy Justice.* New York, 1971.

Nelson, Truman. *The Old Man: John Brown at Harper's Ferry.* New York, 1973.

Nevins, Allan. *The Emergence of Lincoln: Prologue to Civil War, 1859–1861.* Vol. II. New York, 1950.

———. *Ordeal of the Union: A House Dividing, 1852–1857,* Vol. II. New York, 1947.

Newfield, Jack. *A Prophetic Minority.* New York, 1966.

Newton, Huey P. *To Die for the People.* New York, 1972.

———. *Revolutionary Suicide.* New York, 1973.

New York State Legislature: Joint Committee Investigating Seditious Activities. *Revolutionary Radicalism,* Parts I, II. Albany, New York, 1920.

Nichols, Roy F. *The Disruption of American Democracy.* New York, 1948.

———. *The Stakes of Power, 1845–1877.* New York, 1961.

Nordhoff, Charles. *The Cotton States in the Spring and Summer of 1875.* New York, 1876.

Oates, Stephen B. *The Fires of Jubilee.* New York, 1975.

———. *To Purge This Land With Blood.* New York, 1970.

Oppenheimer, Martin. *The Urban Guerilla.* Chicago, 1969.

Osofsky, Gilbert (ed.). *Puttin' On Ole Massa: The Slave Narratives of Henry Bibb, William Wells Brown, and Solomon Northrup.* New York, 1969.

Ottley, Roi. *Black Odyssey*. London, 1949.

———. *New World A-Coming*. New York, 1943.

Ottley, Roi, and William Weatherby (eds.). *The Negro in New York*. New York, 1967.

Owen, Robert Dale. *The Wrong of Slavery*. Philadelphia, 1864.

Owens, Leslie H. *This Species of Property*. New York, 1976.

Painter, Nell Irvin. *Exodusters*. New York, 1976.

Paterson, Thomas G. (ed.). *Cold War Critics*. Chicago, 1971.

Patrick, Rembert W. *The Reconstruction of the Nation*. London, 1967.

Patterson, William L. *The Man Who Cried Genocide: An Autobiography*. New York, 1971.

———. *We Charge Genocide*. New York, 1951.

Pauli, Hertha. *Her Name Was Sojourner Truth*. New York, 1962.

Pease, William and Jane H. *Black Utopia: Negro Communal Experiments in America*. Madison, 1963.

———. *Bound with Them in Chains*. Westport, Connecticut. 1972.

———. *They Who Would Be Free*. New York, 1974,

Penn, I. Garland. *The Afro-American Press and Its Editors*. New York, 1969 (originally published in 1891).

Perry, Lewis. *Radical Abolitionism: Anarchy and the Government of God in Anti-Slavery Thought*. Ithaca, New York, 1973.

Phillips, Ulrich B. *American Negro Slavery*. Baton Rouge, Louisiana, 1966 (originally published in 1918).

Pollack, Norman (ed.). *The Populist Mind*. Indianapolis, 1967.

Pope, Liston. *Mill Hands and Preachers*. New York, 1942.

Pope-Hennessy, James. *Sins of the Fathers*. New York, 1968.

Porter, Dorothy. *Early Negro Writing, 1760–1837*. Boston, 1971.

Porter, Kenneth W. *The Negro on the American Frontier*. New York, 1971.

Powell, Adam Clayton, Jr. *Adam by Adam*. New York, 1971.

———. *Marching Blacks*. New York, 1945.

Preston, William. *Aliens and Dissenters, Federal Suppression of Radicals, 1903–1933*. New York, 1963.

Price, Richard (ed.). *Maroon Societies: Rebel Slave Communities in the Americas*. New York, 1973.

Proudfoot, Merrill. *Diary of a Sit-In*. Chapel Hill, North Carolina, 1962.

Quarles, Benjamin. *Black Abolitionists*. New York, 1969.

———. *Frederick Douglass*. Washington, D.C., 1948.

———. *Lincoln and the Negro*. New York, 1962.

———. *The Negro in the American Revolution*. Chapel Hill, North Carolina, 1961.

———. *The Negro in the Civil War*. New York, 1953.

Quint, Howard H. *The Forging of American Socialism*. Indianapolis, 1953.

Rainwater, Lee, and William L. Yancey. *The Moynihan Report and the Politics of Controversy*. Cambridge, Massachusetts, 1967.

Randall, Dudley (ed.). *The Black Poets*. New York, 1971.

Randall, Dudley, and Margaret G. Burroughs. *For Malcolm*. Detroit, 1967.

Raper, Arthur F. *The Tragedy of Lynching.* New York, 1970.

Raper, Arthur F., and Ira De A. Reid. *Sharecroppers All.* Chapel Hill, North Carolina, 1941.

Ratner, Lorman. *Powder Keg: Northern Opposition to the Anti-Slavery Movement, 1831–1840.* New York, 1968.

Rawick, George P. *From Sundown to Sun Up: The Making of the Black Community,* Vol. I in *The American Slave: A Composite Biography* (19 vols.). Westport, Connecticut, 1972.

―――― (ed.). *The American Slave: A Composite Autobiography* (vols. 2–19). Westport, Connecticut, 1972.

Record, Wilson. *The Negro and the Communist Party.* Chapel Hill, North Carolina, 1951.

――――. *Race and Radicalism.* Ithaca, New York, 1964.

Redding, Saunders. *The Lonesome Road.* New York, 1973 (originally published in 1958).

Redkey, Edwin S. *Black Exodus.* New Haven and London, 1969.

―――― (ed.). *Respect Black: The Writings and Speeches of Henry McNeal Turner.* New York, 1971.

Renshaw, Patrick. *The Wobblies.* New York, 1967.

Richards, Leonard. *"Gentlemen of Property and Standing," Anti-Abolition Mobs in Jacksonian America.* New York, 1970.

Rice, C. Duncan. *The Rise and Fall of Black Slavery.* New York, 1975.

Robeson, Paul. *Here I Stand.* New York, 1958.

Robinson, Donald L. *Slavery in the Structure of American Politics, 1765–1820.* New York, 1971.

Rodney, Walter. *A History of the Upper Guinea Coast, 1545–1800.* London, 1970.

――――. *How Europe Underdeveloped Africa.* London, 1972.

Rogin, Michael P. *Fathers and Children.* New York, 1975.

Rollin, [Francis] Frank A. *Life and Public Services of Martin R. Delany.* Boston, 1883.

Rousseve, Charles B. *The Negro in Louisiana.* New York, 1970.

Rose, Willie Lee (ed.). *A Documentary History of Slavery in North America.* New York, 1976.

――――. *Rehearsal for Reconstruction: The Port Royal Experiment.* New York, 1967.

Ross, B. Joyce. *J. E. Spingarn and the Rise of the NAACP, 1911–1939.* New York, 1972.

Rudwick, Elliot M. *Race Riot at East St. Louis.* Carbondale, Illinois, 1964.

――――. *W. E. B. Du Bois, A Study in Minority Group Leadership.* Philaphia, 1960.

Scheer, Robert (ed.). *Eldridge Cleaver.* New York, 1968.

Scheiner, Seth M. *Negro Mecca.* New York, 1965.

Seale, Bobby. *Seize the Time.* New York, 1970.

Seibert, Wilbur H. *The Underground Railroad from Slavery to Freedom.* New York, 1968 (originally published in 1898).

Sellers, Cleveland. *The River of No Return.* New York, 1973.

Sellers, James B. *Slavery in Alabama.* University of Alabama, 1950.

Seton, Marie. *Paul Robeson.* London, 1958.

Shannon, David A. *The Decline of American Communism.* New York, 1959.

Shofner, Jerrell H. *Nor Is It Over Yet.* Gainesville, Florida, 1974.

Shogan, Robert, and Tom Craig. *The Detroit Race Riot.* Philadelphia and New York, 1964.

Simmons, William J. *Men of Mark.* Chicago, 1970 (originally published in 1887).

Sinkler, George. *The Racial Attitudes of American Presidents.* New York, 1972.

Skolnick, Jerome H. *The Politics of Protest.* New York, 1969.

Smith, Abbot E. *Colonists in Bondage.* Glouster, Massachusetts, 1965 (originally published in 1947).

Smith, Arthur L. *Rhetoric of Black Revolution.* Boston, 1969.

Smith, Elbert B. *The Death of Slavery: The United States, 1837–1865.* Chicago, 1967.

Smith, Homer. *Black Man in Red Russia.* Chicago, 1964.

Smith, Timothy L. *Revivalism and Social Reform in Mid-nineteenth Century America.* New York, 1957.

Sorin, Gerald. *Abolitionism: A New Perspective.* New York, 1972.

Southern States Convention of Colored Men. *Proceedings.* Columbia, South Carolina, 1871.

Spero, Sterling D., and Abram L. Harris. *The Black Worker.* New York, 1968 (originally published in 1931).

Stampp, Kenneth M. *The Era of Reconstruction, 1865–1877.* New York, 1965.

———. *The Peculiar Institution.* New York, 1956.

Starkey, Marion L. *Striving to Make It My Home.* New York, 1964.

Starobin, Robert (ed.). *Blacks in Bondage: Letters of American Slaves.* New York, 1974.

———. *Industrial Slavery in the Old South.* New York, 1970.

Staudenraus, P. J. *The African Colonization Movement, 1816–1865.* New York, 1961.

Steinfield, Melvin (ed.). *Our Racist Presidents from Washington to Nixon.* San Ramon, California, 1972.

Sterkx, H. E. *The Free Negro in Ante-Bellum Louisiana.* Rutherford, New Jersey, 1972.

Sterling, Dorothy (ed.). *Speak Out in Thunder Tones.* New York, 1973.

——— (ed.). *The Trouble They Seen.* New York, 1976.

———. *Freedom Train, The Story of Harriet Tubman.* New York, 1954.

———. *The Making of an Afro-American: Martin Robison Delany, 1812–1885.* New York, 1971.

———. *Tender Warriors.* New York, 1958.

Sternsher, Bernard (ed.). *The Negro in Depression and War, Prelude to Revolution, 1930–1945.* Chicago, 1969.

Still, William. *The Underground Railroad.* Chicago, 1970 (originally published in 1871).

Stowe, Harriet Beecher. *The Key to Uncle Tom's Cabin.* New York, 1969 (originally published in 1853).

Stuckey, Sterling (ed.). *The Ideological Origins of Black Nationalism.* Boston, 1972.

Sugarman, Tracy. *Stranger at the Gates: A Summer in Mississippi.* New York, 1966.

Sutherland, Elizabeth (ed.). *Letters from Mississippi.* New York, 1965.

Sykes, Gresham M. *The Society of Captives.* Princeton, 1958.

Takaki, Ronald T. *Violence in the Black Imagination.* New York, 1972.

Tatum, Georgia Lee. *Disloyalty in the Confederacy.* Chapel Hill, North Carolina, 1934.

Taylor, Alrutheus A. *The Negro in Tennessee, 1865–1880.* Washington, D.C., 1941.

————. *The Negro in the Reconstruction of Virginia.* Washington, D.C. 1926.

————. *The Negro in South Carolina During the Reconstruction.* Washington, D.C., 1924.

Thomas, Benjamin, and Harold Hyman. *Stanton: The Life and Times of Lincoln's Secretary of War.* New York, 1962.

Thompson, E. P. *The Making of the English Working Class.* New York, 1963.

Thorpe, Earl E. *Black Historians, A Critique.* New York, 1971.

————. *The Old South: A Psychohistory.* Durham, North Carolina, 1972.

Toppin, Edgar. *A Biographical History of Blacks in America Since 1528.* New York, 1971.

Tragle, Henry Irving (ed.). *The Southampton Slave Revolt of 1831.* Amherst, Massachusetts, 1971.

Trelease, Allen. *Indian Affairs in Colonial New York.* Ithaca, New York, 1960.

————. *White Terror: The Ku Klux Klan Conspiracy and Southern Reconstruction.* New York, Evanston, and London, 1971.

Tuttle, William M. *Race Riot: Chicago in the Red Summer of 1919.* New York, 1970.

————. (ed.) *W. E. B. Du Bois.* Englewood Cliffs, New Jersey, 1973.

Tyson, George F. (ed.). *Toussaint L'Ouverture.* Englewood Cliffs, New Jersey, 1973.

U.S. Bureau of the Census. *Historical Statistics of the United States: Colonial Times to 1970.* Washington, D.C., 1975.

Ullman, Victor. *Martin R. Delany, The Beginnings of Black Nationalism.* Boston, 1971.

Uya, Okon Edet. *Black Brotherhood, Afro-Americans and Africa.* Lexington, Massachusetts, 1971.

Valien, Preston, and Jitsuichi Masuoka. *Race Relations: Problems and Theory.* Chapel Hill, North Carolina, 1961.

Victor, Orville J. *History of American Conspiracies*. New York, 1863.

Vincent, Theodore G. *Black Power and the Garvey Movement*. Berkeley, California, 1971.

Vogel, Virgil J. (ed.). *This Country Was Ours: A Documentary History of the American Indian*. New York, 1972.

Wade, Richard C. *Slavery in the Cities*. New York, 1964.

Wagstaff, Thomas (ed.). *Black Power: The Radical Response to White America*. Beverly Hills, California, 1969.

Wakefield, Dan. *Revolt in the South*. New York, 1960.

Wallace, John. *Carpetbag Rule in Florida*. Jacksonville, 1888.

Walters, Alexander. *My Life and Work*. New York, 1917.

Ward, Robert and William Rogers. *Labor Revolt in Alabama: The Great Strike of 1894*. University, Alabama, 1965.

Ward, Samuel Ringold. *Autobiography of a Fugitive Negro*. London, 1855.

[Warner, Samuel]. *Authentic and Impartial Narrative of the Tragical Scene . . . In Southampton County*. New York, 1831.

Washburn, Wilcomb E. *The Governor and the Rebel*. Chapel Hill, North Carolina, 1957.

———— (ed.). *The Indian and the White Man*. New York, 1964.

Washington, Joseph R. *Black Sects and Cults*. Garden City, New York, 1972.

Waskow, Arthur I. *From Race Riot to Sit-In, 1919 and the 1960s*. New York, 1967.

Watters, Pat. *Down to Now: Reflections on the Southern Civil Rights Movement*. New York, 1971.

Watters, Pat, and Reese Cleghorn. *Climbing Jacob's Ladder*. New York, 1967.

Weinberg, Meyer (ed.). *W. E. B. Du Bois: A Reader*. New York, 1970.

Weisberg, Harold. *Frame-Up: The Martin Luther King–James Earl Ray Case*. New York, 1971.

Wesley, Charles H. *Negro Labor in the United States, 1850–1925*. New York, 1927.

Wharton, Vernon L. *The Negro in Mississippi, 1865–1890*. New York, 1965 (originally published in 1947).

White, Walter. *A Rising Wind*. Garden City, New York, 1945.

Whitelaw, Reid. *After the War*. New York, 1965 (originally published in 1866).

Wiley, Bell Irwin. *Southern Negroes 1861–1865*. New Haven, 1938.

Willhelm, Sidney M. *Who Needs the Negro?* Cambridge, Massachusetts, 1970.

Williams, Eric. *Capitalism and Slavery*. New York, 1961.

Williams, George Washington. *A History of the Negro Troops in the War of the Rebellion*. New York, 1888.

Williams, John A. *Captain Blackman*. New York, 1972.

Williams, Robert F. *Negroes with Guns*. New York, 1962.

Williamson, Joel. *After Slavery*. Chapel Hill, North Carolina, 1965.

Willis, Garry. *The Second Civil War*. New York, 1968.

Wilmore, Gayraud S. *Black Religion and Black Radicalism*. Garden City, New York, 1973.
Wilson, Joseph T. *The Black Phalanx*. New York, 1968.
Wilson, Theodore B. *The Black Codes of the South*. University, Alabama, 1965.
Wiltse, Charles M. *David Walker's Appeal*. New York, 1965.
Winks, Robin. *The Blacks in Canada*. New Haven, 1971.
——— (ed.). *Slavery: A Comparative Perspective*. New York, 1972.
Wolff, Miles. *Lunch at the Five and Ten*. New York, 1970.
Wolters, Raymond. *Negroes and the Great Depression: The Problem of Economic Recovery*. Westport, Connecticut, 1970.
Wood, Peter H. *Black Majority*. New York, 1974.
Woodruff, James. *Race War in America*. New York, 1972.
Woodson, Carter G. *A Century of Negro Migration*. Washington, D.C., 1918.
——— (ed.). *The History of the Negro Church*. Washington, D.C., 1945.
——— (ed.). *The Mind of the Negro as Reflected in Letters Written During the Crisis, 1800–1860*. Washington, D.C., 1926.
———. *Negro Orators and Their Orations*. Washington, D.C., 1925.
Woodward, C. Vann. *American Counterpoint*. Boston, 1971.
———. *The Burden of Southern History*. Baton Rouge, 1960.
———. *Origins of the New South, 1877–1913*. Baton Rouge, 1966.
———. *The Strange Career of Jim Crow*. New York, 1957.
Wright, Richard. *Black Power*. New York, 1954.
———. *White Man, Listen!* Garden City, New York, 1964.
———. *12 Million Black Voices*. New York, 1941.
[Writers Program, Works Projects Administration, Virginia]. *The Negro in Virginia*. New York, 1940.
Wynes, Charles E. (ed.). *The Negro in the South Since 1865*. University, Alabama, 1965.
Yetman, Norman R. (ed.). *Life Under the Peculiar Institution: Selections from the Slave Narratives*. New York, 1970.
Yette, Samuel F. *The Choice: The Issue of Black Survival in America*. New York, 1971.
Young, Alfred F. (ed.). *Dissent: Explorations in the History of American Radicalism*. DeKalb, Illinois, 1969.
Zilversmit, Arthur. *The First Emancipation*. Chicago, 1967.
Zinn, Howard. *SNCC, the New Abolitionists*. Boston, 1964.

Index

AASS. *See* American Anti-Slavery
  Society
ABB. *See* African Blood
  Brotherhood
ANLC. *See* American Negro
  Labor Congress
Abernathy, Ralph, 168
"Abolition Riot," 44
Abysinnia Baptist Church, 135
Abyssinians, 112
Africa, 1–9, 11, 20, 25–27, 33, 34,
  37–38, 55, 66, 85, 89–90, 92, 93,
  95, 103, 107–112, 118, 124, 135,
  140, 141, 191, 203, 209
"Africa Fever," 85
African Blood Brotherhood (ABB),
  103, 116, 117
African Legion, 108
African Liberation Days, 217
African Liberation Support
  Committee, 217
Afro-American League, 85
Afro-Cuban music, 137
Alabama, 40, 75, 83, 84, 88, 118,
  119, 126, 160, 181, 182. *See also*
  Montgomery, Alabama
Albany, Georgia, 162, 168
Algeria, 191
Ali, Noble Drew (Timothy Drew),
  92, 112, 123, 193
Alkalimat, Abdul (Gerry
  McWhorter), 219
Allah, 124, 154

Allegheny, Pennsylvania, 53
Allen, Richard, 16
American and Foreign Anti-
  Slavery Society, 49
American Anti-Slavery Society
  (AASS), 48, 49
American Expeditionary Forces,
  103
American Federation of Labor,
  119, 127
American Negro Labor Congress
  (ANLC), 117
Americus, Georgia, 94, 162
Amite County, Mississippi, 161
Anglo-African, 64
Angola, 229
Antinuclear movement, 229
Appalachia, 200
Arkansas, 85, 182
Asia, 3, '4, 135
Asian-Americans, 206, 229
Atlanta, Georgia, 112, 114, 117,
  148, 181, 182, 185, 214, 218
Atlantic City, New Jersey,
  167–175, 177, 181
Attica, New York, 214

Bailey, Frederick Augustus
  Washington, 27, 39, 45
Baker County, Georgia, 161
Baker, Ella, 159, 214, 225
Baker, Fannie Lou, 225, 231
Bakke, 228

Bakongo, 3
Baldwin, James, 173
Baltimore, Maryland, 44
Bandung, Indonesia, 149
Baptist, 17, 135, 148, 149
Baraka, Imamu, 215, 216, 219
Barbados, 6
Barbary states, 5
Barcelona, 6
Baton Rouge, Louisiana, 214
Bay of Biagra, 19
Beaumont, Texas, 134
Bennett, Lerone, 127
Berry, Marion, 159, 218
Bevel, James, 159
Biko, Steve, 230
Birmingham, Alabama, 94, 119,
　153, 167–175
Black and White: Land, Labor,
　and Politics in the South, 81
Black Caucus, 218
Black Codes, 73
"Black Committee," 66
Black Consciousness, 220
Black Economic Development
　Corporation, 215
Black Expo, 214
Black Identity, 220
Black Liberation, 206
Black Muslims, 220, 221
Black Panthers, 113, 192, 196, 202,
　211, 218
Black Power, 204, 206, 220
Black Power conference, 194, 195,
　214
Black Reconstruction, 129
Blacksmith, Ben, 41
Black Star Line, 102, 108, 109
Black Studies, 227–231
Blair, Ezell, Jr., 158
Block, Sam, 162–163
Blyden, Edward Wilmot, 85
Boggs, Grace, 225
Boggs, James, 225
Bond, Julian, 159

Boston, 6, 30, 31, 32, 44, 90, 138,
　192
Boston University, 148
Boynton, Mrs. Amelia, 161
Brazil, 6
Bridges, William, 98
Briggs, Cyril, 103, 116
Bristol, England, 6
Brown, H. Rap, 191, 194
Brown, John, 62, 91
Brown v. Topeka, 144–145, 151,
　202
Brown, William Wells, 45
Bruce, John E., 98, 102, 108
Bryant, Rev. M. Edward, 83–84
Buffalo, New York, 49, 40, 192
Byrd, Richard, 23

CIA. See Central Intelligence
　Agency
CIO. See Congress of Industrial
　Organizations
CORE. See Congress of Racial
　Equality
Cambridge, Maryland, 170
Cambodia, 230
Campbell, Grace, 116
Canada, 13, 16, 43, 52, 53, 54, 61,
　91
Cape of Good Hope, 5
Caribbean Islands, 95, 107
Carmichael, Stokely, 113, 182, 185,
　186, 187, 188, 191, 194
Carolinas, The, 6, 7, 11, 24, 25,
　40, 60, 62, 75, 92, 138
Carnegie Hall (New York City),
　109
Carter, Jimmy, 218
Catholic Church, 116
Central America, 107
Central Intelligence Agency
　(CIA), 184, 225–227
Charleston, South Carolina,
　13, 26,　63, 67, 104, 153

Chicago, Illinois, 53, 91–92, 104, 105, 112, 118, 119, 125, 127, 132, 163, 164, 170, 183, 184, 187, 188, 212, 214, 222
Chicanos, 206, 229
"Chief Sam," 92
China, 135, 145, 192, 230
Chisholm, Shirley, 217
Christian Movement for Human Rights, 168
Christiana, Pennsylvania, 53–54, 97
Churchill, Winston, 140
Cincinnati, Ohio, 81
Cinque, 41
Civil Rights bill, 171, 172, 174
Civil War, 63–69
Clark, Mark, 211
Clarke, Peter S., 81
Clarke, Septima, 153
Cleveland, Ohio, 50, 56, 79, 187
Clinton, Tennessee, 152
Collins, Addie Mae, 173
Communist party, 103, 111, 115–121, 123, 124, 125, 127, 133, 139, 141, 142, 148, 153, 157, 206, 215, 219, 229
Condition, Elevation, Emigration, and Destiny of the Colored People of the United States, Politically Considered, 55
Congress of African People, 214
Congress of Industrial Organizations (CIO), 127, 128
Congress of Racial Equality (CORE), 160, 170, 174, 175, 185, 186, 188, 190
Connecticut, 16, 45
Connor, Eugene "Bull," 167, 169
Conyers, John, 218
Copeland, John, 62
Corey, Mr., 39
Corps d'Afrique, 66
Cox, Courtland, 182
Crisis, 91, 101, 129

Crozier Theological Seminary, 148
Cuba, 6, 41, 46, 145, 155, 191, 230
Cuffee, Paul, 21

Daley machine, 184
Daley, Richard, 222
Danville, Virginia, 170
Davis, Angela, 214, 219
Davis, Benjamin, 143
Davis, John P., 127
Davis, Richard L., 82–83
Dayton, Ohio, 92, 187
Deacons for Defense and Justice, 182
Declaration of Independence, 15, 24
Delany, Martin, 45–46, 50, 53, 54–56, 61, 66, 79, 103, 107, 108, 153, 160, 178
Dellums, Ron, 218
Democratic party, 73, 175, 218
Department of Defense, 221
Detroit, Michigan, 112, 123, 127, 134–135, 163, 164, 189–200, 217
Diggs, Charles, 215
Dinka, 3
Dixmoor, Illinois, 174
Douglas, H. Ford, 56, 66, 160, 178
Douglass, Frederick, 39, 45, 47, 50, 54–55, 56, 66, 81, 91, 97
Dred Scott decision, 60–61, 65
Drew, Timothy, 92, 124
Du Bois, W. E. B., 67, 89, 90, 91, 92, 96, 101, 102, 103–104, 116, 129, 132, 135, 141–143, 183, 225

East Indies, 5
East Saint Louis, Illinois, 96, 97
Eastland, Senator James, 142
Egypt, 95
Elmira, New York, 53
Emancipation Proclamation, 65, 66, 68, 147
England, 19, 107, 131
Enid, Oklahoma, 153

Ethiopia, 121, 124, 230
Europe and Europeans, 1, 3, 4, 5,
   6, 7, 9, 15, 93, 94, 98, 103, 117,
   123, 131, 135, 138–139
Evans, Mari, 215
Evers, Medgar, 161, 171
Ewe, 3

FBI, 225–227
Fanon, Frantz, 173, 196
Fard, W. D., 123, 124
Farrakan, Minister Louis, 221
Father Divine, 128
Fayette County, Tennessee, 162
Fire Next Time, The, 173
Florida, 13, 16, 25, 40, 41, 85
Forbes, George, 90
Ford, James, 120
Forman, James (Jim), 159, 215
Fort Appalachiola, 25
Fort-Whitman, Lovett, 116
Fortune, T. Thomas, 81, 82, 85
Fourteenth Amendment, 74
France, 98, 102, 104
Free African Society, 16–17
Free Soilers, 52
Freedman's Bureau, 73
Freedom's Journal, 31, 90
Fugitive Slave Act Law, 52–53, 55
Fulani, 3

GI Bill, 137
Gadsden, Alabama, 170
Garnet, Henry Highland, 45,
   49–50, 61
Garrison, William Lloyd, 48
Garvey, Marcus M., 95, 99, 102,
   103, 106, 107–113, 115, 117, 123,
   124, 153, 154
Garveyism/Garveyites, 107, 112,
   116, 117, 132
Gary, Indiana, 213–219, 231
Gay Liberation, 206, 229
"General Peter," 24
Georgia, 17, 25, 40, 112, 138
Germans, 96, 104

Germany, 120, 121
Gold Coast, 19, 92, 110, 138
Graham, Shirley, 141
Green Corn Rebellion, 97
Greensboro, North Carolina, 157,
   158, 220
Greenwood, Florida, 126, 162
Guardian, The, 90

Haiti, 20, 23
Hall, Haywood, 116
Hall, Otto, 116
Hamer, Fannie Lou, 161, 214
Hamid, Sufi Abdul, 125
Hampton, Fred, 211
Hand of Ethiopia, The, 92
Harlem, New York, 95, 99, 125,
   127, 132, 134–135, 138, 157, 174
Harper, Frances Ellen Watkins,
   215
Harpers Ferry, Virginia, 61–62, 91
Harrison, Hubert H., 92, 95, 98,
   102, 108, 135
Harvard University, 90, 102
Hatcher, Richard, 215
Hattiesburg, Mississippi, 94
Hayden, Lewis, 45
Hayes, Vurtis, 159
Haywood, Harry, 219
Hebrews, 20
Henry, Patrick, 20, 99
Herndon, Angelo, 119
Hitler, Adolf, 121
Hope, John, 88–89, 90, 92
Horne, Lena, 141
House Committee on Un-American
   Activities, 157
Houston, Texas, 97–98, 187
Hudson, Hosea, 219
Hughes, Langston, 45, 117,
   119–120, 215

India, 3, 95, 135
Indians, American, 11, 13, 25,
   40–41, 52, 85. See also Native
   Americans

Indochina, 138, 230
Industrial Workers of the World, 92, 127
Innis, Roy, 113
Institute of the Black World, 225
Isle of Wight region, Virginia, 24
Italy, 120, 121, 124

Jackson, Andrew, 40
Jackson, Jesse, 214
Jackson, Mississippi, 171
Jackson State College, 214
Jamaica, 95, 107, 230
James, C. L. R., 107, 131–132
Jamestown, Virginia, 12, 178
Japan, 124–125
Japanese, 102, 132, 133
Jefferson, Thomas, 16, 19, 20, 99
Jerusalem, Virginia, 35
Johnson, Andrew, 73, 74
Johnson administration, 186, 188
Johnson, Lyndon, 174, 175, 178, 181, 184, 190, 191, 193–194
Jones, Charlie, 159
Jones, Jim, 223–224
Jonestown, 222–224

Kansas, 80, 97, 153
Kansas City, 153
Kansas-Nebraska Territory, 60
Kennedy, Bobby, 211
Kennedy, John F., 173
Kentucky, 60
Kerriem, Elijah (Elijah Muhammad; Elijah Poole), 124
Kikuyu, 3
King, Martin Luther, Jr., 2, 17, 84, 148–149, 150, 155, 158, 159, 168, 169, 170, 175, 179, 180, 181, 182, 183–184, 186, 187, 188, 190–191, 197, 198–199, 200, 202, 211, 212, 213, 214, 216, 222, 223, 224, 225, 231
King, Slater, 161
Knights of Labor, 81–82, 84

Knights of Liberty, 50
Knoxville, Tennessee, 170
Koran, 124
Korea, 144, 230
Ku Klux Klan, 73, 76, 87, 104, 151, 220

Langston, John Mercer, 45
Lansing, Michigan, 187
Latin America, 139, 230
Latinos, 229
League of Struggle for Negro Rights, 117
League of Nations, 102, 111
Lee, Canada, 141
Lee, Don L. *See* Haki Madhubuti
Lenin, Nikolai, 99
Letter from Birmingham Jail, 169
Levitt, Joshua, 48
Lewis, John, 159, 172, 181
Liberia, 85, 111
Lincoln, Abraham, 62, 64, 65, 66, 69, 73, 178
Lisbon, 6
Little, Malcolm. *See* Malcolm X
Little Rock, Arkansas, 152, 153
Liverpool, England, 6
Loguen, Jermain, 45
Longview, Texas, 104
Look for Me in the Whirlwind, 105–113
Los Angeles, California, 134, 183, 184, 218. *See also* Watts
Louis, Joe, 126
Louisiana, 13, 23, 24, 40, 75, 77, 80, 182
Louisiana Purchase, 23, 52
L'Overture, Toussaint. *See* Toussaint L'Overture
Lowndes County, Alabama, 161, 182
Lowndes County Freedom party, 182

McCain, Franklin, 158

McCarthyism, 148
McComb, Mississippi, 162, 182–183
McDew, Charles, 159
McKay, Claude, 105, 106, 116–117, 120, 125, 215
McKissick, Floyd, 188
McNair, Denise, 173
McNeill, Joseph, 158
McWhorter, Gerry. See Abdul Alkalimat
Madhubuti, Haki, 215
Malcolm X, 154–155, 164–165, 173, 180, 181, 195, 202, 216, 221–222, 223, 224, 225, 231
Malcolm X Liberation University, 220
Mandinka, 3
March on Washington, 133–134, 179, 217
Marianna, Florida, 134
Marxism, 115, 132, 209, 214, 215, 219–220, 230. See also Communist party
Maryland, 27, 39, 40, 41
Massachusetts, 138, 154
Memphis, Tennessee, 84, 186, 189–200, 212, 213
Meredith, James, 185–186
Messenger, The, 99, 116
Mexicans, 52, 60
Mexico, 38, 61
Michigan, 138
Middle East, 230
Milwaukee, Wisconsin, 192
Mississippi, 36, 40, 41, 43, 153, 162, 163, 170, 173, 174, 175, 177, 182, 183, 185, 186, 187, 188
Mississippi Freedom Democratic party, 175
Mississippi Territory, 25
Missouri, 128–129
Missouri Compromise, 52, 61
Mobile, Alabama, 134
Moma Dollie, 161
Montgomery, Alabama, 147–155,
158, 177, 181, 184, 196–197, 199, 203, 205, 209, 210
Montgomery Improvement Association, 149, 151
Moore, Amzie, 153, 161
Moors, 123, 124
Morehouse College, 148
Moscow, 116, 117, 118
Moses, Bob, 159, 160, 173, 179, 214
Moslem, 221
Mozambique, 229
Muhammad, Elijah (Elijah Kerriem; Elijah Poole), 124, 138, 153–154, 155, 180, 220, 221, 222, 223
Muhammad Speaks, 222
Muhammad, Wallace, 221
Muslims, 124, 153–155, 196, 221
Mussolini, Benito, 121

NAACP. See National Association for the Advancement of Colored People
NNC. See National Negro Conference
Nantes, 6
Nash, Diane, 159
Nashville, Tennessee, 160
Nassau, 41
Nation of Islam, 153, 154, 164, 180, 196, 203, 208, 218, 220, 221–222
National Association for the Advancement of Colored People, 91, 92, 127, 129, 133, 143, 144, 153, 168, 171, 174, 186, 190
National Black Political Convention, 211, 215
National Convention of Colored Freemen, 50
National Negro Conference, 127
Native Americans, 206, 229
Neal, Claude, 126
Negro-American Political League, 91

Negro Fellowship League, 92
Negro World, The, 108
Neo-Garveyites, 113
Newark, New Jersey, 92, 134, 193, 194, 195, 215, 218
New Bedford, Massachusetts, 45
New Deal, 137
New England, 15
New Orleans, Louisiana, 24, 41, 72, 75, 77
Newport, Rhode Island, 6
Newton, Huey, 196
New World, 5
New York City, 13, 30, 45, 85, 109, 118, 163, 164, 170, 181
Niagara Movement, 90–91
Nkrumah, Kwame, 132
Nobel Peace Prize, 180, 182
North Carolina State Agricultural and Technical College, 157
North Star, 55

Oakland, California, 218
Oberlin College, 62
Oberlin, Ohio, 62
Ohio River, 43, 94
Oklahoma, 85, 89, 92, 153
Omaha, Nebraska, 112, 187
Organization for a New American Revolution, 225
"Organization for Black Power, The," 182
Orient, the, 139
Ottoman Turks, 4
Owen, Chandler, 99

Pan-African Conference, 132
Pan-African Congress, 89, 102, 103
Pan-Africanism, 6, 31, 85, 89, 90, 98, 214, 217
Paris, 102, 103, 142
Parker, Samuel, 54
Parks, Rosa, 148
Peace Conference (Paris), 102, 103
Peacock, Willie, 163
Pearl Harbor, 132, 133

Peculiar Institution, The, 37
Pennington, J. W. C., 45, 57
People's Temple, 223
Philadelphia, Pennsylvania, 16, 17, 30, 44, 59, 61, 163, 183
Philippine independence fighters, 86
Pine Bluff, Arkansas, 170
Pinkerton, 128
Pittsburgh, Pennsylvania, 45, 170
Pittsburgh Courier, 140
Plessy v. Ferguson, 86
Poole, Elijah (Elijah Kerriem; Elijah Muhammad), 112, 124
Poor People's Campaign, 200
Populist movement, 83
Port Royal, South Carolina, 67
Portugal, 5
Powell, Adam Clayton, 125, 135–136
Prattis, P. L., 140
Progressive party, 141
Prosser, Gabriel, 21, 26, 34, 35, 68
Prosser, Martin, 21
Prosser, Solomon, 21
Puerto Ricans, 200
Purvis, Robert, 47, 61

RAM. *See* Revolutionary Action Movement, 192
Radical Republicans, 73
Randolph, A. Phillip, 99, 132, 133, 172, 190
Ray, Charles S., 45
Reagan, Cornell, 159
Remond, Charles, 47, 61
Republican party, 62, 69, 71, 73, 74, 75, 76, 218
Revolutionary Action Movement, 192
Richmond, David, 158
Richmond, Virginia, 21, 41
Robertson, Carol, 173
Robeson, Paul, 131, 132, 135, 141–143, 152, 183, 225

Rochester, New York, 97
Rock, Dr. John, 64
Rock Hill, South Carolina, 162
Rockefeller, Nelson, 214
Rogers, J. A., 140
Rome, 116
Roosevelt, Franklin D. 134, 143
Rotterdam, 6
Ruggles, David, 45
Russia, 120, 121, 131, 142. *See
also* Soviet Russia and Soviet
Union
Russian Revolution, 99, 120
Rustin, Bayard, 172, 175, 190

SCLC. *See* Southern Christian
Leadership Conference
SNCC. *See* Student Nonviolent
Coordinating Committee
Saint Louis, Missouri, 50, 80
Sacramento, California, 192
Sahel, 230
Saint Domingo, 23; San Domingo,
20; Santo Domingo, 26
Salaam, Kalamu ya, 215
Sanchez, Sonia, 215
Savannah, Georgia, 17, 85
Scottsboro Affair, The, 119
Sea Islands, Georgia, 24
Seale, Bobby, 218
Seay, S. S., 161
Selma, Alabama, 83, 170, 180, 181
Sharecroppers Union, 127
Shaw University, 159
Sherrod, Charles, 159, 214
Shreveport, Louisiana, 94
Shuttlesworth, Fred, 153, 161,
167–168
Sixteenth Avenue Baptist Church,
Birmingham, 172
Smith, Ruby Doris, 159
Socialist party, 91, 92, 98, 99, 116,
206
Socialism, 91, 142
Soledad brothers, 214

South Carolina State College, 199
Southampton County, Virginia, 33, 36
Southern Christian Leadership
Conference (SCLC), 168, 170,
179, 181, 186, 198, 213
Southern Tenant Farmers Union,
127
Southern University, 214
Soviet Russia, 139, 141
Soviet Union, 142
Soweto, 230
Spain, 41
Spanish-Cuban war, 86
Stampp, Kenneth, 37
Stono, South Carolina, 13
Student Nonviolent Coordinating
Committee (SNCC), 159, 160,
161, 162, 163, 170, 172, 173, 174,
175, 181, 182, 185, 186, 190, 191,
194, 218
Students for a Democratic Society,
205
Sturgis, Kentucky, 152
Sumpter County, Georgia, 161
Supreme Court, United States, 60,
86, 144, 149, 151, 228

Tampa, Florida, 192
Taney, Roger, 60
Tappan, Lewis, 48
Temple People, 124, 193
Tennessee, 25, 60, 73, 138
Texas, 40, 60, 182
Third World, 191, 196
Third World Press, 225
Thirteenth Amendment, 71
Toure, Askia, 215
Toussaint L'Overture, 20
Treaty of Versailles, 102
Tribune, 72
Trinidad, 131
Trotsky, Leon, 116–117; Trotskyite
movement, 131
Trotter, William Monroe, 90, 91,
102, 103

Troy, New York, 49
Truman, Harry S., 143
Truth, Sojourner, 47
Tubman, Harriet, 59
Tulsa, Oklahoma, 153
Turner, Nat, 2, 27, 33–36, 37, 62, 68
Turner, Henry McNeil, 85, 89, 108
Tuskegee, Alabama, 88
Twenty-fourth Infantry Regiment, 97

UNIA. *See* Universal Negro
  Improvement Association
UMW. *See* United Mine Workers
Underground Railroad, 43
United Nations, 139
United Mine Workers (UMW), 82–83
United States Steel, 167
Universal Negro Improvement
  Association (UNIA), 107, 108,
  112, 115, 117, 149
University of Mississippi, 185
Urban League, 186, 190
Valdosta, Georgia, 94
Verdun, Battle of, 104
Vesey, Denmark, 25, 26, 27, 34,
  35, 68, 135
Vietnam, 174–175, 178, 182, 183,
  188, 189–200, 202, 212, 230
Virginia, 12, 15, 16, 23–24, 27, 35,
  56, 59, 187
Walker, David, 31–32, 33, 45, 50,
  62, 63, 108, 135
Walker, Wyatt T., 179–180, 184,
  197
Walker's *Appeal . . . to the
  Colored Citizens of the World
  But in Particular and very
  Expressly to those of the United
  States of America*, 31–32, 33, 63
Wall Street, 118, 123
Wallace, Henry, 141
Washington, Booker T., 88–89, 90,
  91, 110

Washington, D.C., 104, 105, 106,
  153, 163, 165, 170, 172, 173, 177,
  199, 200
Washington, George, 62
Washington, Madison, 41
"Watergate," 226
Waterloo, Iowa, 192
Watkins, Hollis, 159
Watts (Los Angeles, California),
  183, 184, 187, 188, 193
Weathermen, the, 205
Weber, 228
Welfare Rights Movement, 206
Wells-Barnett, Ida B., 84, 91
Wesley, Cynthia, 173
West Indies, 103
White Citizens Councils, 151–152,
  153
White, Walter, 133
Wichita, Kansas, 153
Wilkins, Roy, 186, 190
Williams, Robert F., 145, 147, 155,
  182, 192
Wilmington, North Carolina, 31
Wilson, Woodrow, 96
Workingmen's party, 81
World Community of Islam, 221
Wretched of the Earth, The, 173
Wright, Richard, 119
Wynn, Prathia, 159

Yarmouth, 102
Young, Andy, 218
Young, Whitney, 186, 190

Zellner, Bob, 159
Zimbabwe, 229
Zulu, 3